W9-BON-030

PRAISE FOR

Arrogant Capital

"You'll enjoy *Arrogant Capital*. Kevin Phillips's view of Washington as a political swamp where a venal elite cashes in even as it lets the nation sink into an economic abyss. . . . Many of Phillips's observations about Washington's political gridlock are on target, and he offers appealing solutions."

— *Business Week Magazine*

"Another great book from Kevin Phillips."

— "CBS This Morning"

"Unusually wise to the dodges of Washington's rich and powerful, *Arrogant Capital* gives new vibrancy to the political cliché that Washington is out of touch with the average American. . . . Phillips is a brilliant reader of the political tea leaves."

— *Kirkus Reviews*

"*Arrogant Capital* is full of the interesting analogies across space and time that set [Phillips] apart from anybody who has written about American politics in recent years."

— *New Republic*

"Our modern Thomas Paine has written another readable volume that deserves widespread attention."

— *Library Journal*

"A provocative, timely, often convincing jeremiad that accurately diagnoses many of the country's ailments and prescribes some tough remedies."

— *Chicago Tribune*

"Political analyst Kevin Phillips, known for his prescient predictions, senses revolution in the air. In this small but densely packed book, he describes our current predicament and offers a diverse menu of 10 proposals for unlocking the grip of money on politics and financiers on the economy."

— *Raleigh News & Observer*

"*Arrogant Capital* assails the permanent government and its New Class clientele ... posing the big questions and pondering the big picture that frames [Phillips's] prophetic reading of the American prospect. This is his best book, and announces Kevin Phillips as one of the very few who have gone to the source of the American debacle."

— *Philadelphia Inquirer*

Arrogant Capital

ALSO BY KEVIN PHILLIPS

Boiling Point

The Politics of Rich and Poor

*Staying on Top: The Business Case for a
National Industrial Strategy*

Post-Conservative America

*Mediacracy: American Parties and Politics in the
Communications Age*

Electoral Reform

The Emerging Republican Majority

Kevin Phillips

Arrogant Capital

Washington, Wall Street, and the Frustration of American Politics

Little, Brown and Company
Boston   New York   Toronto   London

Copyright © 1994, 1995 by Kevin Phillips

All rights reserved. No part of this book may be reproduced in any form or
by any electronic or mechanical means, including information storage and
retrieval systems, without permission in writing from the publisher, except by
a reviewer who may quote brief passages in a review.

First Paperback Edition

Library of Congress Cataloging-in-Publication Data
Phillips, Kevin P.
   Arrogant capital : Washington, Wall Street, and the frustration of American
politics /Kevin Phillips. — 1st ed.
      p.   cm.
   Includes index.
   ISBN 0-316-70618-3 (HC)   0-316-70602-7 (PB)
   1. Political corruption — United States.   2. United States — Politics and
government.   3. Lobbying — United States — Corrupt practices.   4. Pressure
groups — United States.   5. Social movements — United States.   I. Title.
   JK2249.P48   1994
   320.973 — dc20   94-10035

10   9   8   7   6   5   4   3   2   1

MV-NY

Published simultaneously in Canada by
Little, Brown & Company (Canada) Limited

Printed in the United States of America

To my mother

Prudence, indeed, will dictate that Governments long established should not be changed for light and transient Causes; and accordingly all Experience hath shown, that Mankind are more disposed to suffer, while Evils are sufferable, than to right themselves by abolishing the Forms to which they are accustomed. But when a long Train of Abuses and Usurpations, pursuing invariably the same Object, evinces a design to reduce them under absolute Despotism, it is their right, it is their duty, to throw off such Government, and to provide new Guards for their future Security.

THOMAS JEFFERSON,
in the *Declaration of Independence*, 1776

Contents

III The Revolutionary 1990s and the Restoration of Popular Rule in America

Preface to the Paperback Edition

THIS BOOK came out in hardcover in September 1994, just in time to help fuel the gathering popular blast at Washington that helped make the November elections into at least a small revolution. The public turned out to be as livid as the book suggested. When *Time* excerpted it that same month, the magazine also ran a special poll on what voters thought of Washington and a number of the proposals to bring it under control. The results, obtained too late to be included in the book, were a massive affirmation of the *Arrogant Capital* thesis.

People thought the city was controlled by special interests, including — but hardly limited to — corporations, Wall Street, and the rich. Fully 61 percent thought it wasn't even enough to change the *faces* in the capital; the *system* itself had to be changed. Asked what George Washington would think of the city that bore his name, just 7 percent said he'd be proud. An 86 percent majority said he'd be disappointed. By 76 percent to 19 percent — four to one — voters preferred that laws be made by the people themselves through nationwide referenda. Revolutionary *was* a fair description.

There is little debate now about the public's anger at 1990s Washington. But America's leaders must understand two other critical dimensions: first, that disillusionment has *not* been put into the past tense, because the 1994 elections served to worsen about as many circumstances as they improved; and second, that ongoing voter resentment is justified by the capital's interest-group bias and poor performance, which continues (though partially in new veins). The failure of the federal city and the related malfunctioning of U.S. politics confirms warnings voiced by Thomas Jefferson and others in the great debates of the early Republic. The depth of these problems goes far beyond what Republicans circa 1995 were willing to admit — once they had won their Capitol Hill majorities, patronage, and spoils.

Jefferson's passage in the Declaration of Independence proclaiming the right of a citizenry to change its form of government after "a long train of abuses" is the first of many citations in which this book will quote our third president on the dangers of an overgrown Washington, a grasping judiciary, a too-powerful financial establishment, and the like. Awareness of the reemerging relevance of Jefferson's warnings and of America's need to reawaken the radical spirit of the Declaration of Independence has grown in the last few years. Signs are everywhere — in national polling, in the contempt for Washington so visible in the 1994 elections, in grassroots movements and coalitions, in the unusual new alliances for purging the capital and empowering ordinary Americans, and in the demand by even conservative Republican leaders in 1994 for resurrecting the boldness and antiestablishment insurgency of the founding fathers. After starting the book in mid-1993, I was steadily surprised to see how the themes now expressed in these pages have struck unexpected chords in unexpected places. None of this crept up on America, unseen and unwhispered, and the nation's reaction is a long way from being over. Unfortunately, extremism is already visible on the fringe — witness the bombing in Oklahoma City.

The election of a Republican Congress last November produced several important changes, ranging from reform in the House of Representatives to restraints on how much unfunded spending Congress could impose on the states. But economic and regulatory areas have seen a reactionary drift. An important shift in U.S. politics *is* involved, especially in the House of Representatives, hitherto under Democratic control for forty years. We can call this a *small* revolution. But its shortcomings are also important: it is no renewal of the U.S. economy; it is no framework for middle-class revitalization; it is no political realignment of the historic American variety, in which the party winning control of the government in a "watershed" election has thereafter occupied the presidency for most of the next twenty-five to thirty-five years. That kind of generation-long national political domination is a thing of the past. Nor was November 1994 the sort of deep revolution needed to break up the fifty-year stranglehold that lobbyists and special interests have gained over Washington. If anything, the role of the lobbyists has strengthened. This central malfunction — and critical challenge — of American politics remains. Another needed political change is already being outlined.

When *Arrogant Capital* was first published in September 1994, the national revolt against Washington laid out in these pages was starting to come true. In the seven weeks up to the elections, voter anger grew. Discontent with Washington was almost a forest fire. But Republicans preferred to insist that the electorate's disdain of the arrogant U.S. capital city and political class described in the book should be taken (and narrowed) as a mandate to reduce the size of government — in particular response to the business and financial community — partly by cutting regulations and programs that included many benefiting ordinary voters. The lesson that established-party-linked politicians, once elected, will reform only superficially is valid not just in the United States but also in Japan and the rest of the G-7 nations. The cynicism that is justified in response to Washington is also justified in London, Tokyo, and Rome.

A first caution about the November 1994 elections is the extreme volatility of America's disenchanted electorate. Voters no longer have faith in Washington or in the two-party system of Republicans and Democrats. Over the last four years, voter opinions have bounced back and forth like Ping-Pong balls. Between March 1991, after the Gulf War, and August 1992, Republican President George Bush saw his job approval ratings drop from 90 percent to 30 percent, and in November he received just 37.5 percent of the total vote for president, the lowest share received by a Republican president running for reelection since 1912. Then, by the summer of 1994, eighteen months after his own inauguration as president, Democrat Bill Clinton saw *his* ratings for trustworthiness and support for re-election drop into the thirties. The vote of no confidence on November 8 was massive; no newly elected president has seen his party lose so many seats in Congress — fifty-three in the House and eight in the Senate — since Warren Harding in 1922.

Part of Americans' anger with Washington and its entrenched political classes is cultural, part is economic — fear for the American Dream and worry that children may not have today's living standards. As this concern continues, politicians now have less and less time to fulfill public hopes and expectations. Georgia Republican Congressman Newt Gingrich, the new Republican Speaker of the House of Representatives, told a late 1994 meeting that if the 104th Congress degenerates "into the usual baloney of politics in Washington, then the American people, I believe, will move towards a third party in a massive way." Yet at the end of the first one hundred days of the new GOP Congress in April 1995, polls showed this was just what 60–65 percent majorities of Americans believed: that the new Congress presented politics as usual. The national majorities calling for a new party *grew*.

As voters told national survey takers, the new Republican Congress may have been too ambitious. History has shown that each of the four previous midterm landslides in the last fifty years of U.S. politics were reactions *against* the party and president in power — against recessions, scandals, wars, and civil unrest — rather than votes *for* any specific agenda of the opposition party. Perceiving such endorsements has usually been a mistake. The 1994 election is of roughly the same magnitude as those of 1946, 1958, 1966, and 1974; and these didn't produce clear and tangible ideological or legislative mandates, either.

The Republicans have insisted that things are different this time, that the vote against Bill Clinton, the Democrats, and Washington was actually a vote for the GOP "Contract with America," with its Balanced Budget Constitutional Amendment, tax cuts, and other pledges. But, as postelection 1994 *Time*/CNN survey data illustrated, even Republicans did not believe that voters were motivated by support for GOP programs. One midterm landslide should be a particular caution. The Republican 80th Congress elected in 1946 exaggerated its mandate, especially in tax policy, and the Democrats regained control two years later.

After its critical first hundred days, national reaction to the performance of the new Republican 104th Congress was closely divided — some 40–55 percent of voters were positive, but similar numbers said the Republicans were trying to do too much too quickly and favoring the rich at the expense of ordinary Americans. And other voter skepticisms are also revealing.

Statistic after statistic reaffirmed the deep roots rather than the transience of the disillusionment of 1994. To begin with, a majority of voters continued to indicate that the new Republicans in Congress were just playing politics as usual. Few saw a new era under way. Voter belief in Washington remained at the record lows reached in 1994 — only 20 percent or so of the electorate said Washington could be trusted all or some of the time. Just like the Clinton Democrats two years earlier, the Republicans who had run against Washington in the election quickly abandoned their criticisms of insiders and influence peddlers and started making deals with them. Almost the first thing the new victors did was to demand money from the capital city special interests and lobbies they had castigated. And almost from the first, pluralities of voters found the new Republican Speaker of the House, Newt Gingrich, untrustworthy, just as they had President Clinton in 1993.

By mid-1995, negative public ratings of the Congress were back to the same level — 60 percent — as they had been through most of 1993 and well into 1994 while Congress was under Democratic control. The new GOP philosophy was no key to national reassurance. In March 1995, national surveys for *Time* magazine indicated that 56 percent of Americans still wanted a new third party — essentially the same ratio as had prevailed back in 1992, 1993, and 1994 — and those favoring such a party included 48 percent of the self-identified Republicans. April's *Times-Mirror* polling found the highest support for a new party in that survey's history: 57 percent.

The minirevolution in the House of Representatives, in short, has not been a real revolution in Washington. Excessive Republican and Democratic Party interlocks with the capital's interest groups make that almost impossible. Congress's new Republican leaders have not been any more anxious for genuine reform in regulation of lobbying and campaign finance than were the Democrats. What we have seen instead is the *pretense* — a *pseudorevolution* in which the winners make a great deal of noise about change, but the principal reality is that one set of politicians hustling money from special interests and doing their bidding in legislation has simply been changed for another, although this time, the new legislators and interests are more conservative and pro-business. Japanese readers may find the pattern familiar. Or Italians. Or Canadians.

One key to the next wave of U.S. voter frustration in 1996 will lie with the behavior of the U.S. economy. The economic recovery that began in March 1991 started its fifth year in March 1995. Few recoveries last much longer, which would suggest that the next downturn is not far off. Besides, the political division between a Democratic president and a Republican Congress also suggests caution. During the last confrontation, back in 1947–48, the duration of the ongoing economic recovery was roughly three years, presumably shortened by the jockeying between Congress and the president on tax and budget issues. Current tax and budget conflict between Congress and the president could do the same thing. However, if a recession does begin this year or next, it is not clear which side voters would blame: the Republican Congress or the Democratic president. Usually, the president's party gets the blame, but because voters think that the Republicans now control Washington, the GOP may again be more at risk, just as it took the brunt in 1948. Voters could also get angrier with the *whole* political system.

The extent to which popular revulsion at our own capital parallels the anger at other capitals and political elites from Ottawa and Paris to Tokyo is also cautioning. Part of the contempt for political elites is deep enough to be shared across the G-7 nations. Then there are the historical lessons of other abusive and entrenched elites — well known to America's founding fathers — in seats of government from imperial Rome to imperial London. But if reforming, even purging, Washington has this larger legitimacy, the critical challenge is specific and national: the need for major changes in the capital to make the U.S. party system and even the broader U.S. political and governmental system come alive again. Failure in mid-1990s Washington goes far beyond simplistic talk of grid-lock. The increasing ineffectiveness of American government is part of a larger reversal of fortune — of how the grass roots of America have been losing national influence to a permanent political, interest-group, and financial elite, located in Washington, New York, and other centers. Just as the new administration only confirmed this trend, instead of reversing it in 1993, the new Congress has itself kowtowed to a major part of entrenched Washington power. This book has a simple premise: *it's time to take that influence back.*

It would be surprising if this sad state of Washington and the ineffectiveness of national politics were not making voters indignant. Americans are the products of the most important and, conceivably, the most enduring revolutionary tradition in modern Western history. Our revolution is part of our success. Revitalizing it is still essential; the elections of 1994 made only a few of the needed changes.

So the overriding question of the 1990s, with politics and government in such disarray, is elemental: can the nation's citizens rise to the further challenge? Will twenty-first-century historians remember Americans as angry but helpless in facing Washington's dug-in interests and the increasing inadequacy of the party system? Or will the public, responding to the mystic chords of ancient insurgencies and shrugging off the unnerving precedents of earlier great-power declines, somehow keep punching toward another national renewal — a broad political and governmental update of the first American Revolution?

Conclusions won't be possible until the twenty-first century. But in the meantime, history's die is not yet cast. Suspicion of governing elites, capital cities, and what they represent is more powerful in the United States — and has been over two centuries — than almost anywhere else. The muskets of the Revolution were not even cold before Americans were fighting over moving state capitals farther into the homespun hinterland and away from the fleshpots, countinghouses, and salons of the coastal cities, as well as over locating the national capital away from New York and Philadelphia in a place of less sophistication and corruption and nearer to the frontier. Even now, no president — or House Speaker — can be complacent.

Today's voter dismay, then, reflects an old bogeyman and suspicion. The foreboding is of what citizen anger must now overcome: a huge new, entrenched, and bipartisan governing elite, one that in some ways approaches those who mis-governed Rome. Over the last half century, a Washington swollen by expansions in peace and war has become what ordinary citizens of the 1780s and even some architects of the U.S. Constitution feared — a capital city so enlarged, so incestuous in its dealings, so caught up in its own privilege, that it no longer seems controllable by the general public.

Yet aroused Americans rightly sense that the country as a whole is still vital, and that a substantial part of the problem is specific to Washington. The citizenry has its faults and the nation itself many weaknesses, but a historical case can be made that the capital cities of great powers — ambitious, swollen populations clumped together in pursuit of money and power — start to rot or atrophy before the grass roots lose their own vitality or capacity. This book will make that case. Reformwise, the 140-year-old Republicans and the 170-year-old Democrats aren't sufficiently distinguishable.

There is no point in mincing words. Aging great-power capitals often become parasitic cultures. The term *parasite* was frequently used in seventeenth- and eighteenth-century criti-cisms of the Spanish and Dutch capitals. Washington, in dif-ferent ways, has begun to resemble these wayward governmental centers of previous declining empires, from Greece and Rome to Hapsburg Madrid and The Hague. This book develops the parallel, which is chilling — and which is also a warning. The lessons of history could not be more relevant. Too much of what happened then is happening again now.

In the United States, though, it is essential to underscore how the outsider groups and grassroots movements that snap and snarl at 1990s Washington exemplify a mindset unmatched in any preceding great power: a revolutionary awareness and tradition that Americans quickly reworked during the nineteenth century into a uniquely successful style of national politics. Whether the insurgent groups of the 1990s can still play yesteryear's essential renewal role — whether another bloodless political revolution is possible — will tell us a lot about America's place in the new century.

There is a case for optimism. The greatest obstacle, however, lies in the rise of a massive, special-interest-driven Washington and its tightening death grip on what has been the unique genius of American politics. This genius, which must be rescued and restored, has rested on the U.S. ability to stage political revolutions or watershed presidential elections every generation, thereby putting the nation on a new course and sweeping the old regime's exhausted interest groups and elites from Washington.

That was easy at first, with the federal district of 1800 or 1828 so thinly populated that vacant lots outnumbered buildings. Electoral waves swept in the new and swept out the old. As we will see in Chapter 1, this hosing down of the corridors of power kept the spirit of the American Revolution alive at the ballot box. It prevailed again in the great sectional tension surrounding the election of the Republicans in 1860 and the subsequent breakup of the Union, and then once more with the victory of the Democrats in 1932 and the coming of the New Deal. The idea of a massive, Permanent Washington — a fortress powerful enough to turn aside a presidential-level electoral wave — was only a dim, abstract worry. The most important thing about this politics of national renewal was supremely practical: it kept succeeding.

No longer. Yesteryear's easy transformability started to vanish as Washington expanded in the 1930s; then the larger system's political fluidity and openness to a capital-city purge began to dissipate as Washington mushroomed into the power center of the world during the 1940s, 1950s, and 1960s. This, as we will see, is when the Permanent Washington took shape.

In *The Emerging Republican Majority*, written in 1967–68 and published in 1969, I argued that the country was ripe for another of its generational upheavals in Washington, setting out the thesis of America's periodic electoral revolts. Through them, the book argued, U.S. politics had renewed itself — and by the yardsticks of cyclicality, another such upheaval was due. Yet despite Republican control of the presidency for twenty out of twenty-four years between 1968 and 1992, this occupancy of the White House was not, as events turned out, matched by the ability to take control of Congress or to create a new establishment, as GOP strategists originally hoped. Washington's influential classes had been sinking their roots too broadly and deeply — history's familiar danger signal — to be displaced as before. The U.S. political system was losing the capacity for a broad transformation, which was what had made it work.

A generation later in 1990, I predicted in *The Politics of Rich and Poor* that the post–1968 GOP era would soon end in a populist reaction against both the increasingly unresponsive Washington elite and the economic redistribution of the 1980s in favor of the nation's rich. But while the book foresaw a populist upsurge and some new political cycle beginning in the 1990s, it did not try to spell out its form or depth of success. There was enough wear and tear in the aging two-party system, enough citizen dismay with Washington becoming a citadel of special interests and shopworn officeholders, that too many uncertainties crowded the stage. Possibly the old pattern could no longer repeat.

These skepticisms were justified by the three-way election of 1992 and the eventual triumph of Bill Clinton following a campaign flavored by one brand of outsiderism after another. Once in office, though, Clinton abandoned his outsider postures to compromise with established lobbies, power brokers, and Congressional leaders, even as his job-approval numbers collapsed to low levels unprecedented for a newly elected president. But there were times when he had no choice. Like Nixon two decades earlier, albeit in different circumstances, Clinton was overwhelmed and constrained by the Permanent Washington as well as by his own mistakes. His narrow successes in enacting critical tax and trade legislation depended on deals with key lobbies and concessions to interest groups represented by pivotal legislators. Old New Deal Democratic lobbies — labor, minority, and urban — found themselves decreasingly relevant as Clinton abandoned yesteryear's "interest-group liberalism" for a new "interest-group centrism" of collaboration with the capital's new business-financial-international power axis.

Which brings us back to the thesis of this book, namely, that as Washington has become entrenched, the old two-party system, revitalized by once-a-generation bloodless revolutions at the ballot box, no longer works. The Republican takeover of Congress in 1994, produced by national disdain for Clinton, turned out to continue cynicism at the grassroots level despite the cheers of conservative lobbies. Governmental mechanisms, too, are losing their responsiveness. The American people, more or less aware of this, are grasping for a solution to what is clearly a larger, deeper problem, for all that opinion molders cannot agree on a definition. The naive perceive nothing more than gridlock or control by the wrong party, an ineffectiveness that is merely superficial, in which the mechanisms and processes of Washington can be unlocked by the right lubrication and the right leadership. But as we will see, it is difficult for politicians — not just late-twentieth-century U.S. politicians — to develop the needed debate over what no longer works for a nation and then to weigh history for appropriate remedies.

As Chapter 2 will pursue, Washington is now too big, too rich, too pride-set in its ways as arbiter of the postwar world, to accept another of the upheavals and housecleanings that Thomas Jefferson predicted would be necessary every generation. Special-interest power just keeps consolidating. Besides, in one respect Washington is a particularly prominent tip of a much larger problem. The emergence of a rich and privileged capital city is part of a broader transition in America toward social and economic stratification, toward walled-in communities and hardening class structures, toward political, business, and financial elites that bail each other out, toward an increasing loss of optimism, and even toward hints of European cultural stratification and economic polarization. The United States of 1937 or even 1951 could not have produced either this kind of transition or so smug a capital city; the Washington–New York–Boston corridor of the 1990s could and did.

As a corollary to the emergence of a fortresslike Washington unconquerable by angry winds blowing in from Idaho or Long Island, the U.S. financial sector has also developed its own unprecedented size, power, and uncontrollability. On this dimension, too, the country has paid a price. Just as the political fluidity of the United States from the 1790s to the 1930s made possible the turnover of Washington and the renewal of an effective party system, there have been parallel benefits in how the national economic panics and downturns of that period scythed through the U.S. financial sector, cutting away failures and abuses. If over a hundred congressmen and senators lost their seats in the elections of 1894 and 1932, the carnage was many times greater among banks, investment firms, and other financial institutions. Thousands went under. But chaos and destruction also served to renew vitality, as subsequent U.S. economic growth showed.

No longer. By the late 1960s and 1970s, yesteryear's cleansing operation of market forces on political and financial elites had become unacceptable to national decision makers. The Permanent Washington circa 1970 could not be drummed out of town like the defeated friends of John Quincy Adams, or even the forgotten underlings of Herbert Hoover. Within a few years, corporations like Lockheed and Chrysler, also too big to fail, would qualify for a pioneering form of assistance: the government bailout. So when the economic bubble of the 1980s popped as the decade ended, no one should have been surprised that so few of the major financial institutions that had carried speculation to new heights were left to drown in their own failed investments. Instead, the national political power structure bailed out the shaky financial sector, and on a large enough scale that in the end, the banks and S&Ls rescued through federal insurance payouts represented a higher share of the nation's deposits than the institutions forced to close their doors in the economic hurricane of the late 1920s and early 1930s!

The crash of the 1930s had been revitalizing, in a bloody and purgative sort of way, because many of the too-adventuresome financial organizations and techniques of the twenties failed or were forced to change. Part of the reform impetus came from stock and asset values crashing, but part also reflected the new political and regulatory climate of the 1930s. Wayward financiers became whipping boys. The bailout of the early 1990s, however, followed a different script. Financed by massive borrowing and further enlargement of the federal deficit, it served largely to hold harmless bank investors and assets. The result was not just to prop up the stock market but to allow it to keep hitting new highs, while Wall Street firms achieved new record earnings with new products, services, and speculative devices. The private-sector architects of the 1980s bubble, in short, survived to retain their influence over the nation's finances. As a result, what we will call the financial economy, with its pinstriped cowherds, megabyte marauders, and derivative instruments able to speculate on everything short of war with Mars, continued to eat the real economy, in which ordinary breadwinners who once relied on the American Dream of a home, a job, and a pension faced the future with churning stomachs. As Chapter 4 will examine in depth, reining in the Frankenstein Monster of the financial economy has become another central challenge of the 1990s. From municipal disasters like that of Orange County, California, to global waves of currency speculation, derivatives and electronic speculation have already justified this book's skepticism.

It is this destructive convergence of forces — signs of national decline in the United States, along with political fortification by interest groups and financialization of the economy — that casts doubt on turn-of-the-century U.S. vitality. Yet just as Americans must face the prospect of major changes in government and politics now that the Cold War is over, so do citizens in most of the other leading economic powers, from Britain, Germany, and Japan to Canada, France, and Italy. Upheaval is everywhere. The surprise success stories of the early twenty-first century will be the Western nations that rise to the challenge.

A common hardening of the arteries is particularly evident in the Anglo-Saxon nations, where practices that came to dominate the world in the nineteenth and twentieth centuries are now losing their world sway. The risk to the United States is substantial. But as we will see in Chapters 7 and 8, the

United States has physical dimensions and renewal possibilities that the earlier great economic powers, Holland and Britain, did not. Thus, it remains plausible to offer a blueprint by which the United States can revitalize its political and governmental systems, and these suggestions are set forth in the concluding chapter, in the same form as they were in 1994. There are two sets of proposals: one sweeping and quasi-revolutionary, the second more moderate and achievable, but less remedial.

I should underscore that this book is written with only a small infusion of Washington insidership and a much larger commitment to Washington outsidership. My interest in politics over three decades has not been one of sympathy for the quiet collegiality of America's richest metropolitan area or empathy with its institutions and maneuvers, but one of commitment to the populist processes of American electoral realignment and renewal. As set forth during twenty-five years in *The Emerging Republican Majority*, *The Politics of Rich and Poor*, and *Boiling Point*, these forces surge up from the grass roots or they do not come at all. Washington, in a nutshell, must periodically be attacked and purged, not simply enjoyed and fortified by a capital establishment — and this, as much as anything else, is what has gone wrong with U.S. politics in the forty years that I have been studying it. The time for another wringing out is at hand. The Republican "Contract" has only a small overlap with what this volume suggests.

Not a few politicians and ideologists insist that we don't have to worry about the future because "This is the United States." This is dangerous nonsense. First, because no country is immune from history. Second, because this country's unique traditions and circumstances may make successful change possible if Americans move quickly enough. This is the essential thrust of the book's conclusion. The 1990s must be the decade of action, not some vague time in the future. The previous nineties — the 1790s, then the 1890s — were also decades in which popular democracy rallied against special interests and changed history. There is, admittedly, a danger in overromanticizing America's revolutionary past as the source of national renewal mechanisms. The genius of American politics and government, perfected in the era of steamboats and wildcat banks and already middle-aged when Alexander Graham Bell invented the telephone, may not work in the era of tele-democracy and megabyte money. Even so, the question of whether old political renewal methods can come alive again in some kind of new U.S. political revolution and whether the capital of these United States can be reclaimed for the people from the interests may be the biggest test of American democratic institutions since the Civil War — and perhaps since the Revolution itself.

Kevin P. Phillips
Bethesda, Maryland
May 1, 1995

Acknowledgments

NO BOOK has only a single architect, and this one is no exception. Particular thanks go to my agent, Bill Leigh, who helped *Arrogant Capital* take shape not just as a political concept but as a book idea, and to my editor at Little, Brown, Jim Silberman, who saw the book in the idea and helped it grow. In my office, important research and word processing assistance was performed by Michelle Klein, Rebecca Palmer, and Liz Abruzzino, and at Little, Brown, Miki Packer provided assistance on almost every dimension.

And finally, within the fabled Washington Beltway, there are tens of thousands of residents — some well known — who share the anger at the nation's capital felt in the hinterland. To those who quietly helped or provided encouragement, my thanks.

Part I

The End of Self-Renewal
in Washington
and in American Politics

Chapter One

Washington and the Late-Twentieth-Century Failure of American Politics

When all government, domestic and foreign, in little as in great things, shall be drawn to Washington as the center of all power, it will render powerless the checks provided of one government on another, and will become as venal and oppressive as the government from which we separated.

— THOMAS JEFFERSON, *1821*

In this atmosphere, politicians of both political parties have sensed an opportunity. Everyone wants to run against Washington, the Establishment, the insiders, and most of all, Congress.

— WILLIAM SCHNEIDER,
political analyst, 1992

THE WASHINGTON BELTWAY, officially Interstate 495, was begun in 1959 and completed in 1964. For another two decades or so it was simply a ribbon of concrete, a fast road from Bethesda to Alexandria or Falls Church and nothing more. But by the early 1980s "inside the Beltway" started to become a piece of political sarcasm — a biting shorthand for the self-interest and parochialism of the national governing class. Aerospace engineers in Los Angeles and taxi drivers in New York understood well enough. What flourished inside the Beltway, like orchids in a hothouse, was power, hubris, and remoteness from the ordinary concerns of ordinary people.

And those concerns were mounting. By the early 1990s three decades of evidence that U.S. politics and government didn't work — from Lyndon Johnson and Vietnam, Richard Nixon and Watergate, through endless petty congressional scandals to George Bush and a blind presidency defeated by a recession it couldn't understand — had brought Americans to the brink of mass disillusionment. Cities were falling apart, debt was rampant, taxes on the middle class were setting records, and the people profiting were the manipulators, the elites in and around government, finance, and the professions. The leaders of the most powerful government in the world were unable to keep crime from reaching new dimensions: car-jackings at busy urban intersections, random shootings, gang wars in dull, white middle-class suburbs where young people faced a downhill future, foreign terrorist bombings in downtown New York City. Jails in America held almost a million criminals at an annual cost of $22 billion, more than the whole annual budget of the government of the United States until World War II.

It was an unfortunate historical first. Never before had so many Washington regimes for so long proved so incapable of relieving the fears and concerns of the citizenry. The election of Bill Clinton as president in 1992 provided only a brief reassurance. Surveys taken one hundred days after his inauguration found Clinton's ratings weaker than those of any other newly elected president since the beginning of opinion polls, and although he recovered, public doubts lingered.

Disillusionment pervaded the survey data. Even though most Americans were still pleased with their own lives in their private worlds, it was the failure of leadership that worried them. The fear was that the twenty-first century would belong to others, to the economic samurai of Japan or the busy tigers of Korea and Taiwan, and that America's children might not live as well as their parents. National disillusionment with Washington and politics was a staple as the 1990s unfolded. A poll for *Fortune* magazine in late 1990 found opinion ripe for revolt against the rich. In 1991 the Ohio-based Kettering Foundation charted voter outrage that American democracy was being blocked by a Washington "iron triangle" of politicians, interest groups, and journalists. Then, in 1993, the Boston-based Americans Talk Issues Foundation reported Americans so contemptuous of Congress that one third of those sampled thought the offices might as well be auctioned to the highest bidder, while half thought members of Congress could be chosen randomly from a list of eligible voters. Alan Kay, the group's chairman, was stunned: "I don't think I've ever tested any ideas that were so extreme." By the end of 1993, Democratic pollster Celinda Lake reported that 57 percent of Americans thought Washington was controlled by lobbyists and special interests, up nineteen points from two years earlier. And as the graph on the next page also shows, a mere 19 percent of Americans trusted Washington to do what is right all or most of the time.

This frustration wasn't just coincidence. Much of it grew out of something more serious — an aging of America and its institutions, the historical equivalent of arteries clogging up. However, the Washington establishment couldn't accept this, especially the role of the capital city as the political circulatory system's most dangerous clot. Instead, most Washington opinion molders embraced a particularly delusionary and deceptive pretense — that the electorate was only temporarily disaffected, that no historical crisis was involved, that the disarray in Washington, the party system, and the process of government was little more than a matter of "gridlock." The nation's capital would work again when the presidency and Congress were in the hands of the same party and cooperation prevailed.

This interpretation also had other pillars. Election-year criticism of Washington, the argument went, dated back to the city's founding. The grass roots had always grumbled, and the Republic prospered anyway. But in reality, what we have been watching *is* new: a deep-seated anger focused on Washington *in its own right.* As we will see, the real targets of the national watershed elections of earlier times were the sectional and ideological elites — the coastal bankers, then the Southern slaveocrats, and later the Republican business and financial elites — who had used politics to win command of a capital city that was little more than a parade ground for power rooted elsewhere. Win the election, seize the open capital. Even as late as 1964–68, the Republicans under Barry Goldwater, Richard Nixon, and Ronald Reagan lambasted the "Eastern Establishment" of limousine liberals, a runaway judiciary, the New York foundations, the media elite, and remote

National Opinion of Washington: A Portrait in Contempt

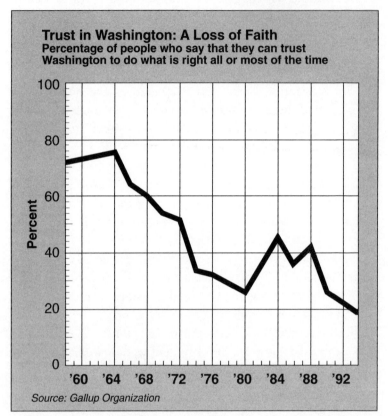

Trust in Washington: A Loss of Faith
Percentage of people who say that they can trust Washington to do what is right all or most of the time

Source: Gallup Organization

January 1994: Nineteen percent trust in Washington all or most of the time.

Public Opinion of Who Controls Washington

Which one of the following do you think really controls the federal government in Washington?

	May 1991	December 1993
The President	8%	6%
Democrats in Congress	19	16
Republicans in Congress	10	5
Lobbyists and Special Interests	38	57

Source: Mellman, Lazarus, Lake for U.S. News & World Report

bureaucrats. Washington was part of it, to be sure, and a useful bogeyman, but office seekers still saw Washington as a city where authority was mostly derivative. The American presidency reflected popular sovereignty: the will of voters. Jefferson's revolutions at the ballot box would work again — or so we believed until, slowly, we learned better. The Washington that now approaches the twenty-first century is an interest-group fortress, essentially unconquered by the public since the walls and turrets began rising after World War II.

Washington and the Workability of U.S. Political Revolutions

Yet entrenched Washington cannot rest easily. No other Western electorate confronts its established seat of government with so deep a skepticism that goes back over two centuries. Poetry and prose may commemorate the rights of free-born Englishmen, but they had no say in approving London as their capital. Americans, by contrast, were arguing over seats of government and condemning official arrogance even before the Revolution. They wore suspicion of the ruling classes like a cockade, urging that colonial capitals be moved from plantation, merchant, or ship-owner country closer to the frontier and its democratic values.

In the last years of the War of Independence and for a decade thereafter, state after state heatedly discussed where its lawmakers would locate. Or where they could be trusted to reside without cozying up to the interests and forgetting the average citizen. New York, after hastening its officials out of a Manhattan recaptured by the British, finally settled its capital in Albany. The Commonwealth of Pennsylvania moved its seat west to Harrisburg on the brawling Scotch-Irish frontier. Virginia transferred its government from colonial Williamsburg, haunted by its royal governor's palace, to upcountry Richmond. Both Carolinas, in turn, shifted their capitals from coastal New Bern and fashionable Charleston to the raw, new piedmont towns of Raleigh and Columbia.

Discussion was even more heated on where to put the capital of the new United States. Would there be a single seat of power — or two separate ones to share responsibility? Would it be in a major city, tainted by urbanity and wealth, or would it be in a small place, closer to the people? Would it be in the North or South, or in between? And where was "in between" — along the Delaware River between New Jersey and Pennsylvania, along Pennsylvania's Susquehanna River, or somewhere on the banks of the Potomac between Maryland and Virginia?

In 1790, Treasury Secretary Alexander Hamilton resolved the issue by striking a bargain with Southerners in Congress: if they would support him on a key financial issue, he would agree to placing the new capital on the Potomac River, well into the South. The federal establishment would move there in 1800.

If seats of government were so easily changeable in the United States, one reason was the fundamental changeability of government itself — drawing its legitimacy from "the People," as the noun was capitalized in the Declaration of Independence. Thomas Jefferson went so far as to say that revolutions are as necessary in politics as storms in the physical world; and forty years after he wrote the Declaration, he restated his view in a more peaceful but time-specific context:

> Each generation has a right to choose for itself the form of government it believes most promotive of its own happiness. . . . A solemn opportunity of doing this every 19 or 20 years should be provided by the constitution.

Without this flexibility, he warned, frustration would breed force, and then an endless circle of oppressions, rebellions, and reformations would follow. Jefferson's once-a-generation restructuring of government was never inserted into the U.S. Constitution, but the succession of national political watersheds from 1800 to 1932 served essentially the same purpose. In 1800, 1828, 1860, 1896, and 1932, five "electoral revolutions" were attempted. Four succeeded. As long as Washington stayed small, no citadel on the Potomac could stand athwart change.

In the early years, winning and losing presidential contenders openly described their confrontations as revolutions, claiming the prized mantle of 1776. Years after Jefferson was elected in 1800, he contended that "the Revolution of 1800 was as real a revolution in the principles of our government as 1776 was in its form." The new president's intention had certainly been bold enough — not just to beat the incumbent Federalists, but to destroy their future political effectiveness and create a new party system. The new seat of government was not an obstacle. Jefferson's capital included just 599 houses, a handful of government buildings, and several dozen warehouses, hostelries, taverns, and retail emporia. Pennsylvania Avenue, the main link between the White House and the Capitol, was "a streak of mud newly cut through woods and alder swamps."

By Andrew Jackson's inauguration in 1829, the population had risen to almost forty thousand, including several thousand local federal patronage holders. But the half-empty city, sneered at by foreign visitors, provided almost no resistance of its own to the incoming swarm of muddy-booted Westerners in Jackson's coalition of outsiders. The campaign of 1828 had been an ugly one, and the term "revolution" was used almost as readily as in 1800. As inauguration day approached, Margaret Bayard Smith, a social arbiter, noted that she had never seen Washington so gloomy, its drawing rooms so empty, dark, and dismantled. Another observer likened the arrival of the Jacksonians to "the inundation of Northern barbarians into

Rome. . . . Strange faces filled every public place and every face seemed to bear defiance on its brow." And Daniel Webster said, "I never saw anything like it before. They really think the country is to be rescued from some dreadful danger." After their hero was sworn in, this same crowd boiled through the White House, smashing china and glasses and forcing dignitaries to escape through the windows. Jackson's tenure continued to imitate revolution. Looking back in 1837, Henry Clay — no Jackson admirer — allowed that the Tennessean "had swept over the government, during the last eight years, like a tropical tornado."

America's third great electoral upheaval — and once again, few politicians were in doubt about its significance — came in 1860, when a 39 percent minority of voters, mostly Northerners, elected Abraham Lincoln president. No state or county within forty miles of Washington gave the nominee of the new Republican party serious support. Soon thereafter, eleven Southern states seceded from the Union and launched the Confederacy. This sequence made the Republican political takeover of Washington highly unusual: Most of the Southerners, civilian and military, who dominated the city during the Democratic 1850s, were leaving or had left as the Republicans arrived. In particular, Southerners had come to control the army and navy, but most of them decamped. Otherwise, the change of power in 1861 might not have been so easy.

At the opening of the Civil War, Washington *was* a Southern city. After deciding to put the capital on the Potomac, Congress let George Washington choose exactly where, and after various inspections, he chose the southernmost site just across from his own plantation. Yet, ultimately, it made little difference. Maryland did not secede in 1861, and thus it did not trap the federal capital inside a larger, extended Confederacy. The exodus of many Southern military officers, senators, congressmen, and senior government officials left society hostesses to sulk in their parlors but no meaningful political establishment to fight the transfer of power. Besides, although the city had grown to a population of sixty thousand, it remained visibly incomplete. Henry Adams recalled that "as in 1800 and 1850, so in 1860, the same rude colony was camped in the same forest, with the same unfinished Greek temples for workrooms, and sloughs for roads." Pigs were common in the streets, and disgusted congressmen and officials joined foreigners in cataloging other deficiencies that ranged from oppressive summer humidity to inadequate rail connections. It was not a national mecca.

Let me underscore: to describe the elections of 1800, 1828, and 1860 as revolutions was and is no great overstatement. Jefferson reused the revolutionary words of his youth too freely in later years, as even admirers admitted. But for early and mid-nineteenth-century Americans, the confrontation of 1775–83 remained a powerful living memory, and the founding fathers themselves had been earlier influenced by the two successful revolutions of English history in the seventeenth century.[1] Far more than now, Americans of Jefferson's day — or, for that matter, Americans of Jefferson Davis's day — were taken with revolution. It was a national heritage. Two of the first three U.S. political watersheds even flirted with violence — in 1801, when angry Jeffersonians, worried that their presidential victory of the previous November might be stolen, threatened to bring in the militias of politically friendly Pennsylvania and Virginia, and again in early 1861, when defeated Southern Democrats, still holding the executive branch, pondered whether to try to block Lincoln's inauguration.

The next great watershed, coming in 1896, had an important difference: it was a revolution *avoided*, not *achieved*. The agricultural depression that followed the Civil War inflamed the farm states and the West to rise against the industrial and financial dominion of the East by nominating William Jennings Bryan of Nebraska on a fusion ticket of Democrats and Populists. There was an echo of Jackson in the air, as Cleveland factory owners and Boston bankers worried that another radical hour might be at hand. Clarence Darrow, who would mock Bryan two decades later in Tennessee's famous Scopes trial, announced his support of the Great Commoner in "a year in which we are to fight the greatest battle of modern times between the plutocrats and the producers." "Most of my friends think Bryan will be elected," noted former secretary of state John Hay, "and we shall be hanged to the lampions of Euclid Avenue." Besides the Democrats and the Populists, a half dozen radical minor parties also endorsed Bryan. On the other side, Mark Hanna, the Republicans' chief strategist, all but tithed Wall Street and the U.S. manufacturing community. By election day, the GOP had raised and spent $16 million, unheard of in that era (and four or five times what the Democrats could command). Some businesses in the Great Lakes region and the Northeast published notices to employees not to show up if Bryan won; the factories and mills would be shutting down. After the election, allegations of stolen votes and falsified counts were widespread.

By 1896, Washington was no longer a place that scarcely mattered. The last serious attempt to relocate the capital — to St. Louis in 1870 — had failed because of opposition by President Grant. The hundreds of Civil War battles fought from Antietam to Fredericksburg had given the capital and the Potomac Valley greater meaning for Americans through songs, memories, and inscriptions on the tombstones of fathers, brothers, and husbands from Maine to Texas. The city was also bigger, some two hundred thousand people in the 1890 census, and the government buildings were complete. Henry Adams's open Greek temples now had telephones as well as completed roofs, and the directory of government was sounding more modern, with the Interior Department and the Interstate

Commerce Commission. Yet Washington was still not an *independent* power center. Both parties concentrated their campaign headquarters, their money, and their effort into the Midwest and three swing states in the Northeast. As the political armies of 1896 deployed, this time the Potomac was far from the fighting.

Was this yet another of Thomas Jefferson's revolutions taking the form of a watershed election? I think so — despite the failure of Bryan's presidential bid. In the end, he could not win beyond the South and much of the West, losing narrowly in the nation as a whole with 47 percent to McKinley's 51 percent. Yet when statisticians took a second look, they advised that Bryan's losing vote was larger than that of any previous presidential victor — and a shift of just 19,346 ballots in California, Oregon, Kentucky, North Dakota, West Virginia, and Indiana would have elected him. Over the next two decades, much of what Bryan and the Populists sought became law. Once again, the storms unleashed reinvigorated the U.S. political system.

The last of the five electoral watersheds able to tame Washington and gain political revolution status came in 1932. By this time, however, the American Republic was a hundred and fifty years old, and presidents no longer claimed the legacy of 1776. Franklin D. Roosevelt in some ways emerged as a mild revolutionary, at least of the American electoral sort, in his successful effort to overcome the Great Depression and cement the 1932 election as a Democratic watershed. Certainly by 1936 most upper-class Americans disliked him as their tax rates soared and inheritances shrank. However, in a way that could not be said of Jackson or Bryan, FDR was also a conservative — himself a man of the upper classes staving off a larger revolution, the kind of upheaval Oklahomans or Carolinians associated with Karl Marx, not with Patrick Henry or prairie political gospel-singers like Bryan.

Another kind of transformation was also under way in the nation's capital. When Roosevelt came to town in 1933, it held half a million people and a growing federal establishment, even though the future power structure, to which we will turn in Chapter 2 — the Permanent Washington able to thumb its nose at grassroots anger — was only a vague glimmer on the horizon. The neighboring Virginia and Maryland counties of still-voteless Washington had contributed two- and three-to-one Democratic majorities to the 1932 wave that swept out Herbert Hoover. And even in 1940, commentator David Brinkley recalls, the District of Columbia was "a town and government entirely unprepared to take on the global responsibilities suddenly thrust on it. The executive branch, despite its expansion during the New Deal, remained relatively small, its employees more concerned with egg prices and post office construction than with the war clouds gathering in Europe and Asia."

That would change, and with a roar heard around the world. Washington and the nation were about to ride a crest that would be exhilarating, enriching, and uplifting, yet also dangerous. The unique genius of American politics, proven over a hundred and fifty years, would be put at risk.

The Endangered Genius of American Politics

Bloodless revolutions have been the key. Some academicians contend that U.S. politics has an unusual cyclical quality, which is true. Electoral cycles *have* played an important role in guiding America across the continent and into world leadership. However, to describe these ups and downs alongside the dry-bones rhythms of global wheat prices, Venetian trade routes, or capitalist development misses the point. American politics has a star-spangled singularity.

If this genius is now in trouble, which it is, then a vital

transmission fluid is draining out of the American system. During the period from 1800 to 1932, the American people did something no other nation's population has ever done — they directed, roughly once a generation, revolutionary changes in the nation's political culture and economic development through a series of critical presidential elections. It only sounds commonplace; as a successfully executed politics, it was *extraordinary*. Britain's elections during the nineteenth century were much less democratic and less influential, and no other major European nation bears mentioning. On the Continent, violent revolution remained the usual agent of change.

The United States, by contrast, took the most successful revolution of the modern world and continued its spirit, especially during the nineteenth century, through the (relatively) peaceful pattern of insurrections fought in polling places instead of in the streets and on the barricades. By institutionalizing the American Revolution in electoral upheavals, the Jeffersons and Jacksons helped keep it going; so did the conservatives, who called the people a great beast and saw blood-red banners in any agitated assembly.

The result, up until the mid–twentieth century, was that Americans could plausibly look to the watershed or revolutionary election to substitute for actual *revolution*, which became deplorable and un-American — as patriotically unacceptable to Boston Irishmen (whose cousins were enthusiastic revolutionaries across the Atlantic) as to the suburban Anglo-Saxon clubwomen calling themselves Daughters of the American Revolution. The national impact of these revolutionary elections was increased by how long they lasted and how deep they went. Since 1800 the party that has won one of these watershed elections has gone on to hold the White House for most of the next generation. The Jeffersonians were in occupation for twenty-four of twenty-eight years between 1800 and 1828; the Jacksonian Democrats for twenty-four of thirty-two years between 1828 and 1860; the Republicans for twenty-eight of thirty-six years between 1860 and 1896; the Republicans for twenty-eight of thirty-six years between 1896 and 1932; and the Democrats for twenty-eight of thirty-six years between 1932 and 1968. The twenty years out of twenty-four for which the Republicans held the White House from 1968 to 1992 is half a continuation of this pattern, half a crippled variation to which we will return.

Setting in motion these eras of accomplishment has been a genius of U.S. politics. No other major Western nations can point to a similar succession of generation-long presidential regimes of one party lending themselves, in orderly and usually peaceable fashion, to define one national era after another: Jefferson and consolidation of the new nation; Jackson and the rise of the trans-Appalachian west; Lincoln and the era of the Civil War and Reconstruction; the post-1896 Republicans and the emergence of a modern industrial nation; and Franklin D. Roosevelt's ability to combine the New Deal and America's emergence as a world power. Party political tenures or groupings of prime ministers elsewhere provide no match; the parallel significance, aside from the occasional Bismarck or Churchill, is in the reigns of monarchs or in the sweep of royal dynasties.

The watersheds also had other achievements. Geographically, they usually established some new supremacy — of the coast, of the frontier, of the North, or of the cities. Needless to say, such watersheds rearranged the locus of power, shuffled regional elites, and changed national directions in ways that less deep-acting elections elsewhere could not manage. Watersheds also promoted different national cultures. Usually they began as eras of the common man, of log cabins, or of forgotten Americans. Each upheaval set up the framework for a new elite, but then the next watershed would come along.

Each generational redefinition also performed surgery on

clogging arteries in the U.S. party system. Sometimes a party moved toward the political graveyard or a new one emerged (1800, 1828, 1860); sometimes third parties helped key constituencies to shuttle between parties (the Populists of 1896, the George Wallace supporters of 1968); less frequently, the two major parties simply realigned themselves (1932). Darwinian survival-of-the-fittest processes were at work. At least through the 1930s, watersheds meant the chance for the two-party system to reinvent itself and to point Washington in the new directions. No Washington infrastructure was big enough or sufficiently dug in to reject the electorate's pointing.

By the end of the 1960s, however, one was big enough, and it deemed unacceptable a transfer of national power to the 57 percent of Americans who had voted for Richard Nixon and George Wallace in 1968 or to the combined 61 percent who supported Nixon in 1972. Part of the hesitation involved the unacceptability of Nixon the individual politician — and ultimately, of course, of Nixon the lawbreaker. By itself, this reluctance, even loathing, on the part of defeated capital insiders was nothing new. The Federalists of 1800, the Adamsites of 1828, the Southerners of 1860 had all felt as hostile to those unseating them; in 1896, some fearful Republican businessmen and financiers talked about not accepting a Bryan victory; and the political losers of 1932 within two to four years were using words like "fascism" and "dictatorship" to describe the presidency of Franklin Roosevelt. Losers' outrage was old stuff. The difference after 1969 involved two new circumstances: Factor number one was the enormous enlargement and entrenchment of the capital from the 1930s to the 1960s, which I will describe in Chapter 2 and which had finally created a governing elite large enough to stymie an ambitious new president. Factor number two, of course, was the vulnerability the new GOP president brought on himself by turning to political espionage to overcome the intra-Washington

Nixon's

opposition — and being caught. Nixon became the first president forced to resign.

So the electoral revolution of 1968 succeeded at the polls, but it became the first of its kind to fail in Washington. It would be twenty years before the Kettering Foundation survey found Americans describing the Washington complex of politicians, interest groups, and media as an "iron triangle." But there was at least some tactical precedent in the opponents that the new Republicans occupying the White House found blocking them in 1969–70. No one will ever agree on how much democracy was thwarted or advanced during the Watergate years 1972–74. Some of each, presumably. But for our purposes, it is an unnecessary debate. What is clear is that a Republican presidential watershed, one ultimately producing GOP control of the presidency for twenty of twenty-four years between 1968 and 1992, was crippled or crippled itself in its early critical stages. Thus the Democrats held the House of Representatives for twenty-four years out of twenty-four, the Senate for eighteen out of twenty-four. As government divided, special interests multiplied. The Permanent Washington created during the quarter century after World War II, far from being dislodged, grew faster than ever; the theory of Washington as a neutral parade ground for presidential election victors collapsed.

But something more was happening: Henry Adams's raw and empty capital was changing into the Washington of the imperial presidency, the imperial Congress, and an interest-group explosion that linked and also obstructed them. And the genius of American politics was becoming no more than a phrase from books of a happier era.

Good Countries Can Have Bad Capitals

The basis for hope, to which we now turn, is that great nations and their capitals do not decay or atrophy at the same speed.

Capitals rot first, and the more completely that they are citadels of political, governmental, and interest-group inbreeding — as with Washington — the larger the mushrooming effect and the greater the psychological distance of the governmental elites from the rest of the country. For a people with Americans' traditions and sensitivities to the abuses of capital cities, the decade of the 1990s is still time enough for reform.

The evidence of past leading world powers, from Greece and Rome down through Hapsburg Spain and eighteenth-century Holland, is that bloated and unresponsive capital cities tend to get that way while the rest of the nation is still vital politically, with the capitals becoming part of the decline process. As we will see in Chapter 2, Washington is already starting to resemble them. What's encouraging is that such capitals can be — and several times have been — reformed or moved, which can have a beneficial effect. The caveat, though, is that great powers have rarely reformed or relocated capitals once the latter have entrenched and become major drains on the rest of the nation.

Logic and history both argue that nations do not age uniformly within themselves. The eastern part of the Roman Empire, based in Constantinople, took up the lead as the western part declined. The downhill slide of the British Empire between the world wars and afterward didn't stop the growth of London suburbia. American railroads declined in the 1960s as U.S. economic power reached its twentieth-century peak; the U.S. computer software industry soared in the late 1980s and 1990s as the U.S. flag was being lowered at military bases from Spain to the Philippines.

In nations, the political and economic aging processes are not the same and do not go at the same pace. Great economic powers have often grown in waves — early emphasis on agriculture, shipbuilding, fishing, or mining, then a move to manufacturing, then a shift away from manufacturing to financial services. Major cities are free to shift their roles: like Pittsburgh going from fur post to steel center and to medical complex.

For the political nerve centers of nations, the aging process is different. Scientists might find parallels in the physical world. Bridges ice before roads. Hearts fail before capillaries. The basic political evolution in a great power or empire is similar: the general public — in modern countries, the electorate — doesn't spend much time thinking about politics, so that the nation's basic hopes, traditions, and myths tend to live on. Capital cities, by contrast, are humid cultures for the intensive, tropical growth of political forces, schemes, bureaucracies, parasites, and interests — and for greed and institutional corruption. This occurs even before the capital city takes on international status, but the effects are five to ten times as great where a global power center is involved. The examination in Chapter 2 of the evolution of Washington's parasite culture since the end of World War II will also look at previous great-power capitals and how they, too, played rot-at-the-core to their nations' slowly fading greatness. However, because Washington has gone wrong in an accelerated hothouse time frame, the rest of the United States still has its ability to generate grassroots activism and reformist revolution that can force the capital to heel.

Cynics will scoff: this panders to Middle America; it upholds the myth of American exceptionalism while sidestepping the realities of national decline and ignoring the hard truth that Washington simply mirrors the greed, fatigue, and apathy of an equally self-centered public. Yes and no. Yes, there are powerful signs of decline, and there are also many ways in which the special-interest emergence and entrenchment of Washington does reflect the civic fatigue, entitlement smugness, and special-interest tendencies of ordinary Americans.

More than a hundred and fifty years have passed since Alexis de Tocqueville described the penchant of our citizens for political and civic associations. For much of U.S. history, that has been a strength. But now what has always been a vital force at the grass roots — willingness to join together in volunteer causes or in the Masons, Elks, and Ohio League of Insurance Agents — is becoming a source of blockage at the national level.

On the other hand, no, it doesn't pander to Middle America to say that the remoteness of Washington has been intensifying, that the city's parallels with previous bloated capitals are disturbing, and that Washington, like others before, serves as a kind of breeder for congestive disorders in the nation's politics, culture, and economics. Besides, warnings come from more than history books. Similar complaints are echoing around the world, in current publications and broadcasts describing abuses, arrogances, and parasitism from Tokyo and Ottawa to Rome and Paris. Out-of-touch capital cities are a global problem.

And so are the obstacles to reform. In this era of capitalism, the market forces ascendant in commerce do not apply in politics. Automobile companies and pharmaceutical firms have competitors, but capital cities do not. Most of their functions are reserved for government. In the United States, the two-party system itself enjoys elaborate, codified systems of legal preference, preferred ballot access, postal subsidies, and other dollops of public financial assistance. From electoral cradle to political grave, national officeholders here and abroad are coddled with the best medical care and pensions. And when the officials of Washington or another national capital run out of money, they can borrow it — or they can simply print more of it. When a capital city is also the governmental seat of the world's leading power, the interested parties and preference seekers flocking in are almost limitless — and so, often, is the hubris of the city's officeholders, functionaries, and backstage arbiters. It is, literally, parasites' heaven. Major reform is possible in theory, but minimal in reality. As part of the process of entrenchment and decay, great-power capitals frequently continue to enlarge and prosper, their residents hiring, consulting, favoring, and wining and dining one another, long after the tides of national decline have become apparent. The air does not go out of the capital balloon until its damage has been done.

The capitals of past leading world powers have always produced critics or observers who could see what was happening, and at a point — usually when it was starting to be too late — reform programs were offered. In Rome. In early seventeenth-century Spain. In eighteenth-century Holland. In pre-World War I Britain. None of these efforts succeeded in reversing history, as we shall see.

The challenge for the United States of the 1990s is to break the pattern. Fear of national political and economic decline has aroused the public, if not the elites. Demand for reforming, even purging, the nation's capital is enormous. The national election process has become a call to arms. This decade has seen presidential candidates liken a sitting president of the United States to King George III and call their insurgent supporters "minutemen"; the independent who ran for president in 1992 is a billionaire so immersed in the tradition of Anglo-American political upheaval that he owns a copy of the Magna Carta as well as some land on which Philadelphia's Independence Hall sits. If history is any guide, though, it is difficult for a great nation to reach back two hundred years into its past and resume youthful vigor and political vitality. None ever has.

On the other hand, no other country has a record of being so suspicious of its capital and political elites — or a record of so successfully, for so many years, institutionalizing its revolutionary origins in a continuing wave of national political upheavals. This, above all, frames the critical question: can we mount another such upheaval, this time against a seat of government and an interest-group-crippled politics that is beginning to mock the two-hundred-year-old precepts of American democracy?

Chapter Two

Imperial Washington: The Power and the Glory — And the Betrayal of the Grass Roots

Twelve days before the Inauguration, we may be able to predict the fate of Bill Clinton's promise to free American government from the grip of special interests: Broken by Day One.

— *NEW YORK TIMES,*
January 1993

If ever this vast country is brought under a single government, it will be one of the most extensive corruption, indifferent and incapable of a wholesome care over so wide a spread of surface. This will not be borne, and you will have to choose between reformation and revolution. If I know the spirit of this country, the one or the other is inevitable. Before the canker is become inveterate, before its venom has reached so much of the body politic as to get beyond control, remedy should be applied.

— THOMAS JEFFERSON, *1822*

CAPITAL CITIES that become world centers have usually managed to fulfill Jefferson's fears of venality, which he drew from the examples of Greece and Rome, as well as from the London of King George III. For America's seat of government, though, the transformation has only been recent. Through midcentury, its performance still honored its marble halls, granite statues, and alabaster shrines.

Imperial capitals don't become notorious until they display wealth and develop serious, parasitic elites, not true of Washington until it came of age in the late 1960s and 1970s. The jokes about its Northern charm and Southern efficiency began to fade; its old pattern of open racial segregation became covert. Expensive stores from New York and elsewhere opened local branches. French restaurants spread into the suburbs, replacing fried oysters with *moules provençals*. The staffs of the White House and Congress exploded. The influx of lawyers, corporate representatives, and trade associations began to turn K Street — "Gucci Gulch," as it would soon be named — into the leading interest-group bazaar of the Western World. In 1969, Congresswoman Edith Green of Oregon, ranking Democrat on the House Education and Labor Committee, described a pattern of making public issues into private opportunities that would repeat in future decades: "Probably our most enduring monument to the problem of poverty has been the creation of a poverty industry. There are more than

100 companies in Washington, D.C., alone which specialize in studying and evaluating the poor and the programs that serve them." With each decade, the census promoted more Washington-area counties into the ranks of the nation's richest. By the 1990s no other part of the United States matched metropolitan Washington in per capita income — or matched its pomposity and abuse of power, if you listened to the average American in Duluth or Chattanooga.

This chapter will assess what has happened and its importance. Late-night television jokes about the capital city go beyond acid humor; the larger crisis of Washington and its wayward role within the United States is a crisis of effective government and politics. The emergence of overbearing, overstuffed seats of power has been a relentless historical warning for aging nations, and while other countries share some of this problem in the 1990s, the United States has the greatest urgency — and, unfortunately, probably the greatest obstacle.

The Crowning of Imperial Washington

Franklin Roosevelt finally brought Washington to the big time. On one hand, the New Deal pushed government into new activities from securities regulation to agricultural supports and home loan guarantees, increasing the number of federal employees in the area from 75,000 in March 1933 to 166,000 in 1940. The federal presence was looming larger. But it was the Second World War that gave the city its global preeminence. London, Berlin, Tokyo, and Moscow were largely or partly in rubble; Washington bestrode the world like a geopolitical colossus, yet also like a gangly teenager — growing awkwardly in every direction.

When the world gets a new political or commercial capital, that city usually experiences a major population spurt. Rome and London were exceptions in their days, growing into global prominence less abruptly. But seats of government in ancient Greece had boomed, and Madrid was little more than a fortress town in Castile until the fifteenth-century union of the Spanish crowns and the sixteenth-century rise of the Hapsburg Empire. Then the new imperial capital mushroomed from a population of 4,000 in 1530 to 35,000 in 1594 and at least 100,000 in the mid-1600s before fading again when the great days were over. Comparable increases came in Amsterdam and The Hague (the official seat) during the rise of the Netherlands. Ambition was the beacon light. Fortune seekers came — clerics, bureaucrats, refugees, penniless jobhunters, ambitious nephews and cousins of the powerful, ambassadors, bankers, money changers, and merchants. The magnetism of a great capital is hard to overstate.

So, too, in Washington from 1945 to the late 1960s. When architects were designing the huge Pentagon in 1941, a cautious Roosevelt suggested modifying the design so part of the building could become a storage facility, if necessary, when the war was over. For forty years, though, the war never really ended — and neither did Washington's expansion. The ongoing Cold War, heated up by combat in Korea and Indochina, kept the Pentagon humming and the ratio of gold braid rising. Over in Foggy Bottom, the personnel roster of the U.S. Department of State included 6,438 employees in 1940; 25,380 in 1950; and 39,603 in 1970. Global preeminence was one of the capital's prime jobs machines.

Yet if Washington was enlarging the staffs by which it looked outward to Vienna, Panama City, and Bangkok, practicality had also ballooned the political staffs by which Congress and the White House cultivated Brooklyn, Kansas City, and Boise. A new self-importance was everywhere. Back in McKinley's day, the president personally hired and paid the small White House domestic staff. On the first floor, only the dining room was closed to public visitors. Even in the 1930s, a motorist on Pennsylvania Avenue could drive under the White House portico to put up his convertible top in a rain shower. By 1950, although comparative numbers can be misleading, the White House staff had grown to over three hundred, and public access to the building was shrinking; by 1970, the place was a fortress.

Congressional staffs were growing even faster. In 1933, members of the House were allowed a staff of two persons and a total clerk-hire budget of only a few thousand dollars. By 1957 that had climbed to five aides for each member and $20,000; and by 1976, a total of fifteen assistants could be paid $255,000.[2] Individual staffs expanded just as rapidly in the Senate, as did committee and subcommittee staffs in both houses.* The combined overall staffs of the U.S. House and Senate soared from 1,425 persons in 1930 to 6,255 in 1960 and to 10,739 in 1970.

Such expansion soon overflowed the existing House and Senate office buildings, and additional ones were constructed. The Rayburn House Office Building, finished in 1964, was a ponderous concrete slab built to mirror the self-importance of former Wauwatosa city councilmen who had become guardians of the world. One critic suggested that Washington was launching a new architectural style: he called it "Early Mussolini."

The 1930s had brought new government "alphabet agencies" like the Civilian Conservation Corps and the Works Progress Administration, and the postwar years continued the trend. Between 1945 and 1970, four new federal departments

---

* In 1930 the various Senate and House committees, subcommittees, joint committees, and special committees had a combined staff of 285. By 1950 these units had 480 staffers; by 1970, 333 of them were manned by a staff of 1,700. No other legislature in the free world commanded such an elaborate support structure.

were created: not just the Department of Defense, which combined the old War Department and Navy Department, but also the Department of Health, Education and Welfare, the Department of Housing and Urban Development, and the Department of Transportation. By 1970 that expansion had raised the number of federal employees in metropolitan Washington to 327,000, up from 223,000 in 1950 and 73,000 in 1930.

Imperial analogies had more and more validity. The "imperial presidency," Arthur Schlesinger's apt coinage, became an indictment in the 1970s; the term "imperial Congress" rang accusingly in the 1980s. The global context also lent a laurel wreath or two. The United States was the new Rome: Pax Americana stretched from U.S. military bases in Britain, Germany, Spain, and Morocco eastward to Turkey, Ethiopia, and Arabia with greater pomp and power than Pax Romana had displayed seventeen hundred years earlier, although embarrassment in Vietnam was already bringing unacceptable talk of decline. Speculation that the slain John F. Kennedy might ultimately be remembered as the American Trajan, Rome's emperor at its zenith, was dismissed; the new Rome on the Potomac was only getting started.

The ballooning of federal employment, however, was nearly over. A more influential and better-paid second growth was now coming from private-sector lobbyists, association executives, lawyers, consultants, media, economists, and experts. Journalists earned their spurs as the Fourth Estate, lobbyists as the Fourth Branch of government, and so on. With this buildup, private enterprise was paying tribute to public power. As wave after affluent wave washed into the better neighborhoods and suburbs, the metropolitan-area population boomed from 908,000 in 1940 to 2,076,000 in 1960 and 2,861,000 in 1970. The first metropolitan suburban counties made their way onto the Census Bureau's envy list of the twenty with the nation's highest per capita incomes — Arlington, Virginia, and Montgomery, Maryland, qualified in 1960. Then three more Virginia jurisdictions, Fairfax, Falls Church, and Alexandria, made the 1970 list.

In one respect, that era's talk about "imperial" Washington was premature. The city's wealth, even more weighted with high-income professionals and more distant from the average American, would be much further advanced by the 1990s. Even by the 1960s, however, the U.S. capital, now also the de facto capital of the world, had become home to an unprecedentedly powerful elite that regarded itself, with some cause, as the nation's proven guardian class. Its largely Democratic senators, consuls, and tribunes bridled at the mere thought of turning over the White House, Congress, and the Supreme Court to the equivalent of Vandals, Huns, and Visigoths: Republican political outsiders from Long Island potato fields, Omaha chambers of commerce, and Orange County, California, GOP clubs that sent "Happy birthday" telegrams to Barry Goldwater.

All of which brings us to a critical transition: by the end of the 1960s, the political fluidity of 1800 to 1932 was gone. Three decades of national success had produced, for the first time, a capital elite large enough to challenge a political change that threatened its power. The continuing enlargement of Permanent Washington over the next quarter century would further confirm the trend's ultimate power, but it was probably far enough along in 1972. We can only say "probably." Because Watergate, too, played a role in undoing the Republicans, we can't know whether their antiestablishment upheaval could have succeeded without that scandal. Perhaps the Washington elite could have repulsed Nixon's transformation in any event, but perhaps not.

By 1972 Nixon was saying in speeches and, more bluntly, in private meetings that the "Liberal Establishment," having failed in both urban America and battle-torn Vietnam during the 1960s, should be replaced. Building a new establishment would be the objective of his second term. How far he could have moved, no one will ever know, because any possibility of upheaval was soon cut short by the foolish 1972 White House attempt to wiretap its foes at the Democratic National Committee headquarters and its devastating aftermath. Kindred tactics, illegitimate offspring of the imperial presidency, had already emerged under Democratic presidents Kennedy and Johnson. However, the Nixonites, who saw themselves embattled, even beleaguered, in a hostile city still controlled by opposition forces, took the politics of surveillance a fatal step further — into disaster. Democrats soon realized their opportunity, and in the summer of 1974 Nixon, weeks or months away from being removed from office, became the first U.S. president to resign.

As to whether Washington's Democratic elite, including bureaucrats, opinion molders, and leaders of Congress, worked to reverse the Republican electoral verdicts of 1968 and 1972, one thing can fairly be said: human nature would have made them want to try. If the Federalists of 1800 had commanded such resistance, or the Quincy Adams forces of 1828, they might have stymied the Jeffersonian and Jacksonian revolutions. And imagine if the Southerners who controlled Washington and the U.S. military back in 1860 had decided to fight politically rather than secede. By the Nixon years, the new size and clout of the capital made acceptance of expulsion especially difficult. Twenty thousand egos and careers were at stake, not the three or four thousand of 1932.

Besides, the new power elite so unhappy on Richard Nixon's inauguration day had especially prideful origins. This was an establishment unlike any other, built not just by the capital's coming of age but by America's. During the three decades after the Democrats took over in 1933, America climbed out of a deep economic depression to become the center of the mid-century world, and it was to the doorsteps of the Washington Democrats who had guided that climb that the world had come to beat a path. Here were the architects, gatekeepers, and chroniclers of the New Deal Democratic cycle: congressmen and ex-congressmen, lawyers, lobbyists, former ambassadors, deputy CIA directors, columnists, think-tank officials, and evening newscasters. Not all were Democrats, because the Washington establishment had a few green book pages of socially and ideologically acceptable Republicans — senators like Clifford Case of New Jersey and John Sherman Cooper of Kentucky, Eastern Republican lawyers and Ivy League investment bankers who had run the CIA or had been part of the bipartisan foreign policy of the 1940s, as well as others of an internationalist and collaborative bent. However, the Democratic predominance was overwhelming; even for the next two decades, commentators would joke about the difficulty of finding acceptable Republicans for dinner parties.

The Republicans this Washington establishment *especially* did not like were the GOP's dominant majority: the heirs of the regulars who had fought the New Deal, opposed U.S. involvement in World War II until Pearl Harbor, given little more than lip service to the civil rights movement of the 1960s, adorned their cars with anti–Supreme Court bumper stickers, and criticized the failing war in Vietnam with a blunt "Win or get out." Probably 75 percent of the Americans who voted for Nixon in 1968 shared at least one or two of those disagreeable views; the 13 percent of those who preferred George Wallace in 1968 (and then largely flocked to Nixon in 1972) were even more belligerent. The possibility of another electoral revolution was in the air — and fashionable Washington didn't like it. This is the second, less-remembered, context of Watergate.

When Nixon resigned, the imperial presidency was over.

Less auspiciously, so was the late-twentieth-century ability of
the U.S. system to reinvent itself through successful electoral
revolutions. In retrospect, the watershed of 1968, which initi-
ated Republican control of the presidency for twenty of the
next twenty-four years, was shallow and incomplete. The
deeper Republican gains that took shape in 1972, especially in
the South, dissipated in 1973–74. Republicanism in the post-
Watergate years appeared to be a ship that was sinking, not
one spreading more sail. Yet because the Democrats had failed
in Vietnam, and because the public verdict that slowly
emerged over two more decades also took issue with their government spending, their permissive sociology, and their weak
foreign and military policies, the Republican post-1968 watershed had a historic dimension. That also is more clear in retrospect than it was at the moment. The Democratic Party paid
its price by being kept out of the White House, save for the
four-year term following Watergate, although its control was
left more or less uninterrupted in the states and in Congress.
The long-term result of this split, we can now see, was a destructive interest-group entrenchment in Washington and loss
of vitality in the nation's two-party system.

We will return to the party breakdown in Chapter 5, but
the election of 1968 produced more than the first watershed to
transfer control of the presidency without changing the guard
elsewhere in Washington. From a political science standpoint,
this in itself was a major change — and, of course, its causes
went beyond Watergate. The other damage was less obvious.
To divide government, setting the executive branch against the
legislative branch in the new Washington, also set the scene
for what turned out to be an enormously counterproductive
further buildup of interest groups and influence peddlers —
and a further confusion of government.

This had not happened in the late-nineteenth-century periods when one party often controlled Congress while the

other occupied the White House. But those were low-pressure
years close to the peak of *laissez-faire* in the United States,
when the federal government didn't have many functions.
During the activist 1970s, by contrast, intensified rivalry
spurred Congress to create new offices and capacities — from
a Congressional Budget Office to an Office of Technological
Assessment — to counter a hostile executive branch. Moreover, the labyrinthine qualities of divided government, from
the need to drop seeds of hoped-for legislation in several different decision-making bodies to the multiple procedures and
conferences required to guide provisions into the statute
books, only increased the unfolding opportunities for lawyers,
lobbyists, and interest groups. In contrast to the watersheds of
1800, 1828, 1860, or 1932, with their interest-group turn-
overs, Washington was not purged and revitalized by the election of 1968 and its aborted follow-up of 1972.

On the contrary. The Democratic establishment stayed, always commanding at least the House of Representatives as a
base (and usually the Senate, too). Meanwhile, Republican influence peddlers proliferated to deal with the executive branch.
What had already been an interest-group *expansion* soon became an *explosion*. And by the 1990s, the new layers of bipartisan lobbying and law firms in existence — "You take the
Senate, Harry, and I'll handle the Treasury" — had produced a
capital establishment big enough to dwarf the one that had
rolled back Nixon's threat a generation earlier. New presidents
would find the city an impossible nut to crack. Reform would
have to look for unguarded entryways and alleys.

This is the evolving crisis to which we now turn: the coming together of interest groups in an unprecedented magnitude and role in the nation's capital. Those circumstances only
added to Americans' contempt for their capital city, and then,
in the 1990s, it aroused their support for multiple presidential
challenges by radical outsiders and third-party candidates.

These campaigns, in a phenomenon not seen before, took aim at a bipartisan failure centered in "Washington" — not in the South, not at Harvard and the Ford Foundation, or in Wall Street, or in the long-ago coastal mansions of Federalist merchants, but right smack in the now-bloated capital itself.

The Rise of Washington's Parasite Culture

The facts — the cold statistics of growing infestation — support the public's intuitive anger. Sagas of great capitals filling up with privileged classes and parasites are as old as history. Reformers in early seventeenth-century Madrid put the ratio of parasites to actual productive workers as high as 30:1. Current-day Japanese and Italians have similar, if milder, complaints about Tokyo and Rome. However, some of what is now happening to Washington had been predicted many years before — and political scientists should have been paying more attention to the implications of the extraordinary interest-group and lobby buildup underway since World War II.

From 1783 to 1789, in Congress and then at state and federal constitutional conventions, a minority of delegates had nightmares about what a permanent American seat of government would become. One day, they said, the new federal capital might hold two or four million people and a wealthy elite that would live on the fruits of others' labor and jeopardize the new republic just as the aristocracy had in Rome. Over the next 150 years, of course, most of the "parasite" charges raised against Washington were just politics, trivial in a world historical perspective. The U.S. capital was just too relaxed, too unformed. In early 1942 an angry Franklin Roosevelt, aroused by the criticisms of newspaper magnate Cissy Patterson, offered *his* definition of capital parasites: socialites living in twenty-room mansions on Massachusetts Avenue and not doing anything for the government or the war effort. But the *New York*

Herald Tribune countered with its own intriguing statistic: the first parasites to leave, the newspaper argued, should be the federal government's 2,895 press agents. The outlines of a serious debate were beginning to dance across the horizon.

As the federal government's agenda grew during the 1960s and 1970s, Washington drew power brokers and courtiers in numbers that began to constitute another of history's danger signals. Some of the parasites were government employees, but given private-sector demands and late-twentieth-century civil service restraints, the notable expansion in the Washington parasite structure during the 1970s and 1980s came from *outside* the federal government — from an explosion in the ranks of lawyers and interest-group representatives out to influence Uncle Sam, interpret his actions, or pick his pockets for themselves or their clients. The gunslingers, card sharks, and faro dealers were checking into Gucci Gulch.

It was no coincidence that other major cities, too, were adding white-collar professionals during the 1970s and 1980s. The United States was shifting economic gears, enlarging its service sector, and polarizing. Miners, farmers, and blue-collar workers were losing ground as the nation's respect and income shifted toward capitalists and what political economist Robert Reich called "symbolic analysts" — the manipulators of ideas and concepts. Money was concentrating at the top, inheritance was bulking larger in people's economic well-being, and more of the best jobs were going to graduates of the best schools. Elite growth in Washington was *leading* a national trend, not *bucking* one. From Sacramento to Columbus, Indianapolis, and Albany, *state* capitals, too, were among the nation's fastest-growing metropolitan areas.

By the 1990 census, the growth of Washington's new private and nonprofit jobs — centered in what academicians were starting to lump together as the lobbying or transfer-seeking sector — had raised its metropolitan area to the highest per capita income of any in the United States. Seven of its jurisdictions were now on the list of the twenty U.S. counties with the highest median family incomes. Now it was no longer just Bloomingdale's moving in; Tiffany's came, too, and its new store in wallet-heavy Fairfax set opening-year records. A huge ratio of professionals produced local income statistics that stood out even in an era of national socioeconomic polarization: Washington exceeded any other major U.S. city in the spread between the average incomes of its richest 10 percent ($101,831) and poorest 10 percent ($12,661).

Lawyers were an especially prominent growth sector. Statistics show what can only be called a megaleap: in 1950 not quite a thousand lawyers were members of the District of Columbia bar; by 1975, there were twenty-one thousand; and by 1993, sixty-one thousand. About forty thousand actually worked in the metropolitan area. No other major U.S. city matched the capital's per capita concentration of attorneys. The comparative lawyer overload of ancient Rome, which we will discuss further in Chapter 5, paled by comparison.

Congressional payrolls were also soaring. The annual staff salary allowance for each congressman, small potatoes in 1930 and $20,000 in 1957, reached $515,760 in 1990. The total staff of Congress, about eleven thousand in 1970, had climbed to twenty thousand in 1990. No other major nation's legislative branch employed a staff even one quarter the size.

The number of national trade associations in the entire United States had climbed from 4,900 in 1956 to 12,500 in 1975 and 23,000 in 1989. Meanwhile, the percentage of U.S. trade and professional associations choosing to make their headquarters in metropolitan Washington increased from 19 percent in 1971 to 32 percent in 1990. This rapid centralization at the seat of federal power was no coincidence. Each of the great postwar public policy waves — urban, environmental, health, and so on — forced more associations to pack their bags for Washington to locate where the legislative and rule-making action was. In 1979 the National Health Council found 117 health groups represented in Washington; by 1991 they listed 741. The nature of representative government in the United States was starting to change, so that more and more of the weight of influence in the capital came from interest groups, not voters — a danger we will pursue in Chapter 5.

Skeptics will say Yes, but the role of interest groups is the same now as it has always been. But that is not true. At some point, probably in the 1970s, the buildup of interest groups in Washington reached what we could call negative critical mass. So many had come to Washington or been forced to come that the city started turning into a special-interest battlefield, a competitive microcosm of interest-group America. When policy decisions were made, attendance would be taken, checks would be totaled, lobbyists would be judged, mail would be tabulated — and if a group wasn't on hand to drive its vehicle through the Capitol Hill weighing station, that organization was out of luck. Few organizations could afford to stay away, and very few did. It is at this point that the institutions of politics and government — and of American democracy — began to bend under the burden. The pressure worsened as industries and groups of Americans began to worry that the tides of America's postwar economic zenith were beginning to recede, which only increased their need to hasten to Washington to try to prolong the good times for themselves, if necessary at others' expense.

Trade associations, congressional staffers, and lawyers, of course, are only part of the Washington influence and opinion-molding complex. "Interest group" is a broad description. Any comprehensive list must also include representatives of domestic and foreign corporations, government relations and lobbying firms, think tanks, coalitions, public interest and nonprofit groups, and representatives of other governments and governmental bodies anxious to keep in touch with Washington. No census is taken of these functions — any accurate official count would make voters boil. However, one 1991 estimate of eighty thousand lobbyists by James Thurber, a professor of government at American University, touched off a storm, especially when he admitted, "[It was] off the top of my head." Lobbyists scoffed, saying the figure was more like ten thousand. Thurber, responding to the challenge, undertook a more systematic sampling and came up with a still higher figure: ". . . ninety-one thousand lobbyists and people associated with lobbying activities in and around Washington."

Thurber's number, while extraordinary, seems all too plausible if you try the addition. The combined ranks of trade and membership associations in greater Washington had about 69,000 people working for them in 1993. The number of U.S. corporations with offices in Washington grew from under a hundred in 1950 to more than five hundred in 1990, at which time they probably employed from 5,000 to 7,500 people. Foreign corporate giants were just as interested in Washington outposts as the U.S. megafirms. Of the fifty largest foreign multinationals, two thirds have offices in Washington, including giants like Siemens, British Petroleum, Rhone-Poulenc, and Toyota. Close to four hundred foreign corporations have some kind of representative on hand. We should also count the foreign embassies, about 150 of them with perhaps 10,000 employees. Many have been nerve centers for lobbying campaigns using hired government-relations consultants, lawyers, lobbyists, and trade experts. Then there are the various functionaries of state and local government charged with monitoring the federal government: representatives of two thirds of the states, two dozen cities, a number of large-sized counties, and several state legislatures (the Republican New York State Senate and the Democratic New York State Assembly both had Washington offices in 1990). Even a few local water and power authorities were on the muster roll. Prior to the early 1990s recession, which devastated both California and its budget, some 90 people in Washington, including retained lawyers, were said to be representing some element of government — state, county, municipal, and local — of the state of California alone.

The capital's think tanks, coalitions, institutes, foundations, and centers added another five hundred or so organizations of various age, subject matter, and staff size. Here, too, the total numbers, budgets, and nose count of nonclerical staffers involved — some five thousand — represented a roughly five-fold increase since 1970. Like the trade association and lobbyist explosions, the boom in think tanks, coalitions, and centers reflected their growing role. On one hand, these auxiliaries are increasingly useful to special-interest lobbies and to the various backstage opinion-molding networks — defense, tax, environmental, trade, budgetary — that have evolved. With their origins, funding, and loyalties disguised behind bland labels, many have become powerful forces in reinforcing public policy biases toward elite rather than outsider viewpoints (who ever heard of the Center for Increased Attention to Ordinary Voters or the Coalition of Laid-off Middle Managers?). Just as significantly, though, think tanks and institutes have become vital sources of taint-free employment for ex-cabinet members, ex-commissioners, and even former presidential candidates marking time between platforms or primaries. Twenty years ago, out-of-office Republicans had few such roosting places; now they have dozens, well funded by corporations, investment firms, and multimillionaire individual donors. When the Bush administration left town, several former cabinet members interested in running for president in 1996 quickly found well-paid niches in these tax-deductible hostelries.

Some do lobbying, some do not. But the collective function of these groups is broader: old-boy and old-girl policy networking that verges on Potomac incest. Moreover, it usually combines with attempts to influence politicians by influencing the press, which has ballooned even more in size and importance.

In 1950, there were roughly 1,500 journalists in Washington; by 1990, the number had climbed to 12,000. The Washington press corps, more narrowly defined, increased from 437 in 1936 to 873 in 1956; 3,000 in 1980; and 5,000 in 1990. The press, or at least its more prominent members, had long since risen to the purple, being decried as the "imperial media" at regular intervals since the 1970s. To the public, Washington journalists and pundits were part of the "iron triangle" complained of to survey takers — the interaction of politicians, interest groups, and media perceived as making the capital unresponsive to the demands of ordinary Americans.

There is no need to overcatalog. The books, chapters, and charts about interest-group buildup are starting to multiply. Suffice it to say that no previous great capital has ever come close to Washington in this regard. The separate governmental enclaves of other nations — Ottawa, Canberra, Bonn, Brasilia — are dwarfed against the backdrop of our own capital like launches and minesweepers bobbing in the shadow of a great gray battleship. Washingtonians themselves understand better than anyone, from watching the daily parade of eight-hundred-dollar suits in the streets, elevators, and restaurants. In 1949 a photograph taken from Connecticut Avenue looking down the same K Street — the Wall Street of Washington's political influence brokers — showed a drab drugstore next to some row houses just beginning to be remodeled. Jeffersonians would call those the good old days. Now K Street is a half-mile-long canyon of high-rise office buildings, with each street directory listing law firms, institutes, trade associations, corporations, and public relations consultants.

The gunslinger portions of this complex *are* venal or corrupt. When foreign lobbying became a political issue in 1992,

Washington influence-mongers watched nervously as voters bridled at how presidential candidates let foreign lobbyists play key roles in their campaigns, and grimaced at reports of how many former top U.S. trade officials and former Republican and Democratic officials have sold their services to the highest overseas bidder. In some of Washington's richest neighborhoods, from Kalorama and Kenwood to Spring Valley and Potomac, there are almost as many registered foreign agents — mostly American citizens so enlisted — as Mercedes, BMWs, and Jaguars, and the ratios are not unrelated. The top gunslingers almost all have some foreign clients, although the purely domestic practitioners are not much different.

For the most part, however, what is wrong with interest-group Washington is that it has become *over*interested — that as more and more groups have come to Washington or been forced to, they have assumed a role that even many spokesmen and association executives query. Decision-making in the city has increasingly come to be a polling of affected campaign donors and interest groups rather than of the people, and the money and lobbying brought to bear in the process has become a symbol of how the capacity of Americans for associations and fraternal organizations has become a political curse as well as a cultural blessing.

That would have been unimaginable a century and a half ago. If self-renewing electoral revolutions were part of the genius of American politics, Alexis de Tocqueville, the Frenchman whose visits to the United States in the 1830s produced his famous book, correctly observed that a second ingredient was also vital. For Americans, he said, democracy was an especially productive form of politics in part because of their talent for forming social and political associations, as well as their enthusiasm for petitioning and confronting all levels of government. The legal right of association had come to America from Britain, but the far more favorable climate of the nineteenth-century United States — universal male suffrage and a much more open society, especially on the frontier — convinced Tocqueville that associations would maximize on this side of the Atlantic. He was right.

The rest, unfortunately, is late-twentieth-century history. Citizens have embraced associations, presidents have encouraged them, and by 1992 the directory of organizations with voices in Washington was a full inch and a half thick with the names of fourteen thousand representatives. Even honest representation of legitimate interests can reach excess. Before World War II, when the U.S. political economy was more local, the bulk of trade associations, then scattered around the country, located their headquarters amidst the concentration of their memberships in New England, the Midwest, or the South and kept only a loose eye on Washington. By the 1990s, as we have seen, with government expanding its scope and trade associations relocating to Washington on a weekly (if not daily) basis, the figurative Western Jeep Dealers, International Lobster Association, and suchlike were deciding, quite correctly, that without a place at the table of national politics, they couldn't fully protect their members. All of which only underscored the irony. Activism and civic involvement that was laudable for individuals became a giant drag on the system as it collectivized and reached critical mass in Washington. One genius of American political success was starting to undercut another.

The result, as we will see in Chapter 5, is that the dysfunction of the nation's capital, accompanied by the increasing incapacity of the two-party system, was starting to produce a new kind of outsider, antisystem, or third-party politics, exemplified by Eugene McCarthy and Ralph Nader, and Jerry Brown, Pat Buchanan, and Ross Perot. Voters were getting angry waiting for promised reform and renewal that never came.

But part of what was making Washington so hard to change was that the entrenchment in the capital was not all perversity. There was also a bipartisan awareness, involving perhaps a hundred thousand people, that the city on the Potomac had become a golden honey pot for the politically involved, offering financial and career opportunities unavailable anywhere else. Washington was not simply a concentration of vested interests; in a sense, the nation's richest city had itself become a vested interest — a vocational entitlement — of the American political class.

The Bipartisan Honey Pot and the Rise of "Interest-Group Centrism"

Most Washington influence wielders, policy shapers, and opinion molders would bridle at being referred to as parasites. They are, in their own minds, notable contributors to the commonweal. But the question whether the capital needs forty thousand to fifty thousand lawyers and a total of ninety thousand persons involved with lobbying, whether lobbyists for foreign interests should thrive along the Potomac as in no other major country, and whether the U.S. Congress requires a staff of twenty thousand, four or five times as large as any other major national legislative body, is simply not something that most Washingtonians let themselves think about. The status quo is a given, the familiar circumstances of a half century of evolution. And most of all, the capital's intermingling of public service, loose money, vocational incest, overinflated salaries, and ethical flexibility verging on corruption has become such a huge gravy train — which most Washingtonians understand full well — that the prospect of serious debate is unnerving.

Although public sector dollars and decisions are the focus of Washington activity, probably three quarters of the jobs paying $100,000 or $150,000 or $250,000 are in the private or nonprofit sector, and there is no other city where so many of the nation's political activists and brokers could make so much money doing what they do. Washington is Waterhole No. 1 for political Americans just as Ottawa, albeit on a lesser scale, is for Canadians and Canberra is for Australians. The expansion of these federal districts, Washington's in particular, are the product of two eras now ending: the Anglo-Saxon world hegemony that began roughly two centuries ago and the 1946–89 Cold War in which Anglo-American power reached its peak. The extraordinary enlargement and entrenchment of our own capital during those years is what now has become a threat to the nation's larger political and governmental health. If K Street wanted fitting symbols, it would bring back the troughs of the horse era. However, the idea of rolling back the capital city's size and riches, historically sensible in the abstract, is unlikely to happen precisely because of the wealth to which we now turn: the honey pot phenomenon. As we will see in the final section of this chapter, previous great-power capital cities have also become ghettoes for the political and governmental elites built up by the country's imperial hour in the sun. None of these were ever disestablished peacefully. No elite ever wanted to go back to Kansas City.

We have already discussed the principal categories of parasitism: lobbyists, lawyers, think-tankers, consultants, journalists, experts, governmental and congressional staffers, and — in the eyes of the public — most of the elected officials themselves. What the statistics cannot adequately convey, however, is the opportunism, incestuousness, and marginal ethics of so many capital city relationships. Delicate balances just short of legal vulnerability or newspaper outrage have been struck in a way that requires time, experience, and the slow wearing away of concern about the folks back there in Salt Lake City and Terre Haute.

The 1990s have seen a bipartisan flowering. In June 1992 the quarterly magazine of Common Cause ran a cover story, "George Bush's Ruling Class: Who They Are, What They Gave, What They Got," describing the 249 top contributors who gave $100,000 or more to the GOP's "Team 100." Fred Wertheimer, the president of Common Cause, summed up their access to favoritism as effectively "destroying the country's existing anticorruption laws." Then, in April 1993, when it was clear that the Clinton administration was merely favoring a *new* portion of the existing political-governmental elite instead of living up to its election-year housecleaning promises, the *New Republic* described the old-boy and old-girl network of the new Clinton administration as representing "Clincest" because it was so full of Yale Law graduates, well-connected lobbyists, Harvard professors, and Rhodes scholars: "The Rhodes scholar mafia is just the beginning. In Clinton's Washington, the worlds of the government, law and academia are now structurally enmeshed. Most everyone seems to have gone to school with each other, is married to each other, writes about each other or lobbies each other. And boasts about it. Is there any way out of the web?" Probably not, at least without turning back to the GOP's rival elite of $100,000-donor golfing buddies.

New Republican and Democratic administrations are inevitably drawn in. The U.S. capital, after its imperial half century, is a city of cliques, relationships, clubs, coalitions, lunch groups, networks, and cabals that are so powerful — and so largely built around those who have risen through the postwar two-party system — that portions of this Permanent Washington effectively pull (and hold) new regimes like electromagnets attract iron filings. Outsider rhetoric weakens and fades. The entrenched interests to which a Democratic president is drawn are different, of course, from those without which a Republican president cannot rule, although there is also a large overlap. The important thing is that *both* parties are enmeshed; neither is any longer able to fulfill campaign promises about cleaning house in Washington.

More to the point, too much of how Washington operates is incompatible with good government or effective politics. Entrenchment is only part of what's wrong. "Soft" corruption is also rampant. Not only do a fair number of spouses, sons, daughters, and siblings of officeholders find lobbying jobs, but surprising numbers of members of Congress sidestep the nepotism laws by what is called "loophole nepotism," putting sons and daughters on a *colleague's* payroll. An exhaustive eighteen-month survey completed in 1987 by United Press International found seventy-four such examples of sons and daughters in congressional jobs.

This, in turn, is piddling next to a larger problem: that many Washington politicians — in particular senators, congressmen, top executive branch officials, and party chairmen — know that when they hang up their elective hats, the best job prospects are right there in Potomac City selling their connections, lobbying, and expertise. Most don't want to go home; and more than a few start thinking about lobbying and representational opportunities while they are still casting votes for or against potential future employers. All too often, public service has become a private opportunity. In a report entitled "Government Service for Sale: How the Revolving Door Has Been Spinning," researchers for Ralph Nader's Public Citizen found that of 300 former House members, congressional staffers, and executive branch officials, 177 of them — fully 59 percent — had taken lobbying jobs or positions at law firms with Washington lobbying arms. Of the 108 House members who retired or were defeated in 1992, over half stayed in the Washington area, and nearly half were with law firms, doing lobbying work or working "with corporate interests." A few especially hurried enlistments involved apparent violations of the bar on ex-members lobbying their colleagues for a year. Every two or four years, each Congress and administration deposits its new layer of would-be influence sellers. No one has precise numbers, but in addition to the present members of Congress, roughly three hundred *former* members also remain in the capital area. The buildup is incessant; retiring legislators and officials are the Washington equivalent of landfill. Senator John McCain of Arizona, proposing bold new legislation to close the infamous "revolving door," had this to say about its mid-1990s abuse: "Sen. David Boren and I have a list of at least 140 former members of Congress who are currently lobbying their former colleagues. Just from this list, we know that approximately one member of Congress is now lobbying for every six members currently serving. Of all permanent committee staff directors who have left the Senate since 1988, 42 percent have become lobbyists. In the House, the number is 34 percent."

Nineteen ninety-three, however, pushed Washington interest-groupism to a new plane. Not only did the new president bargain with key lobbies almost from the start, but two congressmen actually resigned their offices — without waiting to serve out their terms — in order to take up well-paid and influential lobbying posts. Representative Willis Gradison, Republican of Ohio, resigned to head up the Health Insurance Association of America, while Representative Glenn English, Democrat of Oklahoma, left Congress to run the National Rural Electric Cooperative Association. Nobody could remember anything like it. But senior White House officials were doing the same thing. The White House legislative director left to become the chairman of Hill and Knowlton Worldwide, while the deputy chief of staff left to take over the U.S. Telephone Association. Neither had served a full year in his job, and their departures mocked the president's earlier campaign promises. The exodus from both the legislative and executive branches was unprecedented, and doubly revealing of where Washington's real power had migrated.

In a city where influence mongering is so often the pot of gold at the end of the public service rainbow, we should not be surprised that work-for-anybody gunslinger lobbyists are as lionized — and as little inhibited by law enforcement — as their six-gun predecessors were in the fast-draw years of Abilene and Dodge City. Federal lobbying statutes, meanwhile, have had the stopping power of blank cartridges. They are designed not to matter, especially in the international arena. Estimates in 1992 identified more than two hundred former key U.S. officials representing foreign companies, governments, and organizations, including Howard Baker, the former Senate Republican leader and White House Chief of Staff, former defense secretary Frank Carlucci, and William E. Colby, a onetime CIA director. No one shuns them. Few insiders are even critical. The Center for Public Integrity found that in 1992 most of the presidential candidates, whatever their pretenses, were getting advice from scores of lobbyists, not least those for foreign interests. Four presidential campaigns, those of Clinton, Harkin, Kerrey, and Bush, had a combined thirty-one advisers who were personally registered as foreign agents. George Bush, along with a lot of other people in Washington, couldn't understand the fuss over two prominent lobbyists for foreign interests holding strategic and advisory positions in his presidential campaign. Doesn't everyone do it?

Almost. Ohio University professor Alfred Eckes, chairman of the U.S. International Trade Commission under Ronald Reagan, has lamented that he was the only chairman among the last five who didn't go on to represent foreign economic interests. Still another study, which looked at the ten living persons who had been national chairmen of the Republican and Democratic parties, found that most went on to lobby and

his verb chain —

half had been registered with the Justice Department, either before or after their party tenures, as foreign agents for overseas corporations and governments.

No vehicle by which money can reach politicians' eager hands goes unused. So many U.S. senators have been accused of corruption or ethical infractions that Washington lobbyists can court them by contributing to their legal defense funds. At one point, seven sitting Senators — six of them Republicans — had legal defense funds operating, to which lobbyists could contribute up to $10,000 a year compared to the $1,000 limit on a campaign contribution. Lists of self-interested contributors to the indicted, censured, or about-to-be are becoming regular newspaper features. Congressmen and senators have also taken to establishing personal tax-exempt foundations as a device for tapping expenditures that corporations can no longer deduct as lobbying expenses. Where foundations merely try to educate lawmakers about an issue and do no lobbying, contributions to them remain deductible. The result, according to Ellen Miller, director of the Center for Responsive Politics, is that "these foundations become another pocket of a politician's coat into which companies can stuff money."

The political culture that has legitimized these practices is the same one that has tolerated de facto vote-buying in Congress, winked at the spread of "loophole nepotism," and quietly rolled in the hay with so-called soft money — the astounding $83 million of 1991–92 contributions that poured into the Democratic and Republican National Committees through a legal chink, identified during the 1980s, that permits otherwise illegal corporate and large individual political donations when they are made to support nonfederal state and local party-building activities. And even these flimsy limitations were not honored. Only a quarter of the 1991–92 soft money contributions (from influence seekers and interest groups) actually passed through to the states; most of the money was spent at the national level, further sweetening the honey pot available to officials, consultants, advisers, and pollsters in both parties.

There is nothing partisan about Washingtonians' self-interest in their backyard feeding ground. On the contrary, support for the status quo is intensely *bipartisan* in the truest sense; real access to the honey pot in most cases comes only from service, appointments, and connections within the Republican-Democratic party system. A cynic could even say that the corruption of Washington — because, bluntly, that is what we are talking about — is closely bound up with two-party politics. Influence-peddling access is one of the most important components and privileges of the party spoils system. The most successful Washington lobbying and law firms mix Democratic and Republican partners in flexible ratios so as to reassure clients that they can knock on any and all doors. This would be difficult in Europe, where real ideological and class differences between the parties would at least complicate any such collaboration. It is all too easy in the United States. The principal difference between the Republicans and the Democrats is that the former parade their check-writing lobbyists at their fund-raising dinners while the Democrats are more secretive. The *Washington Post* noted that the Clinton White House banned the press from the 1993 Democratic Senate Majority dinner to keep them from describing the President "consorting with all the fat cats he denounced during last year's presidential campaign."

Clinton may not have been smiling. The accusations he had made in his 1992 campaign that "the last twelve years were nothing less than an extended hunting season for high-priced lobbyists and Washington influence peddlers" almost certainly had sprung from an element of belief as well as politics. But by the end of his first year in office, he had found that the season had been further extended, and that his programs would have been defeated if he hadn't abandoned his election-year populism and started cutting deals — on taxes, trade, and health — with representatives of corporate and financial interests. Lobbyists were no longer the "fourth branch" of government joked about in the 1960s. They were one or two places higher. And in the debris of this transformation, something else was also lost: the ability of Democratic presidents to represent that famous old cement of New Deal coalition-building known as "interest-group liberalism."

If it had weakened under Democrat Jimmy Carter in 1977–81, it expired under Bill Clinton. The Permanent Washington that sounded liberal as it broke Richard Nixon in 1973–74 now has a centrist cast which comes from a mixture of the nation's own ideological shift, the spending constraints of accumulating budget deficits, and the upper-bracket connections and raw self-interest of its pinstriped hierarchs. Almost before it started, Clinton's administration got in trouble for being too close to lobbyists, insiders, and power brokers. But attention has focused not only on these relations, but on the President's willingness to make deals with business and financial lobbies even more quickly than with labor, environmental, and minority groups. Changes like these tell the *real* story of the transition from "Old Democrat" to "New Democrat." What Clinton has done is to shift his party from so-called interest-group liberalism to "interest-group centrism" — away from the pro-spending liberal-type lobbies that represented *people* (labor, seniors, minorities, and urban) to a more upscale centrist (or center-right) group that represents *money* (multinational business, banks, investment firms, trial lawyers, trade interests, super-lobbyists, investors, the bond market, and so on). In short, the new power structure of special-interest centrism. This is the ultimate triumph of Washington's interest-group ascendancy: the party of the people can no longer *be* the party of the people.

The dollar magnitude of the Washington honey pot that commands such fealty — not to say anxiety — from the Washington political classes is awesome. Government payrolls *are* important, especially the twenty thousand congressional staff jobs as well as the four thousand to five thousand top executive-branch jobs at the disposal of a new president. However, the bulk of the cash flow that makes Washington such a cornucopia comes from the tens of billions poured into the city's law and lobby firms and interest groups each year by domestic and foreign seekers of information, access, and favors, as well as from the legal, lobbying, and consulting fees often charged for federal grants and aid being shipped out to Wichita and Walla Walla thanks to this bill or that amendment. The private sector's Gross Influence-Peddling Product is probably $20 billion a year or so. This is enough, as we have seen, to make Washington not only rich, but self-interestedly suspicious of those who would change the all-important status quo.

Newt Gingrich, the congressional Republican firebrand, has offered an insightful, if only partial, rebuttal to accusations that he is a bomb thrower: in Washington, Gingrich explains, the *truth* is a bomb. Exactly. So before we finish describing Washington's governmental culture and corruption, it is worthwhile to look at some of the theorists, academicians, and public policy executives whose writings and activities, whose truths and near truths, have spotlighted Washington's interest groups and parasite economics. Their voices are starting to add up — and they may even be quiet bomb makers for another American revolution.

The Academic Revolutionaries

Most of the presidential campaigns mounted against Washington in the last third of the twentieth century — from George Wallace's down to Ross Perot's — have relied on traditional populist and outsider rhetoric rather than on a sophisticated historical, political, and economic indictment of the seat of government and its abuses. Yet there were signs of change in 1992, spurred by the sheer number and diversity of anti-Washington candidates. Critiques of the capital are beginning to jell. Even academic studies are beginning to load populist or reformist cannon with powerful shells.

Let's look at the growing range of material debunking what Washington is and does. These analyses come from economists who specialize in interest groups, theoreticians of the high cost of economic transfer-seeking, chroniclers of the dynamics of parasitism, and investigators dedicated to spotlighting the ethical underworld of capital influence-peddling. All of them reinforce something else we will look at: the unnerving lessons of past great capitals.

Mancur Olson, professor of economics at the University of Maryland, has written a persuasive book, *The Rise and Decline of Nations*, from a combination of research and simple common sense. Countries that recently have been swept by wars or revolutions — Germany and Japan after 1945, the new United States in the nineteenth century, sixteenth-century Spain after its retaking of the Iberian peninsula from the Moors, Holland in the seventeenth century, Britain in the eighteenth century following Oliver Cromwell and then the "Glorious Revolution" of 1688 — have often made extraordinary strides because their economies are wide open and they have few status quo–minded interest groups to hold them back. Great nations heading into decline, by contrast, can blame much of their slowdown on the interest-group barnacles collected during the long, fat years of their success, smugness, and safety. Thus the onset of stagnation in Spain, Holland, Britain, and the United States within only 100 or 150 years after each nation's emergence. By the early twentieth century, Olson argues, Britain was plagued by interest groups and networks and the current-day United States has an even greater buildup. With careful phraseology, he even acknowledges that "if one happens to be balancing arguments for and against revolution, the theory here does shift the balance marginally in a revolutionary direction."

Economists Donald Laband, Robert Tollison, Gordon Tullock, and Stephen Magee are four pioneers in studies of the cost of transfer seeking in general — transferring rather than creating wealth is clearly one of Washington's leading pursuits — and of lawyering, a particular staple of the nation's capital.[3] Academic attempts to calculate the annual cost to the overall U.S. economy of transfer seeking generally put it in the 5 percent to 12 percent range, which comes to roughly $300 billion to $700 billion. By no means all of this takes place in Washington, but the capital region's combined public and private politico-legal payrolls, consulting, brokerage, and transfer fees may well reach $50 billion to $75 billion a year. Tiffany's knew what it was doing when it put a branch in lobbyist- and lawyer-rich Fairfax County.

Whenever lobbying succeeds, observes Tullock, it is a powerful advertisement for even more lobbying. Most major corporations have found Washington representatives to be good investments, and the transfer-seeking burden imposed by lawyers has been a particular economic red flag to academicians. The University of Texas's Magee has compiled several especially provocative regression analyses. For example, when national ratios of lawyers are plotted against economic growth rates in twenty-eight countries, a depressing relationship emerges: the lower the local lawyer count, the higher the growth. Within the United States, he insists, states where lawyers were thickest also displayed lower growth. Washington, of course, has the highest per capita concentration of lawyers of all major U.S. cities, probably of any major city in the world. Magee also contends that the more lawyers a country has in its legislative body, the more national economic activity suffers. Because lawyers made up 42 percent of the U.S. House of Representatives in 1992, versus an average of 15 percent in eighteen other countries, the Texas professor's formula set that year's cost of Congress's over-lawyering at roughly $220 billion lost to the Gross National Product. This seems absurd when one remembers that the U.S. Congress also crawled with lawyers back in the rapid growth years of the nineteenth century. However, if one uses a calculus that emphasizes the extraordinary overall ratio of lawyers in the nation's capital, not just those in Congress, then the burden is at least arguable.

Analyses like these, however inflammatory in the mouth of a stalwart politician, can be sleep-inducing in the opaque language of academic journals. Jonathan Rauch is a young writer who, at least as much as anyone else, has made the discoveries of the transfer measurers and lawyer watchers come alive in publications like *National Journal*. Rauch's credits include phrases like "*parasitemia economicus*" (the parasite economy), "*demosclerosis*" as a capsule of Mancur Olson's interest-group thesis, a pithy description of lawyers as "a good proxy for the size of the nation's noncriminal parasite class," and a straight-faced discourse on the correlations between capital-city status and unusually high ratios of golf courses and sit-down restaurants.

Charles Lewis is a former CBS television executive who got angry after producing a segment for the show "Sixty Minutes" on the extent of foreign lobbying in Washington. So he went out, raised some money, and established the Washington-based Center for Public Integrity. His organization becomes less popular each year as it combs through lobbying and foreign agent registrations, making telephone calls and churning out reports that poke flashlights into the dirty-laundry baskets of the Washington power structure. Compilations by the center have documented the lobbyist connections of presidential campaign advisers and detailed how many previous senior U.S. trade officials and former national chairmen of the Democratic and Republican parties have signed up as representatives of foreign corporations, organizations, and governments. "In the mercenary culture of Washington," says Lewis, "money and power, access and influence, dominate politics and public discourse. The lobbyist is to Washington what the investment banker was to New York in the Eighties. There are huge sums of money to be made and no real controls." His efforts are at least raising the embarrassment level.

Washingtonians who deal in these exposures are as popular as the proverbial skunk at a garden party. But considering the destructive record of past parasitism in great capitals, the iconoclasts exposing the similar trends in Washington are performing a notable service.

The Lessons of Other Capitals

If the trend to government ghettoization over the last two decades supports a concern about Washington's drag on the nation, so does the evidence of world history. Over the last twenty-five hundred years, arrogant or atrophied capitals have been front and center in most great-power declines.

Two centuries ago, America's own founding fathers, who would have been flabbergasted to hear that the U.S. Congress would one day have twenty thousand staffers, talked with foreboding of ancient history they knew well and we have forgotten. The decline of Athens from its glories under Pericles was common knowledge even for schoolboys back in the nineteenth-century days when Americans named cities for Alexander and Homer, for Troy, Sparta, and Corinth — and filled up their own capital with Henry Adams's Greek temples. Professor Peter Green of the University of Texas recently published a portrait of the subsequent Hellenistic age, which also teems with unfortunate analogies to the present-day United States, including reminders of how Alexandria, Antioch, and Pergamon, in their fattest days, became "governmental ghettoes for a ruling elite."

Rome's later years, in turn, constitute another powerful warning. From the third to the fifth centuries, Roman society polarized as it declined, and the ruling elite grew more preoccupied with wealth and privilege while the middle classes struggled to survive — a dilemma echoed in our own day. Historian Michael Grant, in *The Fall of the Roman Empire*, describes that classic deterioration as speeded by the huge size and declining quality of the civil service, which slowly became hereditary. Corruption, legal malpractice, and excessive lawsuits were everywhere. In the fourth century, after the death of Valentinian, growing public contempt for officialdom convinced the authorities to declare it an act of sacrilege to even discuss the merits of anyone chosen by an emperor to serve him.

As the barbarians closed in, talk about relocating the capital grew. The fourth-century empire was divided into western and eastern portions, with capitals at Rome and Constantinople. Then, after Rome itself was besieged, the emperor Honorius decided to move the court to Ravenna on Italy's east coast because it was protected from attack by marshes. It is worth pointing out how pagan historians, in particular, sneered at most of the late emperors for holing up in luxury in the capital as the country around them crumbled.

The tendencies of imperial capitals to become a focal point of weakness continued in the Byzantine Empire. The next example brings us up to modern history: how Hapsburg Madrid of the late sixteenth century, basking in Spanish glory, drew impossible numbers to seek positions in the church, the universities, the royal court, and the Spanish bureaucracy. For two years, King Philip II transferred his rule to Lisbon, less cluttered and more outward looking, but pressure forced him back. With Madrid reestablished, the households of the nobility swelled not only with servants but with cousins, younger sons, and impoverished hidalgos. The influx was so massive that in 1611 — to quote historian J. H. Elliot — the government ordered the great nobles "to return to their estates in the hope of clearing the Court of parasites." It didn't work, and reformers "continued to fulminate in vain against the unchecked growth of a monstrous capital which was draining away the lifeblood of Castile."

Favor seekers, courtiers, Catholic clergy, and bureaucrats were a third of Madrid's population. And to make matters worse, sixteenth-century Spain established scores of new colleges and universities to prepare students — many more than could ever be needed — for the church or government. Prestigious colleges and universities even maintained representatives at court whose function it was to help graduates get jobs. When no positions were available, favored graduates could wait, often for years, in the comfort of special hostels, presumably the Castilian equivalent of Washington think tanks. In 1623 critics finally convinced the government to undertake serious reform. Two thirds of the municipal offices were to be abolished as unnecessary, while many of the schools that trained unnecessary churchmen, bureaucrats, or educators were to be shut. But once again, interest groups upheld the status quo. As Spain's late-seventeenth-century decline worsened, Madrid began to fade, yet it provides another chilling example of a capital city ridden with parasites and able to prevent change. It also serves as a warning: *No bloated great-power capital has ever made itself over.*

The next great world power, the United Provinces of the Netherlands, only continued the pattern. During its seventeenth-century golden age, the country had two capitals, more or less, and two competing political forces. The merchants and capitalists were based in Amsterdam, the country's biggest city and the capital of the Province of Holland, which furnished 60 percent of the nation's revenues. The national government, under a ruler called the *stadtholder*, was in The Hague, along with the court and foreign embassies.

Even as the Netherland's world economic leadership waned, the government elites flourished. By the mid–eighteenth century, the state customs services had fifty thousand employees in the province of Holland alone. However, the purest governmental culture was in The Hague, which, after quadrupling its population, was the only major Dutch city to continue growing during the nation's decline in the mid– and late-eighteenth century. Let us accept the summary of the leading chronicler of the period, Harvard historian Simon Schama: "The elaborately beautified Hague, where in 1777, the tax roll recorded the stabling of between 40,000 and 50,000 'pleasure' and carriage horses, was seen by the upholders of the traditional virtues of plain thrift and honest toil as a cesspool of luxury and foreign manners."

London's somewhat different role deserves note. The early-twentieth-century Edwardian era, during which Britain's global decline became an issue, was marked by economic polarization, the emergence of a rich class of capitalists, and a resurgence of the aristocracy, all of which centered on imperial London. The capital grew enormously in Britain's heyday, yet having many other functions and having always been the center of Britain's government, it was not transformed into a governmental parasite complex. London's way of smothering change was different. Members of Parliament and senior government officials alike conducted their business in an aristocratic setting made even more so by upper-bracket residential environs and by the overlap of Parliament's summer session with the London social season. Had the capital of the United States been set down in New York or Philadelphia, the founding fathers' fears of a transatlantic London — a capital city swayed by social and hereditary elites — might have come true. Washington, however, is more the elite governmental ghetto run amok, Pergamon-on-the-Potomac. Unfortunately, this is the type of capital city that history most warns against.

The final reason to heed the crisis of our capital city is current history: many other countries are also having troubles with their governmental systems and their capital cities in the 1990s. This is true of the other English-speaking nations, but it is also true of most of the G-7 economic powers. If these other party systems are in deep trouble, so much more reason for the U.S. to query the vitality of its own. And if the aging institutions and misfunctioning values we share with Britain, Australia, and Canada are straining their governmental arrangements, all the more reason to pay attention to strains in the United States, too.

American leadership elites disposed to scoff at the questions posed by our own capital should look at the countries to which the United States is closest. The 1990s, as we will see, have few precedents as a decade of capitals in crisis. Consider the British: significant minorities of voters in Scotland and Wales do not want London as their capital; they favor a devolution of power and new parliaments in Edinburgh and Cardiff. Canada, periodically in some danger of crumbling along Anglo-French or east-west lines, also confronts a very real public contempt for Ottawa, its federal city. Talk about relocating the capital gets cheers, especially in the western provinces. The Germans are in the process of moving their federal capital from Bonn to Berlin. Northern Italians have rallied behind a "Lombard League" movement that opposes rule from Rome and favors dividing the country into a federation of three self-governing regions. The north would prefer to be ruled from Venice. And proposals are being made in Japan to disperse some of the population and power overconcentrated in Tokyo by moving some governmental functions elsewhere or, much less likely, by shifting the capital to Osaka or Kyoto. All of this, history and current affairs alike, supports a blunt message for American leaders: *pay heed.* We shall come back to these current-day parallels in Chapters 6 and 7.

For the United States, however, the failure of Washington is part of something that goes far beyond the post–Cold War malaise and dislocation visible in so many other countries. For Americans, the question of what to do about the capital city is part of a broader challenge of reversing the nation's slow decline into a broad resurgence and renewal. Political and governmental upheaval is heavy in the 1990s air in these other lands, too, but the accumulated burdens and stakes are greatest here.

Part II

The Critical Shortcomings of U.S. Politics, Parties, and Government

Chapter Three

The Crisis No One Can Discuss: U.S. Economic and Cultural Decline — And What It Means

---

We're starting to lose our standard of living, . . . the middle class is starting to shrink. . . . The Wall Street rentiers can make money and are making money out of the decline in the American economy. So long as they are making big profits they'd just as soon see it go on. They don't care. Takeover attempts, putting together financings, trashing companies . . . the transition can go on for years . . . it's killing us.

— RICHARD GEPHARDT,
Democratic presidential candidate,
1988

It's a misdiagnosis to say [America's] problem is economics. It's a cultural decline. Our problems are moral, spiritual, philosophical and behavioral.

— WILLIAM BENNETT,
Former GOP Secretary of Education,
1993

THE AVERAGE CITIZEN, sounding off about what's wrong with politics and government, might grouse about professional politicians remaining in office too long, powerful contributors pulling strings from distant office suites, congressmen awarding themselves pay raises, political action committees (or lobbies) deciding what legislation wins or loses, and so on. These are important everyday provocations; they are also, realistically, just symptoms.

In considering the deeper reasons why American politics and government no longer work, we should begin with the one that most Americans vaguely sense but that national leaders are so reluctant to discuss: the historical decline of the United States from its postwar peak, how far it has progressed, and what it means. Much of the case for decline is relative, measurable against other countries gaining on the United States or moving ahead in a few limited ways. However, there are also areas of absolute decline — in real manufacturing wages and in middle-class job optimism and security. Few worries change a country more or play greater havoc with the success of politics and government than economic insecurity. When a national population senses decline, politics sours, government stumbles. When a leading world power passes its zenith and starts to go downhill, even in a process that is slow and mostly a matter of comparison, the list of strains and weights imposed is a long one: on the attitudes of voters, on the day-to-day confidence of ordinary breadwinners, on government institutions, and on political party systems that worked better in cheerier times.

The unfolding nineties are part of the new focus. Probably because the last decade of a departing century begins to shift peoples' attention to the enormous changes expected to bear down in the new one, such fin de siècle periods have a fascinating record of crystalizing worries already accumulating in great-power populations. The Spanish, so cocky in the 1490s, became hangdog and gloomy by the 1590s. The Dutch, for whom the 1590s had been electric, were perturbed by the 1690s. The British, rightly convinced in the 1790s that against the odds they could whip Bonaparte's French arse, were concerned by the 1890s that Kaiser Bill and the Germans might soon whip theirs. Now it is the Americans, happy horizon-watchers one hundred years ago, who worry that a new twenty-first-century cultural and technological sun is rising over Asia.

Historians may quibble over exact national chronologies, but in general, the public's apprehensions have been prophetic. In the three "nervous nineties" situations just mentioned, each nation's decline in the historical or comparative sense was already underway. Which means that Americans' worries and agitations in the 1990s are to be taken seriously: they are almost certainly a leading indicator.

In the two chapters following this one, we will look at a number of *specific* inadequacies of U.S. politics and government in coping with America's turn-of-the-century circumstances — at obstacles to national renewal posed by ineffective political parties and government, outdated political boundaries and governmental units, an overblown legal sector, and a profiteering financial sector. Then, in Chapter 6, we will conclude this consideration of why U.S. politics and government don't work with another troublesome possibility: that these problems may be part of a larger Anglo-American exhaustion. First, though, it is worth reviewing how the politicians and even presidential contenders of the last two decades have touched upon, although they have never confronted, a vital underlying question: just where is the United States on the trajectory of its own rise and decline as a great power and what does that mean for Americans?

The Late-Twentieth-Century Debate
over U.S. Decline

The issues themselves are all on the table. Over the last thirty years, one or another candidate or official has touched virtually every aspect of possible national decline. In the late 1960s, Henry Kissinger, then White House national security adviser, privately described the U.S. military predicament in Indochina as the beginning of a managed retreat of American power. As things in Vietnam got worse, books started to appear proclaiming the end of the American era.

For many Americans, especially angry conservatives, the U.S. government's 1977 decision to give the Panama Canal to Panama, followed by the 1979 Iranian seizure of the American Embassy staff in Tehran, provided further unwelcome proof. But President Carter's talk about a national "malaise" did not sit well, and Ronald Reagan won the presidency in 1980 partly because he promised to reverse Carter-era decline. By 1984, he was taking credit for having done so. "America is back," he proclaimed, and voters did applaud the return to a bygone era of gunboat diplomacy and saber-rattling apparent in the invasion of Grenada in 1983 and the air strike against Libya in 1986.

In 1988, however, Democrats dismissed the Reagan claim that it was "morning again in America," by saying that economically, at least, it was a deepening twilight. Paul Kennedy's best-seller *The Rise and Fall of the Great Powers* helped bring out national discomfort. What happened to previous powers could be confronting the United States. Foreign debt was mounting, the dollar was plummeting, and key industries were in global retreat. Senate Republican Leader Bob Dole, running for the Republican presidential nomination that year, tried to split the difference between morning and twilight. It was, the senator from Kansas acknowledged, already "High Noon."

The breakup of the Soviet Union that occurred during George Bush's presidency soon cut two ways. It left the United States as the world's sole superpower, but the end of the Cold War also turned Americans' eyes homeward to the country's growing domestic and economic weaknesses. The Gulf War against Iraq briefly looked like a triumph, yet it was fought against a nation with a GNP the size of Kentucky, and left Iraqi leader Saddam Hussein still in power to thumb his nose at Uncle Sam. The punitive expeditions of 1983–91, which at first had reassured Americans, were starting to look like the punitive expeditions of Rome: pleasing and usually triumphant in the short run, irrelevant in the long run.

Thus the debate in the 1992 presidential race edged back toward the delicate subject of decline. Bill Clinton, the winner, described the United States as globally overextended. We were the only nation, he said, without an economic plan. High-technology industries were being lost; the American dream was in jeopardy; the middle class was being destroyed. One of his Democratic rivals, former Massachusetts senator Paul Tsongas, mused that the Cold War had produced a disturbing pair of real victors: "Germany and Japan won."

From Clinton to Democratic rival Jerry Brown, Republican insurgent Patrick Buchanan, and independent challenger Perot, outsider-type candidates also called down national wrath on another symbol of decay: Washington, the out-of-touch capital dominated by lobbyists and special interests dismissive of the views of the electorate. Then there was the huge buildup of debt and the relentless yearly budget deficit, two other corrosive characteristics of troubled great powers. At the August Republican convention, Buchanan and Vice President Dan Quayle touched on yet another worry point, America's moral and cultural decline. These all had one thing in common: a relationship to national erosion.

What was still missing, however, was identification of an overall framework. The pieces of a jigsaw puzzle were being put down, a few here and a few there, but no one as yet was fitting them into a political worldview. Polls showed that voters were fearful, worried about America losing its global economic edge. But although many politicians touched on some particular ingredient of decline, few wanted to set out a full thesis. That was partly because of overall uncertainties, but partly because, like the Romans, Spanish, Dutch, and British before them, most Americans believed that the United States was different, that decline couldn't happen here. America's problems were only temporary. So the nation's political leaders and opinion molders were missing more than an agenda for reform; they also were lacking a basic reading of history — a cold-blooded assessment of what was going wrong and why it was unleashing dangerous forces.

Competing Interpretations of U.S. Decline

Our rival political ideologies have rival theories. To the extent that American leaders, Democrats or Republicans, liberals or conservatives, see the United States plagued by symptoms of national decline — and privately, many of them do — their solutions are separated by tendencies to blame entirely different bogeymen. To most Democrats and liberals, the critical American failure and deterioration of the late twentieth century has been *economic*. To many Republicans and conservatives, however, the emerging weakness has been *moral and cultural*. Although the line between the two alternatives is artificial, it may also be unbridgeable, because both sides have mutually hostile elites and interest groups on top of divergent philosophies.

For Democrats, emphasizing the economic aspect of U.S. decline is logical, both as a belief and as a tactical priority expressed in their winning 1992 slogan "It's the economy, stupid." Recessions and joblessness have been the Democrats' usual national political opportunity. They have also been the jugular vein of Republican vulnerability, especially after GOP regimes that presided over the major capitalist boom-bust cycles. Positions in national elections have been shaped accordingly. Blaming the Republican administrations in power from 1981 to 1992 for U.S. economic slippage is an obvious Democratic approach; it's also a talking point from which to propose more government regulation and activism to offset the alleged neglect by free-market Republicans.

Republicans have been less comfortable with economic issues, having been stung by them too many times. But the late-twentieth-century decline that many do want to discuss, and that makes many Democrats nervous, involves the erosion of America's culture, morality, and family life. To a majority of conservative leaders and pundits, moral and cultural decline far outweighs economic slippage as an explanation of the nation's 1990s trauma. Some also blame moral decline for any ebb in the economy. Are Americans' living standards down in some places? That's because of weak productivity growth, reflecting how our citizens have lost their old work ethic, especially next to hardworking Japanese, Koreans, or Chinese. Is the country's income gap widening? That's because so many high-earning wives in the top tenth now work full time. Central-city crime, in turn, doesn't reflect poverty; it reflects the breakdown of the family. Politically, this emphasis on cultural and moral causations serves a double purpose: first, upholding the priorities of the religious traditionalists and fundamentalists so important to Republicans and conservatives, and second, defending business and financial elites against arguments of economic mismanagement, which Democrats would use to justify remedies like greater regulation or higher taxes. Cultural causation also pushes blame away from industry and Wall Street, and toward minority, urban, law enforcement, educational, and social-welfare issues where voters are suspicious of Democratic programs, judicial interpretations, and interest groups.

Liberal readers would do well to disabuse themselves of the caricature in which fundamentalist preachers or politicians stand before Sun Belt assemblies hung with red, white, and blue bunting calling for a declaration of war against non-believers. In fact, a large body of mainstream conservative thinking also locates the roots of America's problems in social and cultural decline. Economist Milton Friedman flatly argues that "despite the current rhetoric, our problems are not economic. Our real problems are social, and more government isn't going to help." In a recent book entitled *The Dream and the Nightmare*, Myron Magnet, an editor at *Fortune* magazine, contends that the cultural revolution of the 1960s, not global economic upheaval, destroyed the values of the poor. His one-dimensional answer, then, is "to stop doing what makes the problem worse. Stop the current welfare system, stop quota-based affirmative action, stop treating criminals as justified rebels, stop letting bums expropriate public spaces or wrong-doers live in public housing at public expense, stop Afro-centric education in the schools." David Blankenhorn, director _fascists asshole_ of the Institute for American Values, likewise allows no doubt. The central problem "is called family decline. It's not 'the economy, stupid.' It's the culture." And looking ahead, for conservatives the culture-is-responsible thesis enables them to sidestep the speculative bubble of the 1980s and to insist that Reaganomics worked, so tax cuts and deregulation should be renewed, not abandoned, in the 1990s.

In the middle, where practicality outscores ideology, large numbers of voters perceive elements of *both* kinds of decline, without one necessarily being the engine. So do the limited cadres of moderate Republicans and moderate conservative Democrats in Congress. The Clinton administration has given some attention to the crisis in moral values. The mostly Democratic Communitarian movement has been a source of balanced centrist thinking, and few conservative Republicans can match the pithy candor of Democratic U.S. senator Daniel Patrick Moynihan in his descriptions of the decline of U.S. civility and order over the last twenty to thirty years. Among the public, the two explanations are also almost evenly matched. Concern about economic decline appears broader, but polls show that at least 40 percent of Americans see social and economic problems mainly as a decline of moral values.

Yet ideological polarization seems to recur in national party politics, executive branch policy, and congressional voting patterns. The Republicans showed at their 1992 party convention in Houston how the forces of a crusade against moral decline could take control. And the Clinton administration, in its early days, reinforced the notion that Democrats, happy to intervene in the economy, also continued to favor higher taxes and more regulation while remaining inclined to pursue cultural positions, especially on homosexuality and racial preferences, that were disconcerting to party moderates and infuriating to conservatives. It is hard to imagine either party developing a broad centrist position on simultaneous economic and social decline. Yet the historical evidence, to which we will return shortly, is that the two threads of "decline" occur together. Indeed, they draw on each other. Any plausible explanation of the forces at work in the late-twentieth-century United States

Is the man in office responsible for all that occurs?
— Too simplistic

(or in previous great powers) must include *both*, and parties and ideologies with one-dimensional explanations can only feed the breakdown.

The further irony is that *both* major parties and ideologies have actually been part of *both* U.S. decline patterns — economic and social. How can Democrats hand the Republicans sole blame for the decline of U.S. manufacturing, for example, when they have spent much of the 1970s, 1980s, and 1990s promoting increased economic regulation, an expansive (even crippling) level of product liability, and heights of government spending that fanned inflation? Even the boldest party indictment of Reaganomics cannot sidestep these complicities. And the GOP, in turn, shares culpability for moral decline. For all the Republican insistence on liberal responsibility, the first publication of *Playboy* (1953), the first pelvic gyrations of Elvis Presley, and the controversial federal judicial ruling in favor of publication of *Lady Chatterley's Lover* (1959) came during the Eisenhower era. More recently and more significantly, George Bush in 1992 followed up a Republican convention that saluted family values with an autumn campaign in which he happily appeared before crowds with two Hollywood stars most prominently in tow — Bruce Willis of *Die Hard 2*, a movie with a total body count of 264, and Arnold Schwarzenegger, who gunned down 17 policemen in *The Terminator* and bellowed "Consider this a divorce!" just before he shot his wife in *Total Recall*. Social commentator Christopher Lasch has touched on a further hypocrisy: "Republicans may hate what is happening to our children, but their commitment to the culture of acquisitive individualism makes them reluctant to probe its source. They glorify the man on the make, the small operator who stops at nothing in the pursuit of wealth, and then wonder why ghetto children steal and hustle instead of applying themselves to homework."

Despite these hypocrisies, though, what truly reveals the

differences between the parties and ideologies is when their constituencies come into play. The Republicans, collectively, are simply not free to admit that serious economic declines — for the middle class and the American dream, in accelerating national indebtedness, and the eroded competitiveness of key industries — occurred during the Reagan-Bush period. Party economic policies are too closely linked to the interests that profited from the recent era's speculative bubble, tax cuts, bailouts, and trade liberalizations. That includes multinational corporations, Wall Street investment firms and speculators, entrepreneurs and allied lawyers, lobbyists and conservative economists, all of whose affection for the 1980s is understandable. Nor can conservatives reject sermons on moral decline, what with the religious right and the conservative Christian community marshaling as much as 15 to 20 percent of the electorate. But if these basic alignments can be set out in several sentences, printing the full list of the organizations, political action committees, and contributors involved would take an inch-thick wad of pages. That is what words about "interest-group buildup" cannot convey: the hugeness of the infrastructure involved, and how little the politicians can walk away from the structures that finance and support them.

The Democrats face the same problem with a reverse set of interest groups. Criticizing the economic policies of the 1980s is easy, because their party represents the constituencies that suffered most: minorities, the poor, urban interests, social welfare organizations, labor unions, education groups. But discussing the moral and cultural decline that many Americans feel has taken place since the 1960s is another story. Liberalism and the Democratic Party happen to represent most of the constituencies and interests that view the moral and cultural upheaval of the late twentieth century as a national achievement: blacks, gays and lesbians, feminists, civil liberties activists, and others. Many of these groups are just as enthusiastic about their periods of breakthrough as entrepreneurs and stockbrokers were about the economic opportunity of the 1980s — the notion of a "moral decline" is unacceptable. Beyond that, the Democrats, especially in Congress, also represent the institutionalized social welfare, minority, and urban agenda that was at the core of Washington's response to the urban, poverty, and civil rights crises in the 1960s and 1970s. This further traps them in a cultural defensiveness, because conservatives (and some moderates) blame these agendas for the breakdown of the family, the entitlements revolution, and the decline of individual responsibility.

Arguably, a majority of Americans see each party as having a distinctive failing that it refuses to grapple with. In 1968, the Democrats lost a watershed presidential election, principally because of their cultural and sociological positions, and the Republicans lost another because of their economics a quarter century later. Voters have a keen sense of which party is trapped with what interests — and which party has let America down in which direction.

Changes are always possible, but besides each party's determining constituencies and weaknesses, social and cultural, there is a further constraint: the extent to which both parties are so heavily involved with a large group of relatively centrist lawyers, lobbyists, political donors, and interest groups who give money, without any particular ideology, to gain access to power for narrow interests and transfer seekers. This is the heart of the entrenched Washington power structure examined in the last chapter. The electorate, in short, is entitled to regard both parties as being crippled both ways — by ideology and even more by interest groups. In the matter of reversing America's slow decline, both parties have been so prominent a part of the problem that it is difficult to picture them as part of the solution.

As we will see in Chapter 5, no other Western nation has a

party system that is so old and so rooted in various national yesterdays or so closely intertwined with the biggest special-interest and lobbying complex the world has ever seen. In recent years, as this process has intensified, the two parties have also, for other reasons, polarized on a number of ideological matters, even if their competition on other issues is often marked by posturing and superficiality. With their competing narrow interpretations of decline, neither can hope to define the nation's predicament or to implement a realistic national renewal agenda with broad appeal to the midsection of American public opinion — and few failings could be more critical.

The Linkage of Economic and Cultural Decline

This thesis that America's late-twentieth-century political parties and ideologies are too narrow, too burdened by interest groups and past failures they cannot transcend, becomes even more compelling when one looks at the hallmarks of "decline" in the previous great powers and at what might have been done to reverse it. Economic and cultural changes associated with deterioration usually occur together, suggesting that the causes are as much a historical process as the failure of any single ideology. If this *is* the challenge, politics as usual will have a tough time meeting it.

The United States of the 1990s, in displaying familiar economic and cultural changes, is following a pattern broadly similar to that in the other leading world powers we have been discussing. Some of the symptoms are economic, some cultural, some mixed. By using the examples of Rome, Spain, the Netherlands, Britain, and the United States, and listing the characteristics widespread enough to occur in three or four out of the five nations during their decline stages, one comes up with the following:

Economic	Mixed Cultural and Economic	Cultural
Economic polarization	Declining middle class	Increased sophistication in culture and art
Concentration of wealth	Deteriorating cities	
Rising debt	Declining quality of education	Luxury and permissiveness
Higher taxes	Increasing internation- alism of elites	
Relative decline in manufacturing		Complaints about foreign influence and loss of old patriotism
Increasing speculation and the rise of finance	Increasingly burdensome national capital	
		Complaints about moral decay

In short, great power decline, and not simply the separate weaknesses of liberalism and conservatism, is responsible for the new force field that Americans must deal with, and the dilemma is always economic *and* cultural. Consider Britain in the 1890s, when concern about the country's endangered world economic leadership was expressed in the titles of successful books like *Made In Germany* and *American Invaders* — and when the average family's purchasing power was entering a two-decade period of stagnation or decline while the financial sector boomed and the rich grew ever richer. Even as economic doubts were starting to gnaw, the Victorian middle classes were simultaneously aroused by the emergence of dandyism and decadence in fashionable London art and theatrical circles, by the rising tide of feminism, and by the increasing prominence of homosexuals, symbolized by the scandals surrounding the playwright Oscar Wilde. As manufacturing eroded and cultural modernism accelerated during the Edwardian years, steak-and-kidney-pie England was embattled on *two* fronts.

Holland's ebb produced a similar combination of tensions. Fear about how the nation was losing its old economic vigor *too easy to simply argue both for the middle*

and preeminence grew in the later seventeenth century, taking a quantum leap in the 1690s with the demands of the drawn-out War of the Spanish Succession, which further undercut the country's manufacturing and ran up its debt. Dutch pastors were already decrying how the country was being punished for forgetting the puritanism, patriotism, and hard work of its fathers and turning instead to speculation, luxury, and foreign ideas and vices, a criticism that grew in the eighteenth century. A wave of antihomosexual activity spread across the country in 1730–32, amid claims that the practice was spread by the ever-untrustworthy French. "Moral decay" had been much less of an issue in the golden years of an expanding economy.

As for Spain, the spread of concern about the nation's future in the 1590s — seeded by the unexpected defeat of the Spanish Armada in 1588, then aggravated by failed harvests and a great plague — also involved multiple fears. Spain's economic reformers, the so-called *arbitristas*, who favored trying to rebuild manufacturing and the middle class while cutting government jobs and dispersing the parasites of the court, also had cultural axes to grind. When Spain's chief minister, the Count-Duke of Olivares, finally proposed a sweeping national reform program in 1623, it included measures to close the brothels, to reform the sumptuary laws to curb extravagant dress, and to limit the publication of novels and plays.

Rome's parallel is also familiar (even if overcaricatured): the widening gap between the rich and everyone else, the overload of taxes, the decline of the middle class, the luxury and permissiveness of the aristocracy relaxing in their baths and on their couches even as the barbarians were figuratively at the gates.

In theory, serious reform would require some reversal of the changes on *both* dimensions, economic and cultural. In the United States of the 1990s, such politics would be especially appealing to the eroding, embattled middle class. Consider the list of decline symptoms that appears in the table on the pre-

vious page. The middle class would favor reversing most of
the trends cited, from cultural permissiveness to the decline
of high-wage manufacturing, the rise of speculative finance,
and the increasing share of national wealth going to the rich.
But the politics of pursuing these changes — many of which,
for the current-day United States, would involve jumping out
of the two-party system — would run afoul of the country's
most powerful interests.

Conservative economic elites, which have enjoyed the fruits
of polarization and the enrichment of service industries, professions, and finance, would oppose middle-class populist economics. The idea of protecting heavy industry offends them as
outdated. Rather than worrying about broad national economic decline, many conservatives would laud the 1980s as a
golden age to which the United States should quickly return.
And globalization is an economic opportunity, not a threat.
Liberalism's cultural elites, in turn, would feel threatened by
any attempt to roll back the principal social trends of the last
thirty years. Moreover, the distinction between the two elites
is tenuous. Especially in the most sophisticated East and West
Coast metropolitan areas, from Manhattan to Silicon Valley,
there is a considerable overlap between high incomes and social tolerance or libertarian views. Support for gay rights or
(constitutional) equal rights amendments tends to be strongest
in affluent neighborhoods and weakest in blue-collar or lower-
middle-class strongholds. Financial high rollers and speculators
are better known for sophisticated vices than for puritanism.
Culturally liberal constituencies in Hollywood, the communications industry, fashion and the arts, and the gay community
are all high or relatively high income.

Which brings us to some important interest-group sociology: What ordinary people in the mid-range of the population see as economic or social decline is, from a different
perspective, the transition from one set of values and elites to

another. The elites of a nation's heyday — be it early Roman, Dutch, Victorian, or midcentury American — tend to be patriotic, reasonably puritanical, relatively egalitarian, committed to hard work, suspicious of foreigners and cosmopolitan influences. Vocationally, they would be farmers, soldiers, seamen and traders, inventors, religious leaders, manufacturers, or merchants. Generations later, as "decline" sets in, the new values would be aristocratic, languid, tolerant or permissive, cosmopolitan, and elitist. The elites would be the rich, aristocrats, courtiers, financiers, investors, fashion setters, lawyers, bureaucrats, and communicators. But while this changeover sounds like it ought to be highly vulnerable, that hasn't been true. As we will see, reforms or attempts to roll back the clock or restore a prior status quo have generally failed. What this suggests, in a nutshell, is that what history — and a worried middle class — calls decline is, at the same time, an evolution and transition of interest groups. The transition is crippling to large numbers of ordinary people, but it is a process that American politicians and policy makers, most of them responsive to liberal and conservative elites that are benefiting, will have great difficulty framing in crisis terms and confronting.

Great Economic-Power Decline and the Rise of Interest-Group Internationalism

This is a central part of the transition just described. One relentless characteristic of a great economic power at its zenith and then beyond is a taste for foreign culture, sophistication, and business-financial linkages. In contrast, the rise of these nations has usually involved opposite traits and characteristics: puritanism, nationalism, and cultural parochialism. But in two or three generations, the change is usually quite apparent.

For the puritan commercial cultures of seventeenth-century Holland, Victorian Britain, and the midcentury

United States, success would bring common symptoms of cultural transformation: increasing fascination with things French, from cuisine to *haute couture*, much of it hitherto suspect as frivolous, decadent, or both. The rise of French culture and increasing use of the French language among the socially pretentious was a significant resentment in the Netherlands by the late seventeenth century, and two centuries later, a similar, albeit lesser francophilia in cooking, dressing, and vacationing was visible in the upper-middle and upper classes of Edwardian England. The United States itself followed suit in the 1970s and 1980s, as the count of French restaurants in Boston, New York, Washington, Los Angeles, and San Francisco roughly tripled, and President and Mrs. Reagan became caught up in a pseudoaristocratic social whirl focused on New York's Metropolitan Museum of Art and cultural homage to eighteenth-century France, La Belle Epoque, and fashion setters like Yves St. Laurent.[4]

In economic matters, as these nations reached their zeniths and then began their relative decline, they each found more and more of their opportunity in the international arena and less at home, where once-famous centers of commerce and industry were becoming empty shells. Meanwhile, though, this same phenomenon is one of the reasons why decline or nondecline is so hotly debated. History loosely supports the argument that overall "decline" starts more or less around the time a great power's average families start losing the income advantage they had enjoyed over similar households in competing national economies. This usually happens more or less as the particular nation's share of world GNP or share of world manufactured exports starts to decline. But if we turn to the top one percent or five percent elites of these same nations — the financiers, investors, multinational businessmen, bankers, exporters and importers, shippers, brokers, accountants, lawyers, and communicators — we see that their greatest success comes as the circumstances of ordinary folk weaken. Their opportunities, in Holland, Britain, and now in the United States, maximize a decade or two (or even a generation or two) later as emphasis shifts to letting some of the weaker manufacturing slide and taking advantage of national ability and the opportunity to make money out of investments, finance, and the international sale of commercial and professional services.

In the Netherlands circa 1725 or 1750 and Britain circa 1910 or even 1925, these pursuits were still on the uptick even as old-line manufacturing sectors sagged. Not surprisingly, this pattern complicates — and also *distorts* — any debate over national decline. Then and now, many stockbrokers, international lawyers, traders, and multinational businessmen, instead of sharing the ebb so obvious to textile workers or iron masters, find themselves enjoying the best of times. Like the Dutch and the British in earlier days, U.S. policy makers of the 1980s and 1990s have put little priority on trying to protect older U.S. manufacturers or manufacturing wages in order to concentrate on international markets for business, financial and communication services, investments, and a few value-added categories of merchandise (particularly pharmaceuticals, scientific instruments, and entertainment products in the contemporary U.S.). But these emphases are not based entirely on dispassionate governmental deliberations; they also come from one of the least-analyzed buildups in modern world history — the extent to which interest-group dominance in later-stage great economic powers swings to internationalist outlooks and biases.

In the Netherlands circa 1730, the interest-group biases of Amsterdam and The Hague, which did little to challenge the foreign protectionism or cheap-labor competition crippling Dutch manufacturing from every direction, were well enough described by English novelist Daniel Defoe: the "Dutch must be understood to be as they really are, the carriers of the world, the middle persons of trade, the factors and brokers of Europe." They were also, as we will see, the principal investment bankers of Europe, putting money to work from Russia to the Caribbean. By the early twentieth century, British economic interests were shifting in the same direction. For example, in 1913, the last year before World War I, British manufactured exports were in deficit by £158 million as old industries slipped, but shipping and shipbuilding made up two thirds of that, and the overseas profits of banking, insurance, and brokerage services, as well as insurance, more than made up the rest. And an increasing part of British investment was being made overseas rather than at home. Even schoolboy economic histories reached the obvious conclusion: that these international interests tilted the balance for free trade even as manufacturers' pleas for help were growing.

However, what was merely *obvious* in eighteenth-century Holland and early-twentieth-century Britain has become *blatant* in late-twentieth-century Washington, where interest groups are like giant mushrooms in a tropical rain forest or cabbages in the twenty-hour daylight of a south Alaskan summer, reaching unbelievable sizes. In the Washington of ninety thousand persons engaged in or supporting lobbying and two thirds of former party chairmen and top trade officials being registered on behalf of foreign interests, the convergence of this feeding frenzy with the persuasiveness of foreign embassies and international organizations adds up to a massive interest-group imbalance in favor of internationalist versus nationalist economics. Far from representing an antidote to interest-group domination of U.S. policy making, internationalism has emerged as one of the ultimate Washington expressions and consolidations of special-interest power. Relatively free movement of goods, services, capital, and jobs in and out of the United States, obviously beneficial to perhaps 10 to 15 percent of the population, detrimental to some 30 to

50 percent who just want to keep some of the unique midcentury advantage the United States won on European and Pacific battlefields, is no abstract verity; it has become one of the most potent vested interests in the U.S. capital.

Back in 1988, Democratic presidential hopeful Richard Gephardt charged that U.S. financial elites were colluding in national economic decline because they were making so much money out of it. There is still some truth to this, although, ironically, in 1993 the incoming Democratic administration appointed a deputy secretary of the Treasury who worked during the 1980s for a company that located U.S. firms to sell to the Japanese. By the mid-1990s, U.S. authors like Edward Luttwak, James Fallows, and Alan Tonelson were beginning to identify U.S. free trade commitments with the economic self-interest and ideological blinders of professional, multinational, and investment elites.

But in this case no words, and certainly no theories, can convey what a simple 1993 listing of who in Washington lobbies for what foreign interests can underscore. A comparable catalog of the relationships of New York's financial sector — a portrait of what investment firm or bank advises or underwrites on behalf of which foreign organizations — would be equally revealing, but it is not available. By contrast, the list for Washington, setting out some fifteen hundred foreign interests and naming the individuals, law firms, and lobbying groups who work for them, is an extraordinary document — not secret, not clandestine, just extraordinary. Back in 1979, just four hundred foreign interests paid representatives in Washington. Since then, in a massive mobilization, the list has tripled. Almost every major law firm, accounting firm, lobbying group, or public relations company in Washington has three or four foreign clients. On broad matters of economic globalization and internationalism, almost the whole of serious-influence, high-hourly-rate Washington has been bought and paid for: practically nobody well connected enough to belong to the Metropolitan Club or well-heeled enough to eat at Lion D'Or or Jean-Louis is available to represent the anonymous small towns afraid of losing an auto parts plant or to speak for the ten thousand workers Xerox or International Widget are ready to lay off at the wink of a computer. Bipartisan Washington, loyal to its campaign contributions and retainer fees, accepts almost any breach of the postwar social contract premised on international competitiveness and globalization.

Yet the implication is stark: Washington's extraordinary interest-group buildup is not simply a burden on effective government or politics. Too often, it is also a bar to the ability of the federal government to stand up for the economic interests of ordinary Americans against the better-funded commitments of lobbyists, lawyers, investment bankers, multinational businessmen, and trade consultants for whom globalization has become a profit opportunity.

National Decline as a Political Crisis

In the meantime, the impact of America's transition on politics is likely to be enormous. Nations changing so that economic and cultural elites flourish while the average family sees its livelihood and beliefs threatened do not produce happy elections. The political results in other countries have ranged from dictatorship and oligarchy to revolution and a class-warfare reshuffling of the party system.

The degeneration of both politics and government in the later years of Athens and Rome is a staple of ancient history. Spain's politics and government were a caricature by the late seventeenth century, although Castile was too downtrodden to revolt. As for the Dutch, their mid-eighteenth-century ruling cliques were confronted by a movement called the Patriots, which attacked nepotism, corruption, and moral decay and called for a full return to old liberties and values. More than any others in Europe, the Dutch reformers were aroused by the American Revolution. Then, in 1782, the Batavian Revolution broke out in the Netherlands. Though eventually put down, it was an early portent of the revolutions that would sweep across France and the rest of Europe in the 1790s.

Yet the political reaction to economic decline that presumably has the most meaning for Americans is the disintegration of the British party system from the 1890s through the 1920s. For the previous four decades, when Britain was in its heyday, the average British family's income and standard of living had kept improving. The nation's global lead in textiles, steel, and shipbuilding might be putting Italian marble in the great halls of the manor houses of the nouveaux riches, but it also put better food on the tables of the working class. Until the mid-1890s, that is. Then, for roughly two decades, as the competitive circumstances of British manufacturing declined, so did the average family's real income and purchasing power, even while the rich enjoyed unprecedented incomes and invested them in factories, plantations, and railroads on the other side of the world. As this happened, the bipartisan optimism of the 1850s, 1860s, and 1870s — when composers Gilbert and Sullivan could produce lyrics about every English baby being born a little Liberal or a little Conservative — drained out of British politics, giving way to a growing class-warfare agenda and the slow emergence of the Labour Party.

The effect on the party system was shattering. The competition between the Liberal and Conservative parties in the 1870s and even in the 1880s was somewhat like that between Democrats and Republicans in the fat years after World War II: which side was in power did not make very much difference to economic growth, to business, or to the general political and governmental system. But the new Labour Party, with its

In 1935 Britain's opinion-molding classes found themselves pondering the message of a book called *The Strange Death of Liberal England*, which marveled at how far the Liberal Party and turn-of-the-century political culture had unraveled. The example ought to be a caution for Americans convinced that their two-party system will endure where Gilbert and Sullivan's Liberals and Conservatives did not. The turmoil of national decline — the emergence of new elites, issues, and predicaments — never leaves the political or party system the way it was, and the shortcomings of American political and governmental institutions are already souring a disgruntled public.

But before taking up these governmental malfunctions, it is important to look at another critical facet of the change that has overtaken late-twentieth-century America: the rise of an increasingly speculative financial sector, rich and influential enough so that the values of Wall Street are another part of what is driving the values and interests of ordinary Americans from the temples of Washington decision making.

Who the fuck are ordinary Americans

— This chapter illustrates his argument of an inevitable decline / disintegration of the two party system

Chapter Four

The Financialization of America: Electronic Speculation and Washington's Loss of Control over the "Real Economy"

Banking establishments are more dangerous than standing armies.

— THOMAS JEFFERSON, *1799*

I used to think if there was reincarnation, I wanted to come back as the president or the pope or a .400 baseball hitter, but now I want to come back as the bond market. You can intimidate everybody.

—JAMES CARVILLE,
political adviser to the president, 1993

You mean to tell me that the success of the [economic] program and my reelection hinges on the Federal Reserve and a bunch of f---ing bond traders?

— BILL CLINTON,
President-Elect, 1993

THE PERCEPTION that James Carville reveals would have been implausible back in 1969 or 1972 or even 1985. But by the mid-1990s, the bond market — and the overall financial sector —had become a powerful usurper of control over economic policy previously exercised by Washington, and elected officeholders were losing their ability to serve old average-American constituencies.

Reckless government indebtedness, visible in everything from annual federal budget deficits to the rocketing national debt, is the conventional explanation. America's politicians have borrowed and spent their way into fiscal handcuffs. Yes, but there is also *another* reason: since the early 1970s, the clout of the financial sector has exploded as it changed from yesterday's lackadaisical Yale Club lunches, ever-increasing dividends from "Generous Motors," and typewritten orders from Aunt Jane to "sell my three hundred shares of AT&T" into today's trillion-dollar computer-based megaforce. The statistics of its expansion match its technological revolution. Each month, several dozen huge domestic financial firms and exchanges, in many of their practices operating beyond effective government regulation, electronically trade a total sum in currencies, futures, derivative instruments, stocks, and bonds that exceeds the entire annual gross national product of the United States! Investment-sector power over bonds and interest rates has never been greater. Carville is right; that *is* intimidating.

Too few politicians understand the hows and whys of Washington's diminished control of the nation's fiscal helm and what it means. Back in the early 1970s, before the global economy was hooked up to supercomputers and changed to the megabyte standard, the financial sector was subordinate to Congress and the White House, and the total of financial trades conducted by American firms or on American exchanges over an entire year was a dollar amount less than the gross national product. By the 1990s, however, through a twenty-four-hour-a-day cascade of electronic hedging and speculating, the financial sector had swollen to an annual volume of trading thirty or forty times greater than the dollar turnover of the "real economy," although the latter was where ordinary Americans still earned their livelihoods.* The annual trades of Manhattan-headquartered CS First Boston, one of the world's leading bond houses, by themselves exceeded the dollar value of the GNP, and four or five other firms were not far behind. Moreover, the relative volume of transactions kept soaring each year, as financial mathematicians invented newer and more exotic computer programs and so-called derivatives — hybrid financial instruments or arrangements with a particular speculative twist.

Under the best of circumstances, techniques like these would have saddled the workaday economy with a new set of short-term and speculative biases. But dangerous conditions made the trend worse. High-powered electronic trading arrived just in time to catch the U.S. economy in a period of national stagflation, declining competitiveness in key industries, and mounting debt, producing an interaction we now

---

* The major investment firms and banks all have trading desks and traders, but there is no longer an easy definition of "trading." The extent to which it now occurs in so many exotic forms explains why "trading" involves a dollar turnover 30 to 40 times the size of the so-called real economy.

know to have been momentous. On the one hand, the risk management dilemmas unleashed by inflation, high interest rates, and uncertainties of borrowing worked to justify a legitimate role for electronic hedging tactics. On the other, these same volatilities gave electronic speculation what it needed to feed on and flourish beyond the wildest expectations. The consequence, two decades later, is a massive, revolutionized, and largely unregulated financial sector armed with the latest high-tech weaponry and pursuing profits on any battlefield, straining the stock and bond markets, plucking loot from any debacle, shooting the economic wounded, and outgunning the "real economy" in its transactions by huge ratios. This leap in the importance of spectronic finance is hard to overestimate.

In institutional terms, the new role of spectronic finance ranks with Washington interest-group power in helping to explain why politics cannot respond to the people and why the nation's government and policies are so often ineffective. If America's elected officeholders face shrinking control over the real economy, it is partly because they have so little hold over the financial economy — and because the latter is slowly gobbling the former. Instead of being purged and reformed in the wake of the 1980s speculative bubble, as the history of U.S. capitalism would demand, the financial economy only grew larger. People who should have been indicted got honorary degrees. Practices that should have been curbed produced record profits. Derivative instruments only grew more exotic — and commentators missed the most dangerous examples, from options giving a right to buy a bet against the stock market to interest-only strips and tailormade speculative contracts, because of their fascination with superficial acronyms like SLOBs (sale-leaseback obligation bonds) and SURFs (step-up recovery floaters). Speculation, in short, displaced investment. And financiers, as we shall see, more often controlled politicians than vice versa.

financial market gobbles up the Real economy

The Financialization of America

Establishing a definition is important. What can usefully be called the financialization of America goes far beyond its obvious day-to-day symptoms: the proliferating automatic teller machines in suburban shopping centers, the stockmarket books on bestseller lists, the rising ratios of retirees investing in chancy mutual funds. The actual transformation is so much greater. Nor is the late twentieth century the first example, a point we will pursue below, although today's upheaval is by far the biggest. Finance has not simply been spreading into every nook and cranny of economic life; a sizeable portion of the financial sector, electronically liberated from past constraints, has put aside old concerns with funding the nation's long-range industrial future, has divorced itself from the precarious prospects of Americans who toil in factories, fields, or even suburban shopping malls and is simply feeding wherever it can.

Such two-tier economies do have precedents, long before computers, during some of history's other speculative bubbles. They have recurred whenever the siren song of easy money and profits without work lured nations and "financialized" their thoughts and morality. Spain was a glaring example, when its sixteenth-century economy revolved around the arrival of the treasure fleets from the New World. With wealth depending on the flow of gold into Seville and the latest loans from bankers in Venice and Augsburg, Spain's leaders let manufacturing and the real economy languish. Money itself was what mattered. Holland had a comparable mentality amid the seventeenth-century "Tulipomania," then for much longer during its eighteenth-century speculative era. And a further similarity could be found in the United States of the Roaring Twenties, when lunch-hour crowds gathered around ticker tapes, and every shoe-shine boy was looking for stock tips.

These previous waves also invariably involved technological innovation and new financial instruments, albeit nothing like the rise of electronic speculation. This time, in the megabyte era, there may be a greater basis for a *prolonged* split between the divergent real and financial economies.

Beyond America's transition from steel mills to mutual funds and stock exchanges, late-twentieth-century financialization has also depended on a second critical circumstance: the changeover by which money in the United States and elsewhere lost intrinsic value through the end of silver coinage in the mid-1960s and the end of dollar convertibility into gold in 1971. Once this happened, dollars, francs, and marks were worth only what the cold-eyed computers and markets decided, and politicians — and the bewildered electorate they sometimes represented — could not keep control. Fixing the value of currencies passed to the financial centers, and within the United States more specifically to the New York and Chicago stock and futures exchanges, and the leading banks and investment firms.

The interaction of economic volatility and billions of dollars' worth of computers programmed by the country's best mathematical and financial minds put the nation's leading financial organizations into a catbird seat. This power rested on three pillars: The first was financial-sector ability to take advantage of how U.S. and foreign currencies, now lacking intrinsic or real value, could be played with as almost never before. The second, the firms' wherewithal to use their new electronic search-and-deploy capacity to probe every nook and cranny of both the U.S. and the global economies, every bourse and *bolsa*, every market and contract, for transactions and profits that would have been ungraspable in the pre-electronic era. And the third was Wall Street's command of profits and compensation levels high enough to excite lawyers and corporate executives, motivating them to help push more of the real economy into the orbit of finance. To take full advantage, partly for purposes of risk-hedging but more for speculating, strategists for the big investment firms and banks have been inventing scores of new "derivative" instruments and techniques that computer programmers could use to extract profit from any situation — to bet on the most unusual turn of fortune's economic wheel.[5] Note 5 charts the dates when the major derivative instruments were introduced.

The rest is economic history. The rapid emergence of derivatives in the 1980s closely correlated with the booster-rocket stage of the financial economy. Even the stock market crash of 1987, aggravated by derivatives, caused only a temporary slowdown once it became clear that the Federal Reserve was flooding the system with liquidity. As the volume of transactions soared, the dollar turnover came to outpace the dollar turnover of the real economy by an increasingly huge ratio. Much of the new volume was artificial and speculative; many of the trades were simply designed to milk as many dollars as possible from the largest number of situations. For example, McKinsey and Company has estimated that of the $800 billion or so traded every day in the world's currency markets in the early 1990s, only $20 billion to $25 billion was exchanged in support of global trade in goods and services.

There is a perception, carefully nurtured by those enjoying the profits, that high-tech finance is a global cavalcade of progress, submerging clumsy, outdated local and national governments in a new world order, empowering an affluent teletronic democracy in which humming hospital computers in St. Louis or Cincinnati will dial up livers, hearts, and eyes for transplant from Lima or Tashkent, or in which the average Long Islander can order three-caviar pizza or make reservations for Marrakech on a pocket telecomputer. Perhaps, but at the moment, no more than a few hundred thousand Americans are significantly participating. Moreover, the unfortunate experience of the past great economic upheavals, from the sixteenth-century Renaissance and rise of capitalism to the nineteenth-century Industrial Revolution, is that break-through-level finance and technology are *brutal* for several generations before they are *benevolent*. They erode the living standards of the ordinary folk and destabilize governments unable to interpret the complex new political and economic universe. The great bulk of the profits invariably goes to a small elite able to harness and ride the new techniques, technologies, and opportunities. So it was in 1600 and in 1825 — and so it appears to be again now.

Such global upheavals have always been a great feeding ground for finance, but never before with such magnitude and all-powerful technology. The role played in the sixteenth century by the international financiers of Venice, Augsburg, and Antwerp, or even in the nineteenth century by the Rothschilds, Barings, and Morgans, was small potatoes in comparison to the 1990s impact of financiers controlling tens of billions of dollars' worth of computers programmed by the greatest array of math geniuses and quantum-theoreticians since the Manhattan Project. So armed, the major players of fin de siècle Wall Street — the giant investment firms and banks, plus some of the major currency speculators, hedge fund operators, and corporate raiders — became high-tech-era replicas of the infamous "White Companies" that plundered fourteenth-century France or the pirates who looted Spanish galleons up and down the seventeenth-century Caribbean. Not that any of these swashbucklers enjoyed anything like the opportunity with crossbows or cutlasses that the buccaneers of Wall Street enjoy with quotrons and modems. If Blackbeard or Henry Morgan could be reincarnated in the 1990s, they would want to come back as head trader at Goldman Sachs or CS First Boston.

No politician thinking ahead to the twenty-first century

can ignore this emergence of lower Manhattan as the new Tortuga. And it has happened in a virtual vacuum of effective policing, because the rise of spectronic finance overlapped the deregulatory drive of the late 1970s and early 1980s. Government officials did little more than gawk at the new techniques and practices — just as in the sixteenth century, when the pioneering capitalism of the Renaissance flooded across Western Europe on a wave of innovation and inflation, and in the nineteenth century, when British and American economic regulation took some fifty to sixty years to catch up with the abuses of the Industrial Revolution. In the 1990s, we are discovering how costly a kindred lag has been.

That is because part of the impact on the real economy has been pernicious, not least in the transformation of finance from patient capital to impatient speculation. The interaction of computerization with the volatility of the 1970s and 1980s helped replace the old white-shoe practices of selling bonds, splitting stocks, and advising familiar longtime clients with what could be called transaction-driven amorality. In the world of computer programs and tailored derivative instruments, where the money goes or what it does in its brief minutes, hours, or days of electronic existence is morally meaningless: what counts — *all that counts* — is that it returns to its home screen a slightly more swollen slug of green or gray digits than it began. By the mid-1990s, this was the new profit base in investment firms: sweeping the world electronically, arbitraging veins of profit unreachable earlier, taking $172,000 here and adding $1.72 million there, eventually producing what was real money even to thirty-one-year-old megabyte marauders with $6-million annual bonus packages.

In the spring of 1993, as reports showed major Wall Street firms like Merrill Lynch, Salomon, Shearson Lehman, and Morgan Stanley achieving record 1992 earnings that topped their best years of the mid-1980s boom, one explanation recurred: the unprecedented profits being made from trading in bonds and other instruments. For 1993, Merrill Lynch announced that its revenue from trading swaps and derivatives was up 57 percent from the year before. At Goldman Sachs, also big in trading and derivatives, the profit for 1993 increased 87 percent to $2.7 billion. But while the money was electronic, its impact was all too real. As trading profits at Wall Street firms surged from $9.9 billion in 1988 to $16.3 billion in 1992, power in the executive suites shifted to follow. After listing the bond traders taking over corporate helms at these brokerage houses — John Mack at Morgan Stanley, David Komansky at Merrill Lynch, Richard Fuld at Lehman Brothers — the *Financial Times* explained that "since the mid-1980s securities houses and investment banks have increasingly pursued the shorter-term rewards of trading profits more rigorously than they have the longer-term returns from client relationship banking. The arrival of the traders at the top of the management tree can be seen as the culmination of that process." And it may also signal its institutionalization.

For the average American, or for the typical small businessman, the effects of financialization were less auspicious. Much of the economy had become a minefield. Individual investors might not be fully aware, but many popular mutual funds were spiking their payouts by putting part of their assets in derivatives. That increased their vulnerability. Pension funds were also exposed. For corporations, in turn, the rise of megabyte finance had meant, as early as the mid-1980s, that they were not simply at risk from global trends; *they were also at risk from how global trends were being focused, sharpened, and speeded up by the whirling computers of Wall Street and LaSalle Street.* As we will see, the costs were high. Large firms had to add a percentage point or two to their overheads for de facto financial insurance — a top-flight chief financial officer, hedging operations, investor relations, currency speculation, and so on — on

top of more traditional insurance. Some, like Procter and
Gamble, suffered huge losses from derivatives-linked currency
speculation. Worse still, companies that neglected short-term
attention to their stock prices found themselves suffering speculative whiplash — and then sometimes facing frontal attack
from corporate raiders and other takeover and dismember-
ment specialists.

Not a few big corporations chose to enlarge the financial
side of their business, de-emphasizing what they used to man-
ufacture back in the days of the *Saturday Evening Post* and a
contented American workforce. American Can Company,
once the country's leading producer of containers, slowly
transformed itself into a financial services company named
Primerica. Ford Motor Company, in turn, came to depend on
high profits from a subsidiary, Ford Credit Corporation,
heavily involved in global hedging and speculation. And General Electric sold off its consumer electronics division, emphasizing the huge financial and speculative profits of its General
Electric Credit Corporation. Other large firms were more
covert, simply letting their routine hedging operations drift
into speculation.

Smart businessmen realized that corporate finance was taking on the soul of a computer and that a series of Washington
administrations, mesmerized by the financial sector (and enmeshed, as we shall see, in its rapidly mobilizing campaign
contributions), would not interfere. Firms once committed to
long-term thinking now faced money managers and speculators little concerned about existence beyond the life of a
futures contract. Confronting these pressures and others
of a global dimension, many businesses began to breach
another agreement — the social contract that had existed with
American workers since the aftermath of World War II. Corporations purged employees, especially older ones close to re-
tirement, cut employee benefits, slashed real wages, and shut

down plants in Terre Haute or Muncie to move production to Taiwan and Mexico where ninety-five-cents-an-hour employees were just what the stock-price doctor ordered. For the first time in modern U.S. history, stock prices decoupled from the real economy, enabling the Dow-Jones industrial average to keep setting records even as employees' real wages kept declining. Financialization has only a vague definition, but all of these burdens — the erosion of wages, the agonies of families and communities — go into it.

As corporate chief executives stopped thinking of themselves as stewards with a larger public responsibility, however ambiguous, and started embracing the mores of the financial sector — i.e., "If that goddamn corporate finance guy at our investment bankers is making $4 million this year, I should be, too" — prior salary restraints were pushed aside. Employees' inflation-adjusted wages might be heading down, but CEO compensation packages roared off into the stratosphere, expanding from just 30 or 40 times the average worker's wages in 1980 to a stunning 130 or 140 times as much in 1990. Corporate management wanted, in the worst way, its own equivalents of what Wall Street was packaging for the financial markets and for star financial performers, and as a half-dozen bestsellers have chronicled, that's how management got them: through everything from twenty-eight flavors of stock options to golden parachutes and half-baked LBOs. Greed spread like measles in kindergarten. As the lure of financialization reached Toledo and Springfield, tantalizing the hierarchs of Great Lakes Widget or Buckeye Bearings, senior executives jetted off to Manhattan for advice on how to net $60 million in a leveraged buyout while thousands of worried employees asked a different kind of question: how long would they continue to have a job, health care, and a pension?

The press began to note the extraordinary divergence. "America is not doing very well, but its corporations are doing just fine," said Floyd Norris in his *New York Times* "Market Watch" column in 1992. *Business Week* observed, "The trouble is, Corporate America is surviving at the expense of Household America." In a mid-1992 effort before his column disappeared, *U.S. News* economic columnist John Liscio wrote that "corporate America has been maximizing shareholder value on the backs of the working stiff. . . . Easing credit is supposed to spur reasoned investment, but the nearly 70 percent reduction in short-term rates engineered by the Federal Reserve since February 1989 has done nothing but stimulate frenzied speculation. . . . The chasm between stock prices and job growth stretched even wider as the Fed turned more aggressive in lowering rates. Between October 1990 and July of this year — a period that saw the Fed drop the discount no less than seven times — the Dow-Jones industrial average soared 1,000 points, while nonfarm payrolls were winnowed by 1.2 million."

Wall Street's whirling computers were still telling top corporate managers to decimate jobs in 1993. After the Xerox Corporation's December announcement of a ten thousand-person job cut sent its stock value up 7 percent — a paper profit of almost a billion dollars for investors — one angry journalist quoted a former investment strategist for Goldman Sachs acknowledging that white-collar workers were "in the kill zone. The target of the 1990s is middle-management. The Street is convinced there's 15–20% more fat that can be cut off of the Fortune 500, and they see all of it in those white-collar jobs."

Economists friendly to financialization rushed in with ideological support. American corporations existed for their shareholders. Period. Towns and people weren't part of the equation. If the company is worth more broken up, then break it up. Joel Kurtzman, executive editor of *The Harvard Business Review*, a prominent critic, explained why this was a central weakness: to insist on maximizing shareholder value in a speculative economy was as dangerous as demanding that everyone save during a depression. Advice constructive in one context can become antisocial in another. And Kurtzman identified a second problem: the "quants" — the quantitative strategists hired to write Wall Street's strategies and programs — necessarily skew the financial markets toward amorality. Because raw numbers rule, the effect of the electronic economy is to erase social considerations from the decision-making screen.

The irony is that national long-term investment needs also suffer. The real economic values of companies, like unquantifiable social criteria, are often early casualties in a speculative frenzy. And to add injury to insult, gorging financial markets also levy an increasingly hefty charge on enterprise. As a professor at Harvard, Lawrence H. Summers, now a Clinton Treasury undersecretary, had determined that the corporations listed on the New York Stock Exchange enjoyed a combined income in 1987 of some $314 billion. As an offset, he then calculated the basic cost to business of supporting the investment firms belonging to the exchange as being equal to the sum of these securities firms' 1987 annual receipts — a hefty $53 billion. Summers then added another $20 billion as representing what NYSE companies spent on analysts, lawyers, accountants, and investor-relations programs to keep their stocks listed and traded. His conclusion: that in 1987 the financial markets, by directly or indirectly consuming about $73 billion, effectively ate up almost a quarter of the profits of America's major corporations! The implication is powerful even if the exact mathematics are debatable. The more that finance spreads its computerized wings and digs its talons deeper into the real economy, the less that leaves for everyone else.

As we have seen, this is by no means an entirely new

phenomenon. The United States has experienced smaller degrees of financialization before, particularly in the eras when Wall Street speculation broke into a gallop — the capitalist go-go periods of the late-nineteenth-century Gilded Age and the Roaring Twenties. Each time, as national admiration of entrepreneurs and financiers approached its cyclical peak, finance penetrated to hitherto little touched areas of the economy. More and bigger companies underwent financial repackaging. The holding companies of 1928 were more intricate than the trusts of the 1890s. Debt took on more complicated shapes. New techniques and instruments let speculators inflate ever-bigger bubbles. But each time, when the boom turned to bust, finance was discredited and the real economy regained its primacy. The failure of this to happen again after the bubble of the 1980s is central to the problems of the 1990s.

Which brings us to a powerful historical caution about financialization: the evidence that it is not nirvana, but a late stage of great economic powers heading into trouble. Each of the countries we have been examining, as it passed its peak, underwent a transformation in which finance found itself riding high, feeding on investment and speculation as manufacturing lost importance. As overall decline set in, these same great economic powers also displayed a strong service-sector trend — yes, even back in the crossbow or periwig eras. Observers were often struck by the abundance of bureaucrats, brokers, churchmen, and state employees even as others marveled at how money and finance were leaping old and decreasingly meaningful national borders.

Insistence that transnational finance is unique to the late twentieth century would seem foolish to the Spanish of 1575 or to the bankers of Amsterdam two centuries later. Or to the British financial community of 1910. Indeed, the pattern has kept repeating. Spain, as it declined, exemplified transnational finance — not just a system that substituted treasure, bills, and notes for ordinary work and commerce but a nation that made its money in Mexico and Peru, spent it on the battlegrounds of Flanders and the Rhine, and borrowed to survive from the financiers of Lombardy and the German League.

In Holland, as the mid–eighteenth century spread decay across much of the country, observers compared the plight of the old manufacturing towns with the splendid residences of the stockbrokers. Such were the fruits of financialization. The great economic historian Fernand Braudel has concluded that the Dutch elite of that period had become little more than speculators and rentiers who lived on unearned income, lending their money to any foreign prince or company able to pay the interest. And he cites this Dutch observation circa 1766 to underscore that the international power of today's major financial houses is hardly new:

> If ten or twelve businessmen of Amsterdam of the first rank meet for a banking (i.e., a credit) operation, they can in a moment send circulating throughout Europe over two hundred million florins in paper money, which is preferred to cash. There is no sovereign who could do as much. . . . This credit is a power which the ten or twelve businessmen will be able to exert over all the states in Europe, in complete independence of any authority.

Britain was at a somewhat similar stage by the first decade of the twentieth century. Although its manufacturing was losing ground, its financial services had never been stronger — and its elite of investors, bankers, and rentiers, who controlled nearly half of the world's movable investment capital, were confident that finance and investment would make up for any ebb in textiles, steel, and shipbuilding. However, a prominent critic, Colonial Secretary Joseph Chamberlain, put doubts before a meeting of bankers in 1904:

Granted you are the clearing house of the world, are you entirely beyond anxiety as to the permanence of your great position . . . Banking is not the creator of our prosperity, but is the
creation of it. It is not the cause of our wealth, but it is the
consequence of our wealth; and if the industrial energy and
development which has been going on for so many years in
this country were to be hindered or relaxed, then finance, and
all that finance means, will follow trade to the countries which
are more successful than ourselves.

His warning was prophetic. By 1946 the world's leading
capitalist dynamo of 1914 was a chronic international debtor, its
once proud finances in a shambles, heading into a decline that by
the 1990s would push Britain's GNP below that of Italy. The
lesson is obvious: the great economic powers of the last five
hundred years have each gone through a late-development era
in which earlier reliance on seafaring, manufacturing, or bourgeois commerce yielded to a cocksure faith in finance and a
financial services economy. Not once, though, did this lay a
framework for continued national retention of status as the
world's leading economic power. Quite the reverse. For the
overall national economy, *financialization has been a stage of decay,
not triumph.* An important yet small elite flourishes, but the
average citizen is a loser. The odds are that the latest of these
stages in the United States will have a similar effect — and that
the political and governmental failure in the late 1980s and early
1990s to deal with financialization and its abuses will leave a bad
taste in the mouths of twenty-first-century Americans.

The Politics of a Financial Bailout

Rescuing overextended financial institutions and speculators
from their own folly was a national "first" of the 1980s and
1990s — and an ill omen. In previous crashes, they had been

allowed to collapse. Mark Twain was on a speaking tour of the Pacific Northwest when the Panic of 1893 hit the stock market, and he was struck by the damage. Banks in Seattle, Portland, and San Francisco toppled like Douglas fir trees. Fortunes were lost in the collapse of watered railroad bonds.

When the panic hit, not a few of the financiers who had reveled in the prior Gilded Age boom were shattered in the bust, joining farmers and miners who had been losing ground for decades. The federal authorities provided no refuge from the gales of the marketplace. No one bailed out the flattened banks and traumatized investors. Moreover, once politics changed to reflect voters' loss of faith in unbridled speculation, populist-progressive reforms reshaped the economic landscape, reining in the giant trusts, establishing a progressive income tax, and creating the Federal Reserve Board to supervise the banks. But because the creative cycle of American capitalism worked, another generation of entrepreneurs and speculators would roar again in the 1920s.

When the next crisis came in 1929–33, the process of destruction and renewal was even tougher. The coal miners, railroaders, and farmers who had all been losing ground in the 1920s, early victims of the financial boom, were joined by investors, bankers, and financiers. Washington did not move to suspend market forces. The Bank of the United States and thousands of lesser institutions shut their doors; Samuel Insull's giant public utilities holding company empire collapsed. Cartoons showed Manhattan hotel clerks asking pinstriped guests whether they wanted a room for sleeping or jumping. President Hoover, to be sure, made a small attempt to slow the downward spiral with the Reconstruction Finance Corporation and a few other emergency steps. But the administration's dominant philosophy rang out in the famous words of Treasury Secretary Andrew Mellon: "Liquidate labor, liquidate stocks, liquidate real estate . . . values will be adjusted, and enterprising people will pick up the wreck from less-competent people."

And that is how the cycle worked, because the financial purge was massive, with the Dow-Jones industrial average losing 80 percent of its value, commercial real estate values plummeting, and banks closing everywhere. Thereupon, the political countertide of the New Deal proved even more powerful than that of the populist-progressive era. In the 1932 presidential campaign, Franklin D. Roosevelt had talked about driving the money changers from the temple, and in a number of ways, he did. Critics might carp about the president's tenderness toward banks, but the larger effect of the New Deal was to toughen financial regulation, place the SEC as a watchdog over Wall Street, crack down on public utility holdings companies, and increase taxes on the rich through the Wealth Tax Act of 1935. FDR could fairly say, in a 1936 speech, that in his first administration the forces of privilege had met their match — and that in his second administration he hoped they would meet their master.

For over a century, this had been the genius of American political finance. The legacy of these cycles, of the buoyant capitalist expansion that comes first, followed by a speculative excess, a crash of some degree, and then a populist-progressive countertide, is simply this: they have managed to give America the world's most successful example of self-correcting capitalism. Or at least that has been true until now. If, as we saw earlier, the genius of American politics was that once a generation or so the tidal wave of a new politics would sluice out Washington, the comparable renewal process of the modern American political economy was that once a generation or so a wave from the collapse of market speculation and financial excess would wash away the speculators, failed banks, and investment firms and discredited devices of the U.S. financial sector. Then a new public philosophy would complete the reform process. None of these transient speculative financial elites was able to achieve entrenchment. Each time, American capitalism came back stronger — not as the stagnant, hereditary vocation of rentiers or speculators, but as a dynamic culture still broadening the economy, still boosting America's share of world manufacturing and GNP.

This has not repeated in the 1990s, and the change looks dangerous. Financial mercantilism — government-business collaboration calculated to suspend or stymie market forces — has at least partly replaced yesteryear's vibrant capitalism. The eighties, for their part, had mirrored the start-up patterns of previous capitalist-conservative go-go eras, fulfilling ten critical parallels with the Gilded Age and the Roaring Twenties that ranged from conservatism in power and popular suspicion of government to pro-business attitudes, tax cuts, disinflation, concentration of wealth, and record levels of leverage, debt, and speculation. Then, in 1990–91, as the bubble started to burst, even major business and financial publications were unnerved by the abundance of parallels to yesteryear's speculative blowouts: savings and loan institutions were collapsing from New England to California, the junk bond market was reeling, commercial real estate was losing 30–40 percent of its value in major cities, and hundreds of commercial banks, including behemoths like New York–based Citicorp, were failing or flirting with the possibility. Some saw the specter of another decade like the 1930s.

But whatever had happened in Hoover's White House and Mellon's Treasury Department sixty years earlier, no one in the Bush White House or Treasury — or, for that matter, in the Federal Reserve of Alan Greenspan — was talking about stock market liquidation therapy or touting bank failure as the latest fashion in creative Darwinism. Not with the possibility of another huge speculative debacle. Besides, the president and his closest political ally, Secretary of State James Baker, were

Texans who had watched bankruptcy and the failure of financial institutions cut a swath through their home state business circles in the 1970s and again in the mid-1980s; it was no abstraction to them. And Greenspan, as a New York economist and money manager during the 1980s, had been a consultant to high rollers like Charles Keating of Lincoln Savings & Loan.

Tolerance for the purgative side of market forces was also fading politically: the bailout device had been gaining increasing acceptance in Washington for two decades. In the America of the 1890s and 1930s it had still been possible for large enterprises to fail. Since the 1930s, however, a new climate had emerged: *small* enterprises might fail — family farms, let us say, or local hardware stores — but not big ones. Lockheed was saved in 1971 under the Republicans, Chrysler in 1979 under the Democrats, Continental Illinois Bank in 1984 and several big Texas banks during the mid-1980s under the GOP. There would be many more in the late 1980s and especially in the 1990s, as banks and S&Ls by the hundreds had to be rescued by the ambulances of federal deposit insurance.

National leaders do not rush to say so, but the bailout of the early 1990s was the biggest in America's history. Bert Ely, a Virginia-based banking consultant, calculated that the percentage of total U.S. deposits held in financial institutions forced into FDIC and FSLIC rescues in the late 1980s and early 1990s exceeded the percentage of national deposits lost in the institutions that had failed outright and closed their doors in the late 1920s and early 1930s! This time, however, because of the hundreds of billions of dollars spent in federal deposit insurance bailouts, the financial dominoes did not topple as they had in the 1930s. Only a few pieces of the speculative framework collapsed; most of it survived. In the wake of the 1987 stock market crash, some observers had blamed the new electronic speculation techniques — so-called program trading and portfolio insurance. However, the curbs subsequently imposed were minor, so that spectronic devices continued to proliferate rather than being reined in by regulation. By mid-decade, derivatives and program trading were once again dislocating the markets. A similar point can be made regarding the 1989–92 bailout of financial institutions. Abuses were protected. Shareholders did not lose their shirts, and big depositors generally got paid off by federal authorities even when their multimillion dollar deposits were far above the insurable limits. As with the rescues of Lockheed and Chrysler, this was achieved with the public's money. Within a few years, not a few large financial institutions that had been on the edge of the abyss were making record loans to speculators — or speculating themselves.

Other important components of the bailout were less overt. The Federal Reserve, which had rescued the post-crash stock market with liquidity in 1987–88, came through again in 1990–91. Tumbling interest rates expanded the money supply. So-called overnight loans were made to troubled banks to keep them afloat. The Fed's action in driving down interest rates was a particular gift for two sectors: overleveraged corporations, especially those in hock from unwise leveraged buyouts, were able to refinance their debts, while shaky banks reveled in huge gains on the spread between high long-term interest rates and low short-term borrowing costs. This indirect assistance was almost as important as the institutional bailouts. By the mid-1990s, banks and investment firms were not only liquid again, but had enjoyed several years of high profitability. The investment community also buzzed with another rumor that the Federal Reserve, sheltered in the secrecy of its unsupervised, free-from-audit status, had gone even further by quietly buying S&P 500 futures to prop up the stock market on critical days.

There can be no doubt: serious damage *would* have occurred had a willing Washington not joined with a worried Wall Street in history's biggest financial rescue mission. Large banks and corporations guilty of overspeculating and over-leveraging would have gone under, as the capitalist process of destruction and renewal suggests they should have. The stock market would have plummeted; so would Wall Street's ascen-dancy. Instead, overleveraged firms that headed everyone's list of the living dead — from Citicorp, America's largest bank, to RJR Nabisco, the leveraged buyout made infamous in the late 1980s — survived after a year or two of grave-watching. Wall Street had a decent year in 1991 following a bad one in 1990. Then profitability mushroomed. The linchpin was unprece-dented Washington–Wall Street collaboration. Through a combination of monetary policy favors from the Federal Re-serve, help from the first White House in history headed by a president (George Bush) whose family members were mostly in the investment business, and collaboration by a Congress full of senators and representatives who knew the warm, tingly feeling of being able to count on top executives of Goldman Sachs, Bear Stearns, or Merrill Lynch for an emergency fund-raising dinner, the capital city extended the kind of help never seen in any prior downturn.

Cynics worried that the bailout itself was part of a new de-bacle in the making — a bigger speculative bubble blown up around the earlier one that came close to imploding. The last-ing damage of 1989–92 had been confined to savings and loans and commercial real estate. Junk bonds and other speculative devices shuddered but recovered in 1991. The various stock markets bounced back. The shudder of 1990 turned into a 1991–92 surge: major indexes kept reaching new highs, with the help of interest-rate cuts from the Federal Reserve that forced Grandma and Grandpa in Fort Lauderdale to abandon certificate-of-deposit rates nearing 3 percent and put their faith in God and the Fidelity family of mutual funds. The

Dow-Jones, the S&P 500, and the rest continued to set records even when the economic news was bad — and it made no difference to securities traders or brokerage analysts when the governor of the nation's most populous state announced that after two years, California was still in its worst downturn since the Great Depression. The truth, behind a cloud of wordy explanations, was that the financial markets were riding on a different set of shock absorbers: unprecedented federal favoritism. Whatever might be happening to aerospace workers in Burbank or real estate developers in San Diego, bond traders and derivatives marketers thrived as declining interest rates took the pressure off speculative finance, liquidity kept flooding the system, and official Washington backed away from populist gestures.

Worry about a new speculative bubble was well founded. The excesses of the 1980s had only been camouflaged, not pruned. The concerns of the 1990s focused on the hundreds of billions of dollars chased out of bank certificates and accounts into rapidly swelling mutual funds, as well as the trillion-dollar uncertainties surrounding the new derivative products and techniques. Few senior managers fully understood the techniques, risks, or liabilities. E. Gerald Corrigan, the president of the New York Federal Reserve Bank, had warned in 1992 against the complexities and dangers of the new fad: "High-tech banking and finance has its place but it's not all it's cracked up to be. . . . The growth and complexity of off-balance-sheet activities and the nature of the credit, price, and settlement risk they entail should give us all pause for concern." A year later, the International Monetary Fund issued a similar concern about the risks in derivatives such as futures contracts and currency and interest-rate swaps. But most of the financial establishment hastened to offer reassurances.

The second caution lay in the lingering two-tier quality of the economy after the great scare of 1990–91. On one hand, the money that the Fed kept pumping out sloshed around the financial markets, pushing *them* up. But in the real economy, big companies kept announcing reductions of thousands — or tens of thousands — of jobs that no one expected to come back. Economists will never agree on what was happening. However, the case can be made that the unprecedented liquidity and favoritism extended to the financial sector, going well beyond the taxpayer bailout, served to further divide America into two economies. The self-corrective balance had been suspended. Major financial institutions, largely shielded or rescued from the prior decade's mistakes, entered the mid-1990s basking in record profits, political influence, and power. Much of the nonfinancial, noninvestor economy, meanwhile, was left sputtering along on three cylinders amid a pall of gloom over what the future had in store for Cincinnati and Los Angeles.

If this collaboration between government and finance was unprecedented in the twentieth-century United States, so was the scarcity of insistence on the kind of financial reform typical of a post-speculative era — the regulatory accomplishment of both the Progressive and the New Deal eras. Clinton had won the White House in 1992 as an outsider running on a relatively populist platform, including campaign speeches that used Wall Street and the University of Pennsylvania's Wharton School of Finance as backdrops for criticism of the financial elites for the greed and speculation of the 1980s. No one can be sure how much of it he meant. But even before the man from Arkansas was inaugurated, it was clear that strategists from the financial sector, more than most other Washington lobbyists, had managed the Bush-to-Clinton transition without missing a stroke. Well-connected Democratic financiers stepped easily into the alligator loafers of departing Republicans. The accusatory rhetoric of the campaign dried up. The head of Clinton's new National Economic Council, Rob-

Clinton, just like Bush, crawling in th hands of the financial interest lobyists

ert Rubin, turned out to have spent the 1980s as an arbitrageur for Goldman Sachs. The unpurgable Washington was now being joined by part of what was beginning to look like an equally unpurgable Wall Street. Moreover, the distance between the two was narrowing every year as the financial sector turned its huge resources to cementing its influence in politics and public policy. Washington power brokers and exiting cabinet members, in turn, were coming to an important new realization: that the greatest rewards after high government service now lay in the big investment firms or in specialized financial boutiques rather than in law firms as of yore. Even the ambition of politicians was being financialized.

The Burgeoning Political Influence of the Financial Sector

The influence of financiers is as old as money. What is new in the Washington of the 1990s is the breadth and reach of financiers' clout. Back in the Gilded Age, politicians got cash and opportunities to buy stock at favorable prices from that era's robber barons and financial buccaneers. One result was the famous Credit Mobilier scandal. Today's influence is wielded more subtly, and often in new ways. An essential new leverage, as we have seen, is the attentiveness to the capital markets from a federal government all too aware that its solvency depends on keeping inflation and interest rates (and thus overall borrowing costs) down. But too much of the new political power of the financial sector has been obtained in the old-fashioned way: by buying it.

If money is the lifeblood of finance, candid officeholders have called it the mother's milk of politics — and no sooner were huge profits of the 1980s flowing into the financial markets than they began trickling down to political Washington. Campaign contributions to officeholders by political action committees representing financial services, securities, and investment firms soared during the 1980s, trebling to $2.1 million in 1989–1990. But this visible tip of the iceberg was in some ways the least important. The floodgates of political giving were opened in the late 1980s to "soft money" — the exception established for support of so-called state and local party-building that enabled corporations and individuals to make otherwise illegal contributions of more than $25,000.

Soft money is, in its essence, a giant slush fund administered by the two parties. The Center for Responsive Politics, in its study of how eighty-three million such dollars were fed into the 1991–92 election cycle, used the appropriate title "Soft Money, Real Dollars." "Soft Money, Real Clout" would have been just as descriptive, given the extraordinary opening for influence seekers. To no one's surprise, the combined finance, insurance, and real estate sectors led the soft-money list, giving a total of $17.2 million — $10.9 million of it to the Republican National Committee, $6.3 million to the Democrats. Within this group, the securities and investment business ranked as the biggest single industry, with $7.0 million. The individual leaders were Merrill Lynch, Goldman Sachs, Forstmann Little, Kohlberg Kravis Roberts, and Morgan Stanley (and all except Forstmann Little gave to both parties).

A particular opening for de facto corruption came through the $100,000 and up membership clubs established by both parties for their biggest donors. The Republican "Team 100" program was the more important, both in size and because the Republicans, then in the White House, were able to do favors. In a provocative 1992 analysis, "George Bush's Ruling Class," Common Cause pinpointed the real estate and investment sectors as furnishing the largest bloc among the 249 members of Team 100. The major organizations mentioned most frequently were, once again, Goldman Sachs, Kohlberg Kravis Roberts, Forstmann Little, and Morgan Stanley. Common Cause suggests that the Bush administration may have shown favoritism to Kohlberg Kravis Roberts on antitrust issues. The more serious charge was that a half dozen other members of Team 100 were either officers of companies that cut sweetheart deals with the government to acquire failed S&Ls at a fraction of their value or were charged with S&L-related securities fraud or looting.

But in measuring the political influence of financiers, the overt criminal behavior of a few in the S&L scandal is a diversion. We should attach much more importance to the favoritism shown the financial sector in perfectly legal ways — from the S&L bailout itself to the Fed's interest rates cuts, George Bush's persistence in calling for capital gains tax rate reductions, Bill Clinton's top economic policy appointments, and the bipartisan Washington willingness to let corporations raise their profits and stock prices by large workforce lay-offs. These are what confirm the massive changes taking place in the nation's political power structure. Burgeoning outlays by securities and investment political action committees were only a minor force. More significance lay in the ability of financiers to dominate the Washington soft-money charts by contributing sums that, as we have seen, were a mere drop in the spectronic bucket.

Reformers are particularly mindful of the ability of the major contributors from the big investment firms to multiply their political clout by putting their enormous fund-raising prowess at the disposal of friends and allies. Embattled presidential aspirants looking for another $300,000 to keep their ads on television through the New Hampshire primary or senators needing a pair of megadollar fund-raising events to scare off a potential challenger knew that if they could enlist two or three of Wall Street's several dozen top political movers and shakers, it was done. Last-minute help was particularly appreciated. In 1991 the Center for Responsive Politics cited Robert Rubin, then the co-chairman of Goldman Sachs, for excessive contributions to the (successful) 1990 reelection campaign of Iowa senator Tom Harkin, a self-styled populist, but later acknowledged that Rubin had merely snugged up to the limit.

Other important influence was wielded indirectly. Many of the big securities firms — Goldman Sachs, Merrill Lynch, Lehman Brothers — operate Washington government relations offices. So do some of the big banks figuring prominently in the financial derivatives markets. None of these offices are especially notable power centers. However, when broad pro-investment philosophy is involved, a much larger influence network comes into play. Virtually all the big Washington lobbying firms and most of the major law partnerships operating in the capital have on their client list a large investment firm, a big bank, or both. On matters of overall favoritism to the investment sector of the economy, issues where banks and securities firms are allied instead of trying to grab each other's turf, the former assistants to the president, deputy Treasury secretaries, attorneys general, and former national party chairmen prominent on these firms' letterheads become useful cheerleaders.

A different, but also crucial, brand of backstopping comes from the financial community's quiet role in funding many of Washington's think tanks, institutes, and coalitions. When the word "investment" is mentioned, dozens of nonprofit executives stand up and salute. The éminence grise of this network is Peter Peterson, the former secretary of commerce who now chairs the New York–based Blackstone Group. Besides his prominence in investment banking, Peterson is chairman of the Council on Foreign Relations, chairman of the Institute for International Economics, a director of the Committee for a Responsible Federal Budget, and president of the Concord Coalition, a national deficit-reduction group co-chaired by former U.S. senators Paul Tsongas and Warren Rudman.

Although most Washington movers and shakers understand this new alignment of financial and political power,

Republicans are probably the most amenable. Among the surprises of 1991–92 were the revelations of how George Bush's sons and brothers were enriching themselves in the investment business — and in several cases having scrapes with the law. Son Neil, recruited in the mid-1980s to be a director of Denver's high-flying Silverado Savings and Loan, was reprimanded by federal authorities after Silverado failed, requiring a $1-billion bailout. Brother Jonathan, a New York investment adviser, was fined for improper securities transactions by the states of Connecticut and Massachusetts. Brother Prescott, also a New York investment adviser, was blistered on the NBC evening news for having a consulting arrangement with a Japanese investment firm identified by Tokyo officialdom as a local mob front. Investments were in the Bushes' blood: the president's father, Prescott, had been a partner in the firm of Brown Brothers Harriman, and his grandfather, George H. Walker, founded the St. Louis firm G. H. Walker & Co. No chief executive could have been more open to the first great bailout of the U.S. securities and investment business.

Leading Democrats, however, were managing to wind up in the same posture without the benefit of tradition. When House Speaker Jim Wright and House Majority Whip Tony Coelho were forced to resign in 1989, the immediate causes were their controversial dealings with Sun Belt S&L operators and investment advisers; Coelho, who had bought $100,000 in junk bonds from Drexel Burnham with a check from his campaign committee, himself quickly joined the financial sector as a managing director of Wertheim, Schroder and Company. Several years later, when federal prosecutors were weighing an indictment of House Ways and Means Committee Chairman Dan Rostenkowski, another abuse emerged; Rostenkowski, for many years a close ally of the Chicago Board of Trade, a cockpit of futures trading activity, had arranged for two of his daughters to be put on the board's payroll under other names.

In mid-1993, Wright's successor as House Speaker, Thomas Foley, was obliged to end a relationship with a boyhood friend at a Boston investment firm who, over the previous decade, had cut Foley in on quick profits from the purchase and resale of initial public offerings of stock (albeit to the tune of only $25,000 a year or so). When the statistics for the 1991–92 election cycle were tabulated, political action committees in finance, insurance, and real estate led the list in contributions — for a total of $29 million — and a majority of the dollars went to *Democrats!*

It confuses reality to blame Republicans alone for favoritism to the financial sector. Indeed, when the new Clinton administration appointed Rubin of Goldman Sachs to chair the National Economic Council, after some suggested that his past financial dealings barred him from any post that required Senate confirmation, Cato Foundation fiscal studies director Stephen Moore called the appointment the "climax" of Washington hypocrisy: "If any Republican had ever tried to get anyone like Robert Rubin near the White House," Moore claimed, "he would have been savaged."

Probably so. The appointment of the co-chairman of Wall Street's most powerful firm, a selection to make Andrew Jackson roll over in his grave, certainly underscored how financial sector power has eroded old New Deal and Fair Deal era distinctions between the parties. The deepening influence of finance along the Potomac is utterly and completely bipartisan. It is particularly revealing how many Washington politicians have begun to aim their careers where the electronic money is. Small rewards may be possible while still in office, but the big payoff comes with subsequent affiliation and pro-investment influence peddling. So much so, in fact, that more and more Washington politicians are retiring to the financial sector rather than to the prestige law partnerships that were the principal destinations of earlier eras.

No investment firms are more central to the skin trade in ex-officeholders than Goldman Sachs, Lehman Brothers, the Blackstone Group, and the Washington-based Carlyle Group. Besides former Treasury secretaries and Fed chairmen, for whom jobs in the financial sector are logical return trips, the most revealing shift comes from four senior positions: 1) secretary of state, 2) secretary of defense, 3) secretary of commerce, and 4) director of the Office of Management and Budget. Former secretary of state James Baker associated with the Carlyle Group, as did former OMB director Dick Darman, and, much earlier, ex–defense secretary Frank Carlucci. Former defense secretary James Schlesinger went with Lehman Brothers, as had former deputy secretary of state George Ball. Goldman Sachs has such a strong Democratic image (despite its partners' disproportionately Republican campaign contributions) that it lacks recent prominent ex-officials. The Blackstone Group, home base for former commerce secretary Peterson, also enlisted ex-OMB director David Stockman (and sent former Treasury official Roger Altman back to Washington in 1993 as deputy secretary).

How much have these tightening relationships between Washington and Wall Street affected the direction of U.S. economic policy in the last decade? No one can say for sure. The willingness of the Bush administration to bail out the financial sector during the 1989–91 period was certainly encouraged. And perceptions of this new clout undoubtedly helped influence the Clinton administration to abandon hostile 1992 campaign rhetoric in favor of collaboration with the financial sector and rejection of proposed regulatory constraints on the Federal Reserve Board and the derivatives market. Yet the objectives of the financial sector are much more than defensive: by the mid-1990s, plans were afoot to convince Washington to further benefit America's capital-forming class by massively overhauling U.S. tax policy to increase taxes on consumers and slash them on investors. It would be hard to imagine a bolder political bid.

Savings and Investment: America's Partially Phony Crisis

History, however, suggests that there is already *too much* favoritism — and to the wrong sort of investor. If there is any constant of leading economic powers in their late or "financialization" stage — Holland circa 1750, Britain circa 1910, or the United States today — it is that the rich enjoy record incomes while huge piles of cash sit around looking for some suitably rewarding employment even as large parts of the country wither and the incomes of median families stagnate. When much of the domestic manufacturing or agricultural economy no longer seems like a good investment, available money pours into speculation, palatial homes, luxury goods, or investments overseas. Sometimes government has taken constraining action or tried to; sometimes, as in the case of the late-eighteenth-century Netherlands, a powerful investment sector kept getting its way, letting a bad situation fester toward revolution. But the overall lesson of past great economic powers is clear: such concentrations are dangerous.

Circumstances in the United States are surprisingly comparable. The share of wealth and income collecting in the hands of the top one percent of Americans — and more particularly in the hands of the top one tenth of one percent of Americans with at least $10 million in assets — soared during the 1980s, reaching heights unseen since the even more speculative 1920s. The buildup was fed by the huge capital gains registered by America's investor elite, cumulatively over a half-trillion dollars between 1981 and 1992. Yet there is an extraordinary rub. Scarcely a day goes by without economists, investment bankers, or other spokesmen for the financial sector sounding a klaxon: Americans do not save enough; the tax system isn't friendly enough to capital formation; excessive tax rates keep rich Americans from accumulating the money the country badly needs for investment.

Something is out of kilter. The rhetoric of attempting to try to restore the nation's fiscal and economic health has been twisted. By past yardsticks, the savings rate in the United States *is* low, partly because the ordinary American consumes too much of his or her income (although weak consumer spending would push the economy into a new set of troubles). However, a small group of economists has begun to argue that data on savings are seriously flawed. Some critics argue that the huge amounts of money paid into Social Security should be counted as savings, even though other experts worry about the system's solvency.

But a second argument may be more important: that those huge capital gains received by investors during the 1980s and 1990s should somehow be counted. Weren't those fat checks at least *potential* savings even if many of them never made it past a Mercedes dealership, yacht broker, Sotheby's auction, or investment advisers who preferred LBOs, Hamptons real estate, or Lichtenstein? They *could* have been productive investments. Reassessing the classification of capital gains wouldn't make much difference to middle-class saving, which would still be inadequate. From a larger perspective, though, economists Robert L. Heilbroner and Fred Block published research in 1992 contending that when realized capital gains were included as personal income, then the overall national rate of savings in the 1980s did *not* decline. In their calculation, the new wealth of the very richest Americans fattened up the savings data even though the contributions of other Americans declined.

Most economists disagreed because, by current definition, capital gains aren't counted as personal income or savings.

Economic historians, however, might add a broader perspective. Forgetting labels, the United States of the 1990s displays just what the previous great economic powers did as *their* decline set in: enormous wealth concentrated in the hands of a relatively small class of rentiers and very rich investors. In our earlier discussion of the financialization process, we saw how Hapsburg Spain, the eighteenth-century Netherlands, and Edwardian Britain all developed unusually large groups of people living off capital, dividends, and interest. Manufacturing and physical commerce might be weaker or paying lower wages in order to survive, but rentiers were thriving.

After countries have spent a generation or two as leading world economic powers, their patterns of wealth change. Private and public debt jumps into the spotlight; the importance of interest income rises and so does the financial importance of managing and trading public debt instruments. The growing investor class of late-sixteenth-century and seventeenth-century Spain had big estates or held *juros* — the government bonds of the day. The principal historian of the period, Britain's J. H. Elliott, describes "the growth of a powerful rentier class in Castile, investing its money not in trade or industry but in profitable government bonds and living contentedly on its annuities." When eighteenth-century Holland became, in Fernand Braudel's word, a nation of rentiers and speculators, much of the concentrated wealth at the top came from interest and from investment in government debt. Dutch rentiers not only bought their own nation's debt instruments but they increasingly sought out better returns overseas. According to one 1762 estimate, Dutch investors held about 25 percent of Britain's debt as well as about a third of the stock in both the Bank of England and the East India Company. To Braudel, it was a "perversion of capital." By the late eighteenth century, the Netherlands' elite financiers had so much money to invest that they were making the sort of risky international loans that produced a string of bubbles and panics. Sober investments were no longer enough.

Britain entered the twentieth century under kindred circumstances. Ordinary families dependent on employment in manufacturing sat watching their purchasing power decline while the Edwardian rich — a class on whom Britain's years in the sun had bestowed nearly half of the world's liquid capital! — took their enormous profits, gains, and interest income, and if they weren't building huge houses, reinvested much of it outside the country where interest rates were higher or where cheaper labor brought a higher rate of return. Small matter what the British savings rate for that period was or wasn't. When British overseas investments quadrupled between 1900 and 1914, that money went to build up other countries, often Britain's rivals. The result, once again, is economic history.

Unfortunately, though, it's an economic history lesson that reaches out at us like a set of porcupine quills: the United States of the 1990s has another of these rentier and investor elites, fabulously wealthy and inclined to use its rising political power to become even wealthier. Putting aside the debate over what is income and what is savings, a survey of 1989 wealth and income prepared by Arthur Kennickell of the Federal Reserve Board and R. Louise Woodbum of the Internal Revenue Service came up with some extraordinary findings. The top one percent of American families vastly increased their share of wealth and income during the 1980s, as everyone knows. But within that group, there was an important division: the bottom half of the one percent — the $300,000-a-year lawyers, $250,000-a-year suburban orthodontists, and $400,000 executive vice presidents of mid-sized manufacturing companies — more or less marched in place. Virtually the entire gain went to the top one half of one percent, the families with $4-million to $5-million net worths on up. *Their* investment capacity exploded. To get some idea of the enormous additional capital generated, start with government data that shows how the entire top one percent had more wealth than the bottom 90 percent of the country. Data for the top one half of one percent is not available, but the richest one percent owned $1.25 trillion worth of rental real estate, $1.12 trillion worth of stocks and bonds, $221.9 billion in trusts, and $524.6 billion in bank and other accounts for a total of some $3.1 trillion. The earnings were awesome: Edward Luttwak, one of the conservatives now beginning to criticize America's rentier power, points out that at a modest 8 percent return a year, the 1989 rentier income of the top one percent would have been $248 billion, 49 percent of their total income.

Policy makers confronted similar circumstances in Edwardian Britain. The investor class was making enormous sums — and declining to commit the proceeds to restore British manufacturing and infrastructure, which was not unreasonable by a purely financial yardstick. Instead, investment was flooding out to Argentina, Canada, the United States, even Germany. Dutch rentiers had done the same thing a hundred and fifty years earlier. Perhaps large-scale outlays could have rebuilt each nation's crumbling infrastructure, aging factories, and deteriorating competitiveness, but no one will ever know.

Parallel behavior is now visible in the United States. Not just in the speculative reshuffling of corporations in lieu of new domestic plant construction; not just in the hundreds of new derivatives and unprecedented Wall Street profits from trading in government debt; but also in the mushrooming evidence that rich Americans — like their pre–World War I British predecessors — are shipping more and more of their money overseas. In addition to the U.S. corporations building more factories abroad, foreign firms are raising ever greater amounts of their funding from Americans anxious to invest in Stuttgart and Singapore rather than in St. Louis. Between

1988 and 1993, the foreign equities holdings of American investors doubled from $101 billion to $210 billion. The floodgates were opening.

The warning of earlier Dutch and British investor behavior is that any talk of a savings crisis by capital formation advocates must be broadened into a *second* discussion: how a part of the problem lies in letting rich investors ship so much of their capital overseas. Of course, this view is not likely to carry the day. As was also true in Amsterdam circa 1750 and London circa 1910, the U.S. financial sector and markets are simply too powerful to accept such constraint, especially given their leverage over Washington public policy making.

In fact, the debt and savings crises have become a touchstone of those calling for cuts in middle-class entitlements and for more favorable tax treatment of all investors, which is a bold reach. No one can deny the seriousness of annual budget deficits in the $200 billion to $300 billion range and a national debt approaching $5 trillion. However, the evidence is that once a great economic power goes so far down the deficit-and-debt route, Pandora's fiscal box cannot be closed. The Spanish, the Dutch, and the British, each in turn, proved unable to roll back their public debt once it gained momentum because the vested interests involved were too great. This is true again. The middle class of the 1990s looks askance at sacrifice, being too hard-pressed to give up the 5–10 percent of overall income that its largest membership, those in the fiftieth to eighty-fifth percentiles of the U.S. population, receive from government transfer payments. And voters are just as opposed to letting Social Security or Medicare be means-tested. More to the point, as noted, history justifies middle-class cynicism that a declining great economic power's debt will not be conquered and that any sacrifice by the average citizen would go for nought.

Nor does the financial sector have any willingness to sacrifice. For most firms, federal debt has meant gravy, not hardship. Wall Street profited enormously during the era of huge deficits from 1982 onwards. What at first made the 1980s golden was tax cuts, deregulation, and declining inflation. But by the early 1990s, as we have seen, trading in U.S. government debt and assorted speculative derivatives had become the new framework of unprecedented profits at many of New York's most famous investment firms. Which brings us to an important corollary of financialization: *As massive debt becomes a major national problem, it also becomes a major financial opportunity and vested interest.*

There *are* caveats. The financial sector's view of high levels of public debt is schizophrenic. On one hand, that debt is an enormous source of fees, profits, and speculative opportunity, *but only up to a certain, slowly expanding point.* Deficits are only acceptable when they are operating within a familiar, reasonably comfortable range. Too noticeable a surge of debt often suggests inflation and threatens the bond and stock markets. When that happens, an affected nation's financial sector usually presses for fiscal belt-tightening, be it tax increases or cuts in spending, usually at the expense of less influential portions of the population. Consumption taxes falling on the average citizen have been a particular favorite, both with Spain and Holland in the sixteenth and seventeenth centuries and more recently when conservative governments in Canada, Japan, and Britain faced the fiscal pressure cooker of the late 1980s and early 1990s.

Fashioning the twin crises of debt and savings into a double argument for a consumption tax is already a quiet but central 1990s strategy of many in the business and financial sectors. Unprecedented financial-sector influence in Washington is already in place. The profits of trading in government bonds and in related packages of derivatives have built a war chest. In 1993, moreover, far from bemoaning the deficit, which remained in its acceptable range, optimistic bond traders had pushed bond prices up and interest rates down to the lowest level in twenty years, and the stock market was setting records. Federal deficits, strategists were starting to assume, could be locked in the acceptable $200-billion- to $300-billion-a-year range for the foreseeable future through supposed public support for fiscal reform, specifically the possibility of a reduction of middle-class entitlements and a shift in fiscal policy from taxes on *income* to taxes on *consumption*.

Reducing middle-class entitlements was the envisioned key to deficit reduction. But the consumption tax debate, as we shall see, offered the hoped-for avenue to further tax cuts for the rich. Rising financial sector power in Washington even had an unexpected collaborator: the willingness of the Clinton administration not just to discuss consumption taxes, but to break with the past pattern in which watershed Democratic presidencies gained important historical credentials from tackling abuses of financial power. To recapitulate these: Thomas Jefferson had opposed Alexander Hamilton's thesis of a government alliance with finance, and as president, Jefferson did away with Hamilton's first Bank of the United States. Andrew Jackson, in turn, vetoed the extension of the charter of the Second Bank of the United States in 1832, declaring how fine it would be if "all the stockbrokers, jobbers and gamblers (were) swept from the land." William Jennings Bryan, who sought to shape another watershed, ran against Wall Street in 1896 and almost won. Then in 1932 candidate Franklin D. Roosevelt said he wanted to "drive the moneychangers from the temple," and even sixteen years later, when Harry Truman won a surprise reelection, his feisty rhetoric belabored the Republicans as "bloodsuckers with offices in Wall Street." Few themes were more central to party history.

Clinton had criticized Wall Street during the campaign, noting the irony of the stock market climbing as the real economy flagged. Even after the inauguration, his chief political adviser, James Carville, told the *Wall Street Journal*, "I looooove the stock market falling. In the 1980s the stock market rose 300% and real incomes fell. Maybe now the stock market will fall and real incomes will rise." But as 1993 rolled along, Clinton changed: he began citing upward movement in the stock and bond market as evidence of the success of his economic program — and he expressed interest in the idea of a consumption tax on several different occasions, even referring to the possibility that it might replace part of the income tax.

Prominent conservatives and capital formation lobbyists already had their consumption levy picked out. This was the so-called consumed-income tax, in which family income would be exempted from taxation up to some level in the $15,000 to $20,000 range. Above that, however, a new type of federal tax calculation would take over: families would be taxed on their *consumption* but would avoid tax on their *savings* and *investment*. No other major economic power had such an income tax. Its enactment — even its serious debate — would be a stunning affirmation of the power of the financial sector to promote, in modern form, a tax system like those by which earlier great economic powers put the burden of government on the ordinary citizen.

Definitions would be all-important: just what would constitute consumption? What would qualify as deductible investment? Under typical provisions, however, the $4-million-a-year family of a rich investor would pay taxes (perhaps at a 33 percent rate) on, say, the $600,000 a year its members spent on consumption but sidestep tax on the more than $3 million of that year's income which they "invested" in junk bonds, currency speculation, and Taiwanese mutual funds. That would drop the rich family's effective tax rate into single digits, an enormous reduction from its present level. By contrast, the $55,000-a-year family, spending to survive, might pay a 20

percent rate on about $35,000 of nondeductible spending.
That would make its tax on consumed income about $7,000 a
year, roughly what it now pays in income tax. The disproportionate benefit to the richest 50,000 or 100,000 American families would be extraordinary.

Nevertheless, as the early 1990s gave way to the mid-1990s,
the "consumed income" approach was put forward by a commission including influential senators like Democrats David
Boren and Sam Nunn and Republican Pete Domenici, by
prominent Washington lobbies like the American Council for
Capital Formation and the American Business Conference,
and by Peter Peterson, the chief shepherd of the financial sector's antideficit efforts. Yet the real need for across-the-board
favoritism to *all* investors, as we have seen, was at best dubious
and at worst destructive. The much greater case, as Chapter 8
will pursue, was for savings incentives for the $35,000 to
$75,000 group of Americans whose savings rate had dropped
so much during the 1970s and 1980s. For those already rolling
in money, better public policy would suggest less favorable tax
treatment of dollars invested overseas or otherwise outside national interest guidelines.

The political power of America's financial sector undercuts
the prospect of reform. However, based on the behavior of
wealthy investors in the late days of previous great economic
powers, there is another reality: if finance cannot be reined in,
Washington will not be able to regain power over the economy on behalf of ordinary citizens. And in the 1990s, voters
are impatient.

Chapter Five

The Principal Weaknesses of American Politics and Government

We are currently in the process of a massive shift from a representative to a participatory democracy. . . . The demise of representative democracy also signals the end of the traditional party system.

— JOHN NAISBITT,
author of Megatrends, *1982*

The growing complexity and speed of change make it difficult to govern in the old way. It's like a computer blowing fuses. Our existing political decisionmaking structures are now recognized to be obsolete.

— ALVIN TOFFLER,
author of Powershift, *1993*

THE INABILITY of our political leaders to agree on the nature of national decline, along with the related disabilities posed by the extraordinary special-interest buildup in Washington and the growing influence on the economy by a speculative financial sector, represent central weaknesses of American politics and government. But other failures also deserve attention. Four pillars of the political and governmental system, once ingredients of its youthful success, are becoming weak foundations in its old age:

• The separation of powers, in which the executive and legislative branches are kept apart and frequently plotting against each other, is an eighteenth-century miscalculation that has lingered too long. It weakens effective national policy making, especially management of the economy.

• Our Republican-Democratic party system, the world's oldest, is obsolete. The two parties aggravate more problems than they solve. Voters are right to want a new arrangement.

• America's clumsy framework of local government includes some eighty-three thousand states, counties, cities, and other governmental subdivisions. Too many represent outdated units, layers, and even rationales of government fifty, one hundred, or two hundred years old. Like Washington, these lesser layers of bureaucracy won't be "reinvented" without the institutional equivalent of a chainsaw.

• Finally, the two-century evolution of the judicial and legal system has saddled the country with a globally unique and crippling weight of judges, jurisprudence, lawyers, litigation, and rights. Antilawyer comments have become so ferocious that a president of the California Bar Association suggested that such attacks be made hate crimes — only to provoke another round of lawyer jokes.

All four weaknesses share a common worrisome characteristic, the aging of America's institutions. Yesterday's vigor has become today's arthritis. All four malfunctions reveal the change in a government, extraordinary back in 1800, uncommonly successful through the nineteenth century, and still able to guide the United States to the head of the international table fifty years ago, that has now become stiff in its joints. The grand memories, proud speeches, and lingering Fourth of July salutes to old achievements are a misleading facade. Reform becomes more imperative with every day. This is an old story, and, as we shall see, there are unhappy parallels in the later years of other great powers whose politicians also insisted pompously — and wrongly — that this can't be happening to us, that our (Roman, Spanish, Dutch, British) institutions are as good as ever.

Let me stipulate: these four critical failures of politics and government are not the warts and cankers most often reported in the media. But the corruption that angers so many voters in the 1990s is hardly new; it was worse in the nineteenth century, when key industries owned whole legislatures — mining magnates certainly did in Montana, likewise the timber crowd in Wisconsin. Even so renowned a senator as Daniel Webster openly complained when a bank was late in sending his retainer. Public disdain for the skills of current members of Congress is another misperception. Most are better educated and more qualified than their predecessors of 1850 or 1950. What is poorer is their product, which reflects what Washington has become. As for our citizens being unprecedentedly apathetic and disinclined to vote, Americans are not apathetic — at least not when given a chance to rally around charismatic leaders or to vote on controversial ballot propositions. They *are* disinclined to vote for routine candidates in routine elections. But that's understandable after decades of having to choose between Republicans who represent one set of interest groups and Democrats who represent another, with a considerable overlap. Small wonder that voter turnout ratcheted down for thirty years until enlarged by a major independent candidacy in 1992. The gripes just listed, however, are *symptoms* of what is wrong. They grow out of more basic problems.

Three have already been laid out: the near certainty that America's cultural and economic strength has begun a decline of the sort that politicians have great difficulty confronting; the related transformation of Washington into the world's largest special-interest complex; and the extent to which power over economic policy is shifting to Wall Street and the financial markets. These are the critical underpinnings. Now we turn to the next tier of failures — to four mechanisms that were strengths back in the Republic's younger days but have now become yokes. Actual proposals for reform are left until Chapter 8; our subject in these pages is simply the political and governmental malfunctions and how troublesome they have become.

Watchdogs or Attack Dogs? The Dangerous Legacy of the Separation of Powers

No one has ever seen it, bewigged and translucent at five o'clock in the morning, but the spirit of King George III is one of Washington's most persistent ghosts. Separating the federal legislative branch, arranging it to keep an eye on the executive branch even while generally cooperating, might have made sense to the Revolutionary War veterans who drafted the Constitution, men who also remembered the battles between eighteenth-century royal governors and popular colonial legislatures. But those memories so important to the Constitutional Convention of 1787 have little relevance today, while the separation between Congress and the executive has all too frequently turned into a rivalry — to the discomfort of federal authority in foreign policy, judicial confirmations, and, most damagingly, management of the economy.

Moreover, the odyssey of separate powers in the United States didn't end with the eighteenth century. Independent power centers have continued to multiply. Take the doctrine of judicial supremacy, central to elevating the role of the courts and the law. In the 1803 case of Marbury versus Madison, Chief Justice John Marshall cleverly assumed an unprecedented authority: the right of the judiciary to set aside as unconstitutional acts of the government elected by the people. Today's excess of courts, litigation, and lawyers has some of its roots in that far-reaching breakthrough. In more or less the same time period, Alexander Hamilton, over the objections of the Jeffersonians, succeeded in gaining a charter for the Bank of the United States, a central bank partly modeled after the one in London. That process led finally, in 1913, to the creation of the semi-independent Federal Reserve Board. But in contrast to the Bank of England, which is under the thumb of Britain's prime minister and Parliament, the Fed in recent decades has often been a closer ally of Wall Street than of elected presidents.

The result, an ongoing national handicap of the 1990s, is that the chiefs of Washington's four branches — the president, the Speaker of the House, the chief justice of the Supreme Court, and the chairman of the Federal Reserve Board — do not necessarily represent the same politics. Too often, in fact, they reflect a garble of parties and origins. No other major country's top tier of government is so hedged, guarded, and divided.

Even back in the nineteenth century, when the federal government did little and politics were more fluid, separate powers caused friction. The very existence of the Bank of the United States, allied with the conservative money power of the Northeast, was so infuriating to President Andrew Jackson that in 1832 he vetoed the bank's extension. Controversy also surrounded the role of federal judiciary, partly because presidents sometimes tried to pack the courts, but also because justices and judges of a just-defeated party would often work to block new philosophies and programs. Yet for the first century and a half of the Republic, these frictions were as often creative as destructive.

Over the last few decades, though, the separation of powers has come to be a burden. Branches of government arranged to be mutually suspicious were once a valid defense against despotism or an overbearing executive. What they encourage now, however, is a different tyranny — an inability to coordinate effective government policy. With the emergence of late-twentieth-century Washington as an iron triangle of interest groups, the separation of powers became their tactical playpen. Interest groups have seeped into more and more gaps in the divided machinery of government, clogging and blocking it.

Bridging the constitutional and political gap between the executive and legislative branches is the biggest challenge. In the minimal-government years of the late nineteenth century, it mattered little that presidents of one party also often faced Congresses of another. But tension grew in the divided-government years of the 1950s and even more in the Nixon era; and since then, Republican White Houses and Democratic Congresses — Washington has not seen the reverse arrangement in fifty years — have often been at loggerheads.

The burden on efficiency is most obvious in fiscal politics. As we have seen, increasing debt and the need to raise taxes are hallmarks of a great economic power passing its peak. In the United States, the separation of fiscal powers has created its own political chronicle, from bidding wars to budget summits, of how fiscal policy has become more costly and less effective.

Combat trenches were first dug along Pennsylvania Avenue in 1970 when Richard Nixon, convinced that Congress was spending too much money, decided to impound some of it. Prerogative-conscious congressional Democrats went off like burglar alarms. In order to take on the executive branch's Office of Management and Budget, the House and Senate quadrupled the staffs of their respective budget committees and created the Congressional Budget Office. The subsequent quarter century has produced frequent quarrels, the creation of a circuslike legislative machine for simulated deficit reduction (the Gramm-Rudman-Hollings Act of 1985), and several bipartisan "summits," as well as its twin centerpieces — a budget deficit that ballooned from small change to $300 billion a year and a total national debt that leaped from $381 billion to nearly $5 trillion.

Would — could — the same thing have happened in a government in which the executive and legislative branches were joined rather than separated? Probably not. Divided government has encouraged both major parties to devote a large part of their fiscal strategy to scoring political points. Had Democrats controlled both the executive and legislative branches for twenty-four years instead of just four, full governmental responsibility would have stopped them from spending as freely. Instead, with power divided, it was too easy to fund their own domestic spending constituencies, handing the Republican executive branch the economic management headache.

Conversely, the Republicans, who developed a 1980s strategy of "borrow and spend" that matched any past Democratic laxity, would also have been hobbled by controlling both the executive and legislative branches. Facing waves of red ink in that situation, they would have been unable to point, as they happily did, at congressional Democratic spenders and say, "They did it, folks; they're the ones." Ultimately, of course, for the twenty years out of twenty-four of divided government, neither side had the full responsibility for choosing between hungry constituencies and a more sober federal fiscal policy.

Keeping in mind that the annual federal budget deficit rose from $9 billion in 1970 to almost $300 billion in 1992, here is a possible yardstick. During the years of "separated powers" from 1969 to early 1977, the deficit jumped from near balance to $50 billion. Then during the next "separated powers" years from 1981 to 1992, there was a surge from $74 billion to nearly four times that figure. Deficitry was clearly on a roll in both periods. By contrast, during the Carter years from 1977 to early 1981, where Democrats controlled the entire government, the annual deficit increased by only one half, from $50 billion to $74 billion. Had just one party been in charge from 1981 to 1993, it is arguable — hardly certain, but at least possible — that the deficit would have wound up in a lower $150 billion to $200 billion range, with the national debt also $1 trillion to $1.5 trillion slimmer.

This case is not beyond debate. Canada has run up worse deficits and debt under a parliamentary system. Moreover, the prior leading economic nations we have been recalling all managed to increase their debts in grand style without any separation of powers to take blame. Their fiscal excesses, however, always came down to a common explanation: high wartime costs. For the United States of the 1980s to achieve so much budgetary deterioration in peacetime was unprecedented, suggesting that the separation of powers probably had a role. In any event, no one seriously suggests that the separation of powers is *good* for economic management.

We cannot leave this institutional morass — and the question of whether the United States can afford such a clumsy relationship between its executive and legislative branches — without raising a related dimension: the damage done not just to effective government but also to the Republican-Democratic party structure. The two have gone together. Because of the decay of the party system and the ever-rising role of interest groups and Washington influence peddlers in opening up the gap between the White House and Congress, restoration of a close and effective collaboration between the branches — the sort that goes beyond rhetoric about "reinventing government" and ending "gridlock" — very likely requires major institutional reform. Americans must prepare for something they refused to consider on the two hundredth anniversary of the Constitution in 1987: a serious debate over whether the nation's founding document needs accumulated cobwebs cleaned away.

Reformers have long urged presidents to choose cabinets that included several members of Congress, either as advisers on a particular subject or as institutional coordinators. This would be easy and it would help. But for the most part, the broader changes with the greatest significance, such as requiring presidents and congressional candidates to run together on the same ticket every four years, would require modification of the Constitution. Bolder thinkers, rekindling the spirit of Thomas Jefferson, offer an even more radical suggestion: let Congress call a Second Constitutional Convention, then pray that there is still a genius of American politics capable of rising to the challenge. All of this is uphill work, and the proposals for reform are explored in Chapter 8. Discussing them here would be premature, because any separation-of-powers debate must also weigh what is a linked weakness — the problems of the Republican-Democratic party system and what to do about them — to which we now turn.

The Ancient and Exhausted Two-Party System

During my post–World War II boyhood, there were Americans alive who were more ancient than the Republican-Democratic party system. The weekly magazines ran pictures of the last Civil War veterans as their ranks shrank from hundreds to just a handful: the ex-Confederate drummer boys and the sixteen-year-old Yankee farmhands who had fed Sherman's cavalry horses. Now there are no Americans who were alive when the Republicans first met in Ripon, Wisconsin, in 1854, which tells us how old America's twin political vehicles have become.

Our end-of-the-century dilemma is stark: is the Republican-Democratic system itself still vital and worth reinforcing, or is the legal and financial favoritism it enjoys the political equivalent of hospital life support? History itself is not reassuring. No other Western party system is so aged and weary. Britain's Conservatives are as old as the GOP, but the Labour Party, a relative fledgling, has been stumping for only a century, and the center parties are new. Canada's Conservatives and Liberals, in turn, creak about on hundred-year-old legs, but the New Democrats and the new regional groupings all have postwar birth certificates. In the other major powers, Germany, France, Italy, and Japan, the parties all date from after World War II. And even many of these postwar parties are looking out of date as the postwar system winds down.

Americans easily deceive themselves. At the peak of the postwar era, the coalition politics and ninety-day governments of France and Italy were the stuff of jokes and wisecracks. The hoariness of the Anglo-American parties, like the ceremonial maces of parliament and the eighteenth-century pomp at the opening of Congress, seemed a sign of stability and success. To many, it still may. But the message of the 1980s — and especially the 1990s — is that there is less cause to be cocky, and a good deal more reason to fear the underlying inadequacy of the current party system. And as we saw in Chapter 3, the British analogy should actually give us pause; under pressures reminiscent of the present-day United States, Britain's original two-party system came unraveled in the first third of this century.

Bluntly put, there are a half dozen good reasons to doubt the future effectiveness of the Republican-Democratic system. What keeps these doubts from serious national discussions is an almost biblical faith-cum-vested-interest: America has to have the Republicans and Democrats because we have to nurture the two-party system, which we have used for more than a hundred and fifty years and therefore must cherish. The twenty-first century will make mincemeat of such thinking.

Part of why the party system is decrepit involves not just its age but where it came from. The two parties grew out of the economic combat of a now distant era: the mid-nineteenth-century conflict between manufacturing (Northern Republicans) and agriculture (Southern Democrats). The British party system that came out of that same economic battleground was the one torn apart three generations ago. And exhausted parties are the easiest prey for special interests, because there is little heartfelt belief to get in the way.

Scandal has also taken a toll. Watergate caught the GOP at the beginning of its 1968–92 White House hegemony and knocked it sprawling. The congressional and local realignments, mostly in the South, that were taking shape in 1972 as the Democrats moved left with George McGovern almost all stalled or crumbled with the scandal and Nixon's 1974 resignation. Even after national opportunity recurred in 1980, the post-Watergate GOP pursued realignment with a limp, not with what should have been a much bolder stride. The watershed that began in 1968 turned out to be a partial one unable to provide the sort of broad renewal of the system seen in previous realignments.

Weakness number three builds on the first two. Since the 1960s, the national Republican Party, with its expanding presidential edge in the white South and fading presence in the old Yankee North, has been reversing the geography of its Civil War origins. At the local level, a portrait of the rural and small-town county courthouses controlled by the two parties shows that the Republican map is still Northern and the Democratic map is somewhat more Southern. A party system undergoing this kind of schizophrenia suffers in coherence and purpose. Ours does.

Meanwhile, computer executives, teleconferencing consultants, and their like properly doubt that political parties will keep their role in the high-tech communications or information age. Far from being timeless institutions, the party system has a relatively short history. In modern, mass-based form, parties are very much a product of the Industrial Revolution, with its accompanying reform of "rotten boroughs" and rapid broadening of male suffrage in Britain and, especially, the United States. Both developments were important. In the late eighteenth century, when relatively few people had the vote, British and American politics had involved loose factions, not parties. George Washington himself had advised that organized parties would be a curse. But as the Industrial Revolution, democracy, and the franchise spread in both countries, the factions sorted out and solidified into parties in the 1830s and 1840s, quickly becoming powerful cultural forces and vehicles for unprecedented popular mobilization. By the 1890s, some 85 to 90 percent of male citizens over twenty-one and not in jail were voting in hot-politics states like Indiana. Party involvement was important in everyday life.

No longer. Voter turnout in today's media age is a ghost of these former enthusiasms. Parties are less necessary, and less liked. Much of what they and their interest groups now mobilize is voter contempt, not voter participation, and there is good reason to assume that party functions will be at least partly replaced by some new communications forms or institutions. Direct democracy could take hold through a version of telepolitics, instant referenda, or national town meeting. That change is probably underway.

In the meantime, those of us who have grown up watching thirty or forty years of politics see a problem: just what is it that U.S. "representative government" has come to represent? The answer — special interests more than the citizenry — damns both parties. Two centuries ago, the architects of the Constitution rightly agreed that direct democracy was extreme, that New England town meetings weren't adaptable nationally. Instead, the voters would choose representatives to make the decisions, although in doing so they were to represent the interests of the people. This premise was reaffirmed in the early 1900s, after widespread complaint that the senators then being elected by state legislatures were too close to special interests. The Seventeenth Amendment to the Constitution, ratified in 1913, required that senators be directly elected by the people. It was a populist triumph. To allow legislators and parties to represent interest groups instead of voters, Americans decided, went against the very grain of democracy.

Nearly a century later that challenge is back, because the same fundamental strain on the party system and representative government has returned: an extreme of interest-group power. Once again the genius of American politics and the legitimacy of governmental institutions are at stake together.

Theoretically, a member of Congress represents a chunk of Missouri or Connecticut, and these voters alone get his or her mailings, satellite television feeds, and weekend visits: he or she is *their* representative. But the reality of what the average senator or congressman represents is a tailored slice of interest-group Washington: the party caucus or national committee, some contributors and political action committees, and a collection of think tanks and coalitions, associations, corporations, and unions. Grassroots party loyalty being so loose, 75 percent to 85 percent of senators and congressmen can use the right combination of interest-group backing to entrench themselves. To ordinary voters, representative government has become a shell — and behind it, only the influentials are truly represented. The case for direct democracy, in some new communications-age form, is a gamble, but nothing strengthens its plausibility like the inadequacy of the current system.

Meanwhile, in a perverse way, the *failure* of the system is also its *support base*. For good reasons, America's influentials favor the system under which they have flourished, as do most established interest groups, and for most of the last two decades, bipartisan commissions, Congress, and state legislatures have been trying to reinforce the limited choice between Republicans and Democrats as the political equivalent of the Rock of Ages. The entrenchment tools of the status quo range from state laws that give the Republican and Democratic parties automatic ballot position (while curbing access by potential rivals) to a whole range of federal campaign subsidies, assistance to party-affiliated institutions, and preferred postal rates. Stacked alongside the financial support that the Republican and Democratic parties enjoy from their particular interest groups, these favoritisms add up to what economists call a "duopoly" — the two-party version of a monopoly. Independent political movements can surge and become powerful, but they cannot institutionalize; they cannot win the White House or take more than a few seats in Congress.

America's political duopoly has another unique characteristic that makes little sense to politicians elsewhere — frequent bipartisanship. Hallowed in the United States, the practice is observed in few other countries, except in wartime, because those party structures pivot on deep philosophic and interest-group differences. Bipartisan collaboration between British

Tories and Labourites, for example, or French Socialists and Gaullists is rare to nonexistent. Current-day bipartisanship in the United States, however, has its own logic, since the 1980s frequently involving a suspension of electoral combat to orchestrate some outcome with no great public support but a high priority among key elites. In foreign policy, these issues have included the Panama Canal treaties and NAFTA, the North American Free Trade Agreement with Mexico. On the domestic front, bipartisan commissions or summit meetings have been used to increase Social Security taxes on average Americans while the income tax rates of the rich were coming down, to negotiate deficit-reduction agreements lacking popular appeal, and to raise the salaries of members of Congress.

Sometimes the collaboration can be blatant. The pay raise deal involved walking on so many political eggshells that both sides negotiated an extraordinary side bargain: that the Democratic and Republican National Committees would refuse to fund any congressional candidate who broke the bipartisan agreement and made the pay raise an issue! In the House of Representatives' NAFTA debate, in which Democratic president Clinton was supported by more Republicans than Democrats, he produced — on GOP demand — a letter that Republican congressmen's pro-NAFTA votes shouldn't be used against them by Democratic foes. A conclusion is tempting: bipartisanship is too often a *failure* of the party system — a failure of both political responsibility and of representative government — and not a *triumph*.

In the other English-speaking countries, pressure is growing on what have been largely two-party systems. As we will see in Chapter 6, voters want more breadth of representation. But at least those parties generally fight each other, with the opposition party subjecting major government proposals to just what its name implies: *opposition*. The two-party framework in the United States cannot be counted on even for that.

The framework may also be getting shaky. Aspects of Republican-Democratic rivalry can seem as staged and phony as American professional wrestling, yet there is another important trend of the 1990s, seemingly at odds. That is the extent to which the two parties have been polarizing ideologically, especially in the House of Representatives. It is still true, of course, that the Democratic and Republican congressional memberships meet in the middle of the spectrum, frequently with individual legislators' hands stretched out to the same contributors and political action committees. At the same time, however, changing demography has been pulling the two parties' respective ideological centers of gravity leftward and rightward, in ways that make the existing leadership uncomfortable. The Democrats have relatively few conservative Southerners left, while the Republicans include only a handful of Northern moderates or liberals — a far cry from the circumstances of forty years ago when Civil War sectionalism still dominated, so that conservatives were split between the parties and the bipartisanship of the 1940s had an unstaged genuineness. What it usually represents in the 1990s is the overlapping influence of interest groups.

Further ideological polarization would be significant. In many ways, that would pull *both* parties away from public opinion. Yet much of what passes for centrism in Washington is mimicry of establishment viewpoints and fealty to lobbyists in eleven-hundred-dollar suits, so that more ideology on both sides would create the best opening in a hundred and fifty years for a new reform party or political movement with designs on a more vital interpretation of centrism. And such a shake-up could also undercut the current party system's ability to serve Washington's backstage nonideological interests.

If all of this seems like a brief for ending the Republican-Democratic duopoly in order to have a chance at national revitalization, the American people may already be reaching that conclusion. There was an element of spontaneous combustion in public sentiment in spring 1992's sudden surge to Ross Perot, when the polls put him ahead of both the incumbent Republican president *and* the Democratic front-runner. Since then, several different surveys have shown a clear national majority continuing to call for a new political party to contest the Democrats and Republicans in elections from president down to those for Congress and state legislatures.[6]

But it is unclear how much change is actually at hand. Certainly, the 19 percent vote for Ross Perot in 1992 was impressive. So was his ability to operate just as powerfully against new Democratic president Clinton as he did in helping to defeat Republican president Bush. Previous third-party presidential efforts, by contrast, have rarely outlived indignation at a specific administration or broad policy controversy. Also, two independent governors were elected in 1990, a twentieth-century record, and in several states, including California, splinter party candidates drew substantial votes for Congress in 1990 and 1992. Independent officeholders like Connecticut governor Lowell Weicker, as did previous independent presidential nominees like John Anderson and Eugene McCarthy, found themselves in minor spotlights again, trumpeting the failure of the Republicans and Democrats and the possibility of a new centrist party. Deficit-reduction advocates like former New Hampshire senator Warren Rudman ventured a related prediction: that a new party would form if the deficit wasn't brought under control.

If a party breakdown is under way, however, U.S. history as well as current poll data suggests that the dominant pressure would be more populist — outsider politics and themes of fighting Washington and dismantling its elites. From George Wallace to Perot, the last quarter century of presidential politics has been characterized by such attitudes, and the pressures of long-term disillusionment seem to be mounting rather than fading. During the 1993 debate over the North American Free Trade Agreement, commentators who had dismissed the multiple antiestablishment insurgences of 1992 — calling Ross Perot, Pat Buchanan, Jerry Brown, Jesse Jackson, and Ralph Nader center, right, and left phenomena related only at the margins — boggled to see the supporters of all five combining in a broad populist opposition to NAFTA. A few pundits even took the implications one step further, wondering whether this collaboration might foreshadow the emergence of a major new movement of persons convinced that the elites have cast them out of the system and seeking a new framework for economic nationalism, populist values, and governmental reforms. Along with the tentative institutionalization of the Perot vote, this political sociology could be a pivot of the 1990s: if we *do* see a major new political force emerge, will it be in the genteel, white-collar professional mode, or will it march to the angry cadences of a "radical middle"? Precedents, as noted, suggest the latter. What history doesn't tell us, though, is the odds on a *success* — on the prospects for another revitalization of national politics through some version of the unique American genius analyzed in Chapter 1. There are also many possible varieties of failure that could yield a caricature of reform (or worse).

Voter discontent with the present party arrangement is also generating technical pressures to open up the electoral system. If there is to be an upheaval, electoral reform will be a necessary corollary. Lopsided majorities of voters continue to support one such proposal: eliminating the electoral college and electing the president by popular vote. And on the question of increasing third-party ballot access, already helped by Perot's efforts, the gadfly Libertarian Party has filed protests with international human rights organizations contending that pro-duopoly practices by the United States violate the Copenhagen Document, adopted in 1990 by the Conference on Security and Cooperation in Europe (in which the U.S.

Brian Beedham

participates) and which prohibits government-sponsored discrimination against political parties.

A group called Citizens for Proportional Representation has even begun waving that provocative banner, which rejects single-member, winner-take-all districts in favor of a system that assigns seats to parties based on their share of the total vote. On the European continent, proportional representation and multiparty systems go together. Now, as third-party pressures are growing, and as concern over interest-group influence reinforces voter skepticism, the English-speaking nations are also beginning to look at the proportional representation argument, as we will see in Chapter 6.

Pressure for participatory democracy may be the most immediate signal of national disenchantment with the existing party and interest-group structure. Again, surveys show huge majorities of Americans favoring greater use of initiative and referendum devices on the *national* and state levels, and similar majorities favor televised town meetings. Perot's 1992 advocacy of these approaches was well received, and Brian Beedham, associate editor of *The Economist*, has argued in a powerful essay that with the Cold War over, the next logical step for the Western democracies is to partly replace the outdated structure of interest-group-dominated representative democracy with a more *direct* democracy.

If support for enlarging or even bypassing the existing party system continues to intensify in the United States, it would indeed have a restraining effect on Washington's all-powerful interest-group structure. Any new parties, movements, or teledemocracy vehicles, besides disproportionately enlisting the sorts of groups that now feel left out of national decision making, would be loud voices for sweeping political reform in Washington. Chapter 8 looks at some of these possibilities and how they could transform the stagnating party system and reinvigorate U.S. politics. The idea of the Republican-Democratic system in the United States changing as radically from 1990 to 2025 as British parties and politics did from 1890 to 1925 seems less radical and implausible when you put it in those matter-of-fact historical terms.

The Outdated Federal Framework and the Limited Prospects for Reinventing Government

In this chapter and several previous ones, we have tried to identify why Washington-based politics and government haven't been working. For anyone worried about oppressive interest-group buildup, the unsettling forces of national economic and social decline, the burden of the separation of powers, and the arteriosclerosis of the Republican-Democratic party system, talk about "reinventing government" that ignores these central problems is evasive. Minor employee cutbacks, revision of the federal procurement manual, and such measures sidestep the heart of Washington's difficulties.

In fact, David Osborne, whose 1992 book *Reinventing Government* became a bible of the new administration, has always been dubious about the prospect of reinventing the nation's capital. An earlier Osborne volume, *Laboratories of Democracy*, had emphasized the innovations being devised by Democratic and Republican governors, but even as the Clinton White House was embracing many of his terms, Osborne cautioned that "if you want to know where government is heading, Washington is the last place to look." The Democrats, he observed in 1992, were rooted in the 1930 to 1970 big-government era, and the Republicans were even worse: stuck in the antigovernment 1920s.

The 1993 report by Vice President Albert Gore's Commission on Reinventing Government, while received with brief fanfare, happens to be the eleventh that Republican and Democratic administrations alike have released since 1905 on ways to restructure and revitalize the federal government. None have been notable, with Gore's being one of the less ambitious. From Teddy Roosevelt's day to John Kennedy's, the fact is that American government was a success story, which made its inefficiencies unimportant quibbles. And the proposals since then have not seemed to go to the heart of larger national difficulties.

What deserves at least as much attention are the reasons to worry about the federal structure of state and local governments *outside* Washington. Much of it works too poorly to play its role in domestic policy renewal. Room for change and experimentation is still greatest at the state and municipal level, but those governments have their own considerable problems that parallel the divisions, separations, and outdated relationships apparent in the nation's capital. Part of the grassroots equivalent of Washington's separation of powers — besides the obvious parallel of governors tangling with legislatures — is federalism's own bureaucratic thicket: excessive units of government, many with overlapping bureaucracies or with borders that no longer make sense, some with functions that no longer make sense, and a surprising number of them represented and protected by the more than fifty thousand lobbyists registered in states and major cities across the country. The inability of state and local government to function effectively in some areas is beginning to add up to a national problem. And working with, even encouraging, fifty individual responses to major national challenges — as in the state-by-state health care reform that will unfold during the 1990s — could turn federalism into an even greater administrative and fiscal nightmare.

Hardly anyone thinks about them, but state boundaries in the East, often reflecting lines drawn and compromises struck in the late 1600s or early 1700s by British colonial authorities, are now some of the oldest borders in the world. Major cities like New York and Philadelphia, with metropolitan areas divided between three states, find cross-border coordination tricky. By contrast, British metropolitan areas like those of London, Manchester, and Glasgow have been routinely redrawn since World War II. About one third of state boundaries are outdated or controversial enough — California, Idaho, Alaska, and Michigan are good examples — to have produced secession movements. Yet there is no Washington mechanism to redraw their boundaries, whereas the major European nations have been able to remap their various shires, counties, provinces, and *lander* several times over the last two centuries. It is not simply the colonial origins of state boundaries in the East; those of the Midwest go back 150 to 175 years; and even in the West, the typical state boundary was drawn over a century ago. Major suburban counties just outside central cities often have boundaries just as old and sometimes equally rigid.

States often have little control over outdated units and layers of government they have built up over several centuries and never significantly pruned. The state financial crises of the early 1990s drove home how parochialism and duplication added to the high cost of government. Illinois had sixty-five hundred different *taxing* bodies; Pennsylvania was not far behind. New York authorities, in turn, listed some ten thousand governmental entities, from counties down to sewer districts. As revenue demands tightened, once-complacent voters began to wonder what portion of their taxes went for four or five different layers of local authority.

The artificial nature of state boundaries, plus each jurisdiction's independence in tax policy, has also combined to produce not just a patchwork of prosperity next door to a marginal economy, but a perverse drain-thy-neighbor competition. Thinly populated New Hampshire and Nevada have both used their big-state proximity and rejection of state income taxes to become havens for businessmen and high-income-tax-payers fleeing the next-door urban pressure cooker and high taxes of Massachusetts and California. For years, Connecticut, without a state income tax, played a similar tax haven role for New York.

Economic rivalry also has an uglier side. Illinois governor Jim Edgar, criticizing the practice, widespread over the last twenty years, of states giving corporations subsidies or tax breaks to stay put — when other states are willing to bribe them to move — has called for the equivalent of economic nonaggression pacts through which states de-escalate their bidding wars. The biggest horror story is the $300 million in incentives Alabama gave Mercedes to build its first American assembly plant in that state. A perverse minority of politicians sees this kind of competition as useful. John McClaughry, the 1992 Republican candidate for governor of Vermont, predicts that as states try to compete for the new entrepreneurial activity that has begun to decentralize out of the major metropolitan areas into the countryside the uneven results will be therapeutic: "High-tax, high-regulation Vermont and California will miss out on the economic decentralization wave. Low-tax, low-regulation New Hampshire and Idaho will win."

National-minded policy makers cannot accept this federalist version of Darwinism. Urban states forced to bear the burdens of Medicaid, welfare, big-city crime, illegal immigration, and crumbling transportation infrastructure can't keep their fiscal heads above water in a federal system that lets less-developed states turn themselves into tax havens and skim the nation's economic and demographic cream. Few other major nations allow this kind of tax haven to operate within their borders, although some allow them next door — Britain's Channel Islands (not fully part of the United Kingdom and not represented in Parliament), and French-protected Monaco (likewise not legally French).

The fiscal independence of the states is another eighteenth-century ghost, necessary for confederation but troublesome now. In a 1992 book, former Brookings Institution scholar Alice Rivlin reached the glum yet realistic conclusion that America's poor national performance in many economic areas is partly a product of blurred state and federal responsibilities, coupled with the kind of local-option flexibility to tax or not tax just described. Her solution: to hand back to the states a sizeable group of economic and human resource responsibilities — from education, social services, and skills training to aspects of industrial policy and modernization of infrastructure — and then simultaneously force them into a new tax system and larger revenue base. Washington would collect on behalf of the states one or more common taxes, and the revenues would be divided among the states on a per capita basis.

Maneuvering the states into a new framework won't be easy. Just as the malfunctions of government and politics in Washington have their entrenched interest-group proponents, so do outdated state-level structures, boundaries, and techniques. *Lobbying and Influence Alert*, a national newsletter for professional lobbyists, found some fifty thousand lobbyists registered in state capitals in 1993, up from forty-one thousand in 1991. Interest-group power is growing as fast in the states as it is along the Potomac.

As we have seen in Chapter 2, most capital cities now attract an important new group of lobbyists: wary representatives from lesser levels of government. In Washington, not just the governors but also major cities and even major counties have cadres of special pleaders standing by. Membership in the Monday Morning Group of the U.S. Conference of Mayors ranges from a lobbyist who attends for Key West, Florida, and Riverside, California, to a lawyer for St. Paul, Minnesota, and the nine-person Washington office of the City of New York.

Thirty counties also field Washington representatives, including thirteen from California alone. Lobbyists of lesser governments are also thick on the ground in big-state capitals like Albany, Tallahassee, Harrisburg, Springfield, Lansing, Columbus, and Austin. The spokespersons from local counties and cities have colleagues from development districts, independent school districts, and water/sewer districts. It is a growth business. Persons who lobby one layer of government for another increased roughly fourfold during the "New Federalism" years of the 1980s. The state and local portion of the federal system is calcifying like Washington; its boundaries, duplicate layers, lobbying relationships, and complexities are setting and hardening.

This is neither quaint nor harmless. In fact, archaic boundaries and troublesome, out-of-date divisions of authority are familiar hallmarks of a leading world power that has peaked and started on a comparative downslope. Mancur Olson, the theorist of how nations ebb, has pointed out how many of the nations that have risen to become world economic leaders began their glory years with a powerful, almost electric coming together of provinces, states, kingdoms, or territories, all of which also kept some lesser separate identity. Three of the four modern great economic powers had names that began with "United." Spain lacked the name but had the actuality of such a fusion — first, its union of the crowns of Leon, Castile, and Aragon; thereafter the coming together of much of Europe under one ruler as the Hapsburg Empire.

The Netherlands, in turn, was officially the *United* Provinces of the Netherlands — seven of them, from Holland down to remote Groningen on the German border, prickly and semi-independent. Britain, of course, was the *United* Kingdom of Great Britain and Ireland, and at its peak, the British Empire also included four self-governing dominions. The *United* States, in turn, became the third leading world economic power in a row to have its name begin with the adjective that explained its dynamism.

The fusion process is at first a blessing — and ultimately a problem. Each of these confederations brought about the equivalent of a critical mass of territory, talents, markets, animal spirits, and ambitions. During the golden ages of each nation, the internal divisions, squabbling leaders, provincial jealousies, and separate tax systems remained subordinated in the historical equivalent of a new force field — the confederation and the power it unleashed far outweighed the petty divisions and lingering parochialism.

Not for long, however. After three or four generations, as the tide of prosperity and greatness receded, uncovering still-important separations, these complications and parochialisms started to reassert themselves. Internal divisions again became an obstacle.

As Spain's imperial glories were receding, its ministers found themselves haunted by what a twentieth-century observer might call the problems of Iberian federalism — old privileges becoming controversial and fiscal and procedural orneriness breaking out up and down the peninsula. Castile, the heartland of the kingdom, was bearing too much of the financial and military burden. Yet under the existing structure of the Spanish monarchy, the privileges of subkingdoms like Aragon and Valencia allowed their local parliaments to shrug away most of the demands from Madrid for more troops and more money. So could Portugal and Catalonia. Proposals by the king's ministers to conform the laws of the various subkingdoms to those of Castile were mostly rejected. Aragon and Valencia produced no more than minor concessions, Catalonia broke into revolt, and a revolution took Portugal out of the empire. We can posit an unfortunate rule that probably also applies to the United States: fixing these old divisions and separated powers doesn't matter much when things are going well, and it's almost impossible when the heady wines of early success are turning to sour grapes.

So, too, in the United Provinces of the Netherlands. Internal parochialisms didn't matter too much in 1600 or 1650, when the Dutch faced a common enemy in Catholic Spain and shared a common pride in their wealth and far-flung commerce. But a few generations later, amid the decline of the eighteenth century, the old divisions became increasingly crippling. For example, bickering kept the seven provinces' financial contributions to the national exchequer, which had been fixed during the 1609–21 period, from further revision for another hundred and fifty years, despite a pressing need to update them.

The British example is less emphatic but similar. By the end of Queen Victoria's reign, when Britain's comparative share of world manufacturing and trade was already declining, its "federal" problems were growing. The Irish, on the verge of a revolution, wanted Home Rule or full independence. After the turn-of-the-century Boer War, when London asked the dominions — Canada, Australia, and New Zealand — to increase their support of the British navy, minor sums were forthcoming from Australia and New Zealand and nothing from Canada. Within the United Kingdom itself, the internal boundaries and structures of British local government were Victorian right up through World War II. Rutland kept its ancient status as a county despite just eighteen thousand residents.

If these precedents have an eerie resemblance to some of what is also hobbling the United States as it approaches the twenty-first century, that is the unhappy point. Each of these nations had at least as great a need to "reinvent government" as America today, and the Spanish certainly tried. Too little is always done too late, and the challenge confronting the United States in the 1990s is to deal resolutely with internal divisions and federal problems that history suggests could easily become crippling.

Judicial Supremacy and the Lawyer and Litigation Explosions

There *are* too many lawyers. Back in the 1980s, before the Republican administration of George Bush and Dan Quayle embarked on what would be overt lawyer-baiting in 1991–92, Tom Paxton, a singer of humorous and broadside ballads, made a small hit out of a disturbing statistic. Pretty soon, his lyrics noted, the United States was going to have a million lawyers. That level would be reached around the end of the decade, experts predicted, up from 800,000 in 1991 and just 250,000 in the late 1970s.

Which brings us to the fourth major weakness of the U.S. governmental and political system: too much law, too great a role for judges and the judiciary, and far too many lawyers. Attorneys have been hated down through the centuries, but the United States is testing the force of antilawyer emotions at an intensity rivaling fifth-century Rome. The Bush-Quayle administration was blatant in trying to ignite public hostility. In 1991 the vice president told the American Bar Association that "our system of civil justice is, at times, a self-inflicted competitive disadvantage.... Does America really need 70 percent of the world's lawyers? Is it healthy for our economy to have eighteen million new lawsuits coursing through the system annually?" A year later, Bush was snarling that Bill Clinton was backed "by every trial lawyer who ever wore a tasseled loafer." Seventy-three percent of Americans, up from 55 percent in 1986, told a *National Law Journal* poll that the country had too many lawyers.

Things had come a long way since John Marshall's day, but the nation's first chief justice *did* have something to do with the lawyer explosion. In his famous Marbury decision, he took a lawsuit by an obscure federal job claimant and turned it into a classic jurisprudential power grab. He ruled that he didn't have the authority to act as the claimant desired — and here was the cleverness of the strategy — because the law empowering the Supreme Court to do so was unconstitutional. By rejecting one brand of authority, Marshall created enough future clout for the judiciary that law and the courts in the United States have managed to evolve a role, power, and supporting private sector infrastructure that they enjoy almost nowhere else. This helps explain why this country has nearly a million lawyers, and why in 1991, some ninety-four thousand college seniors applied for admission to law school.

In recent years, judicial supremacy — the term academicians use to describe the power Marshall set in motion — has created individual rights and opportunities for litigation that utterly astonish legalists in other nations. Thomas Jefferson had a sense of what Marshall was up to. Looking back in 1821, he worried that "the judiciary of the United States is the subtle corps of sappers and miners constantly working underground to undermine the foundations of our confederated republic. They are construing our constitution from a coordination of a general and special government to a general and supreme one alone. This will lay all things at their feet."

By the second half of the twentieth century, part of Jefferson's forecast had come true. Much indeed had been laid at the feet of the judiciary, and the ranks of lawyers in the United States began to expand at a rapid pace, capped by the extraordinary surge of the 1970s and 1980s. Of the negative effects on public policy and government, four stand out:

Past a certain point, the effects on the economy of the regulatory proliferation and make-work imposed by lawyers is almost certainly negative. But nobody can be quite sure of where that point is. University of Texas Professor Stephen Magee contends, based on international comparisons, that the United States has 40 percent more lawyers than it (or any nation) should, and that this excess reduces GNP by $600 billion a year. One of the worst things about lawyers, he contends, is how those in Congress and the state legislatures make business for the others: "When lawyers artificially stimulate the demand for legal services through politics, we cannot rely on the usual market forces of supply and demand to control their numbers." Magee's numbers have a shoot-from-the-hip sound, but they do furnish some basis for turning the political accusations of 1991–92 into a more serious national debate.

A second criticism, leveled by former Harvard president Derek Bok, is that the high rewards of lawyering lure too much of the nation's talent pool to that already overcrowded profession at a time when the country cries out for more and better public servants, engineers, teachers, and high school principals. True enough.

Then there's the likelihood that the plethora of rights, distinctions, and classifications that lawyers have been so busily creating has reinforced the Balkanization of America, stimulating group demands for quotas and preferences. If the liberal or egalitarian sociology of the 1960s failed in its national application, lawyers are partly responsible for the way in which it was imposed — through judges not trained for those purposes, through abstract classifications, and through "rights" that often wound up creating more litigation than progress.

Finally there's the question of the insidious overlap of America's lawyer explosion and its lobbyist explosion. Not only do those expansions overlap chronologically; lawyers also constitute a fairly high proportion of the lobbyists in Washington and the state capitals, and they do a good job of producing legislation that contrives to enlarge demand for specialized legal services. Rarely does a session of Congress go by without some major legislation, often a tax bill, being nicknamed "The Lawyers' and Accountants' Full Employment Act of 1990" or whatever year. Moreover, it's also fair to say that Washington's ever-expanding role in giving American businesses and citizens detailed statutory and regulatory instructions through judges, lawmakers, and bureaucrats has brought an expansion of federal legislation and lobbying to match the enormous upsurge in federal lawsuits. And it's additionally fair to say that lobbyists, many of whom are not lawyers, have happily settled into the economic ethics of attorneydom: anybody who can pay is entitled to have you, and vice versa. Intriguingly, the major nation with the lowest ratio of lawyers is also the one — Japan —with the least tolerance of foreign lobbyists.

In short, the maturation of judicial supremacy, which encouraged the role of law, courts, and lawyers to balloon in the mid–twentieth century, is at least partly responsible for Washington's ultimate emergence as a citadel of lobbyists, hairsplitters, regulatory specialists, and legislative procurers. Mr. Chief Justice Marshall has more to answer for than he could ever have guessed. And the disbelief that this could have happened to a nation with such a great legal tradition misses the most unfortunate point of all. It seems *especially* likely to happen to such nations. The greatness of Roman law in the heyday of the Republic degenerated so that by the fourth century excessive litigation was a plague, and the historian Ammianus wrote that "the lawyers have laid siege to the doors of the widows and children." Historian Michael Grant has summed up as follows: "The lawyers, almost as much as the civil servants, caused Rome's administration to grind gradually to a paralyzed halt. Between them, the jurists and the bureaucrats bequeathed to the barbarians an Empire which . . . was already dead."

So the parallels we see in all four of the emerging political and governmental weaknesses set forth in this chapter are two-

fold: first, the increasing stiffness in the joints — or worse —
of systems and processes that worked reasonably well when
America and its institutions were younger; and second, the ag-
gravation of this failure as it became entwined with greater
access by and power for lobbies and interest groups, a weakness that crops up relentlessly in American politics and government of the mid-1990s.

But before going on to look at the potential volatility of the
1990s and then at prospects for reform here in the United
States, it's useful to look at another precarious context: how
the weaknesses of politics, finance, and government in the
United States, while in some cases unique, are also confirmed
by significant parallels elsewhere in the English-speaking
world, adding a major historical caution and increasing the
stakes of reform.

Chapter Six

The Fading of Anglo-American Institutions and World Supremacy

Over the last century, the world economy has been dominated by two countries, the United Kingdom and the United States of America. Although the period of Anglo-Saxon ascendancy is often divided into two periods — "Pax Britannica" from 1825 to 1925 and "Pax Americana" from 1945 to the present — the two countries have often behaved as a single agent because of their common cultural and political background.

— DAVID HALE,
economist, 1987

MALFUNCTIONING political and governmental institutions are bad enough. But what threatens to make a difficult situation worse is that some of the problems facing the United States are part of the ebb tide confronting the whole English-speaking world. A global cultural watershed — and one could be near — would add to U.S. adjustment difficulties.

Four centuries ago, the new era of commerce and acquisitiveness that spread across post-Reformation Europe marked the triumph of what sociologist Max Weber has named the Protestant ethic. By the seventeenth century, it was clear that the major Protestant commercial powers, England and the new United Provinces of the Netherlands, stood for a powerful combination of individualism and representative government with market economics and speculative capitalism. And since 1815, when the Duke of Wellington disposed of Napoleon at Waterloo, essentially the same ideological combination has dominated world affairs, under the successive flags of Britain and the United States.

Even today, important elements of politics and economics flow from this achievement and its philosophy. So if the institutions and confidence levels of Britain, Canada, Australia, and New Zealand are flagging like those of the United States — and as we shall see, they are — then besides dealing with the unique circumstances of the United States, Americans must also face the ebb of a larger political culture. The corollary is that Britons, Canadians, Australians, and New Zealanders have a greater stake than they may realize in coming efforts in the United States to renew shared values and institutions in the twenty-first century.

In Chapter 3 we examined the difficulty politicians and opinion molders have in discussing the historical trajectory of the United States: is the country declining, and who, if anyone, is to blame? Now let us do the same for Anglo-America — the United States, Britain, Canada, Australia, and New Zealand. As the year 2000 approaches, this decline is even more obvious, especially in past geopolitical glories. Just picture a map on which all of Britain's lost colonies, dominions, and former military bases around the world are flagged by little Union Jacks, and all of America's former territory — from the Philippines to the Panama Canal Zone — and one-time naval and air bases were marked by miniature Stars and Stripes. The combined red, white, and blue would be eye-popping. In this game of pin the flag on the declining world power, Anglo-America's ebb in the half century since 1945 exceeds any full *century* in the long-ago pullback of Rome.

The retreat is more than physical. From Khartoum to Karachi, from Manila to Panama City, once the proconsuls and generals have gone home, Anglo-American political culture and institutions have been tenuous survivors. The list of the world's twenty-five biggest banks, lopsidedly Anglo-American after World War II, now tilts to Asia and continental Europe. On a grander scale, Chicago economist David Hale has prepared a revealing graph — see page 276 — of the share of Industrial World GNP enjoyed by Anglo-America (including Canada and Australia).[7] After rising from the late eighteenth century through the middle of the twentieth, that share peaked at 65 percent in the 1950s and began to fall, with the decline becoming a major topic of international discussion in the 1980s.

Another signal, if we look at the five English-speaking nations, is some similarity of economic and political arteriosclerosis that is also distinct from the weaknesses of continental Europe and Japan. Besides the Anglo-American nations' common dilemmas in managing representative government and free-market capitalism, there is a disturbing overlap of onetime shared strengths turning into shared national handicaps. Examples include the Anglo-Saxon penchant for interest groups and associations, the common tendency to speculative finance, overabundant (and seemingly unprunable) layers of local government, tired and hoary political parties, too much legalism, and run-amok individualism that has wound up breeding a culture of rights and entitlements, as well as the lesser talents of Anglo-Saxons, relative to Germans, Japanese, and others, for effective state economic planning or business-government collaboration.

In retrospect, we can make too much of Britain's decline in the bleak years after World War II because the principal pain was economic and imperial. Beyond that, British language, communications, service industries, and political institutions — to say nothing of the fortunes of flourishing ex-dominions like Canada, Australia, and New Zealand — all sheltered and prospered under the successor supremacy of the United States.

Which brings us to a third dimension: how the larger political and economic supremacy now in danger goes back nearly four centuries. Any new watershed would be much more difficult than the transition of 1945. Despite the post–World War II discomfort in the haughtier precincts of Pall Mall and St. James, there was a very real Anglo-American continuum. The United States picked up where the United Kingdom left off. The language of William Pitt and Queen Victoria continued to be a lingua franca in the shops of the Rue de Rivoli, the banks off the Bahnhofstrasse, or the hotels of the Ginza. The ships and planes that patrolled the world were still largely captained by people named Jones, Adams, Campbell, and Callaghan; only the accents and insignia were different. It is appropriate to expand this continuum to include the seventeenth- and eighteenth-century Dutch, close neighbors, whose revolution, explorations, and commerce did so much to pave the way for subsequent British and U.S. hegemony. So it is a long era that could be ending.

The world's next leadership transition, presumably to Asia, will be wrenching. No new Anglo-American power is waiting in the wings to uphold familiar values and institutions. Whether or not the twenty-first century continues to reflect these values and institutions may, in the end, depend most on one thing: the renewal — or nonrenewal — of the United States.

The Dutch-English-American Continuum

The reality of what we too narrowly call the American century or Anglo-American era is actually a continuum going back even further. In the years after World War II, when few foreign nations had major investments in a United States at the peak of its power, there were two principal exceptions: Britain and the Netherlands. The United States subsidiaries of jointly owned Anglo-Dutch companies like Shell and Unilever — the latter doing business in the United States as Lever Brothers — were familiar to most Americans and unsettling to virtually none.

Significant Dutch lineage is an unsung part of America's political-economic framework. If you happened to grow up in New York City, Holland's New World focal point, no foreign country save Britain had a bigger local imprint. Old Dutch names, leftovers from New Amsterdam, were the last stops on a half dozen bus and subway lines: Flatbush, New Utrecht Avenue, Canarsie, Bushwick, and Van Cortlandt Park. Actually, Dutch names spread for three hundred miles, from the Battenkill River rising in southwest Vermont to the Schuylkill River flowing through Philadelphia, from the Bronx (named for Jonas Bronck) to Block Island (named for Adrian Block) off the coast of Rhode Island. When the English took over New Amsterdam —in 1664, and quite bloodlessly — they kept most of the local Dutch administrators. The two Protestant, seafaring nations, neighbors across a hundred miles of North Sea from Harwich to the Hook of Holland, shared a politics and culture of hostility to the continental Catholic regimes of France and Spain. In 1688, when Englishmen rose up in what our shared histories salute as the "Glorious Revolution" against King James II, a Catholic who sought alliance with France, the monarchs replacing him set sail from the Netherlands: the English-born Princess Mary and her Dutch husband, William of Orange, who reigned as William and Mary (and have a well-known American university named for them in Williamsburg, Virginia).

Throughout much of the eighteenth century, the Dutch continued to contribute to Britain as the biggest foreign investors in British enterprises. And descriptions of the people and culture of the Netherlands, Britain, and the United States in their formative years use most of the same words: individualistic, bourgeois, legalistic, association- and organization-minded, parliamentarian, decentralized, Calvinist, puritan, entrepreneurial, mechanical, commerce-minded, seafaring, trade-oriented, speculative, and money-worshiping.

The continuum of the Netherlands, then Britain, and finally the United States exercising world economic and commercial dominance is now old and battle-scarred. The Italians, Spanish, and French — the rival Catholic Latin nations and city-states of the European continent — lost their sixteenth- to nineteenth-century competitions, as did the twentieth-century Germans and Russians. So if this long preeminence is about to end, pulled down by the permutation of traits, characteristics, and institutions that were once its pillars, the effects will be far-reaching.

The Shared Political Obsolescence of Late-Twentieth-Century Anglo-America

We have seen in Chapter 5 how critical weaknesses in American government have developed out of what used to be strengths. There are significant parallels in the other English-speaking countries. Later-stage Anglo-Saxon political culture is in retreat, not just the separate genius of our own politics.

Contemporary critics harp on a revealing turnabout: how yesteryear's self-reliant individualism has lost its Calvinistic ethic of hard work, self-denial, and sacrifice, turning instead into a demand for economic rights, entitlements, and guarantees. All five Anglo-American nations — Britain, the United States, Canada, Australia, and New Zealand — have been late-twentieth-century hotbeds of entitlementism, even though pressures to reverse the welfare state are building everywhere. Government office walls are often papered with circulars like "Do you know your rights?" "Are you claiming for this?" "Are you registered for this?" It is a revealing shift.

Judges and courts and their roles have also become increasingly controversial in Britain and Australia, partly as politicians leave policy vacuums for jurists to fill, but also as rising crime creates demand for stopping and jailing criminals rather than worrying about their rights. Legalistic emphasis on group protections and rights also complicates another shared challenge: integrating growing nonwhite populations or coping with ethnic separatism that didn't used to matter. Each English-speaking country confronts at least one such sociological issue — from aboriginal rights in Australia to race relations in the United States, the possible secession of Quebec in Canada, the status of the Maoris in New Zealand, and Britain's problems with Northern Irish and Welsh and Scottish nationalists. Complex legal systems obliged to pursue ethnic rights and equalities often create more complications than solutions.

As for how to reinvigorate systems of representative government increasingly driven by special interests, that is a discussion topic in London, Ottawa, and Canberra, not just Washington. Canadian and Australian voters, annoyed at their own capital districts for having their nations' highest per capita incomes, echo much of the hostility that Americans direct against Washington. All of the separate federal enclaves — Washington, Ottawa, and Canberra — are routinely denounced as ghettoes of overpaid and overprivileged governmental elites. Contempt for Ottawa reached such a level in the early 1990s, especially in Canada's angry western provinces, that citizens cheered references to bureaucrats as "snivel servants," forced the Canadian Senate to rescind an increase in members' expense accounts, and applauded semiserious suggestions by a former cabinet minister to relocate the capital from Ottawa to Winnipeg near the country's east-west midpoint. These complaints are largely postwar, products of the last twenty or twenty-five years. They reflect a frustration and disenchantment hard to imagine back in the 1950s.

Cheerleaders for the U.S. two-party system cannot be pleased with the trends in other English-speaking countries. Increasingly, two-party systems do not represent a broad enough slice of national opinion. Canada's 1993 general election ushered in a political revolution, with the ruling Conservatives reduced from 155 seats in Parliament to just 2, losing officially recognized status. An already shaky two-party system simply collapsed. Four other parties moved ahead of the governing one, despite its history dating to 1867 and its nine preceding years in power. Australia and New Zealand still have two major parties, but minor party roles have been growing. Furor over a proposed 15 percent national consumption tax

focused voters on Australia's two-party battle in 1993, squeez-
ing the minor National, Green, and Democratic parties. But in
next door New Zealand, the election of 1993 produced a
standoff between the National and Labor parties, with two
new groupings — Alliance and New Zealand First — jumping
to 18 percent and 10 percent of the total vote.

In Britain, the 1990s may see the Conservatives and Labour
finally weaken enough that the centrists, stuck at 10 to 20 percent support in national elections since the 1970s, can break
through, probably in coalition with the post-socialist Labour
Party. Even cynics mindful of the centrists' false starts of the
late 1970s and 1980s began keeping serious scorecards in the
mid-1990s, as the Liberal Democrats destroyed Conservative
candidates in one important parliamentary by-election after
another and took over dozens of local councils in Conservatism's thatched-roof-and-vicarage rural English heartland. At
its low point, Conservative control of local government in England was reduced to a single county: fat, squirearchical Buck-
inghamshire. The Labour Party, long a creature of the trade
union movement, was not much better off, because year after
year discontented voters willing to favor the party in public
opinion polls cringed at actually putting it in office.

This larger background of English-speaking voter aliena-
tion backstops the idea of a weak U.S. party system. Confronting the challenge of the twenty-first century with parties
formed back in the nineteenth doesn't make any greater sense
in Toronto, Manchester, or Brisbane than it does in Long Island. The demand for alternatives is increasing.

This disbelief in the results produced by the present party
system is also beginning to stir interest in wider-ranging reforms. One such debate, noted in Chapter 5, is whether it's
time for Anglo-America to give up the old first-past-the-post,
single-member-constituency approach to electing national
legislatures. Choosing legislators this way favors the two-party

system, but with the old major parties losing appeal, the dilemma is stark: whether to further entrench the existing parties despite their failings or to accept the transformation and establish a system of proportional representation designed to sort out (but also facilitate) the emergence of new groupings. Beyond Anglo-America, most nations already employ a form of proportional representation in their national legislative elections and accept the multiparty results. For the English-speaking countries to change in this direction would break with long-standing tradition, but debate is rising.

New Zealand shifted to the German system of proportional representation in 1993, when parliamentary elections were already increasing minor party strength. Gains for Britain's third-party centrists have spotlighted the issue there, and commentators have been predicting that introduction of proportional representation will come about in the 1990s to seal a coalition bargain between the Liberal Democrats and Labour. In Australia, a form of proportional representation is already used in elections to the Senate. And in Canada, the nation's leading newspaper, the *Toronto Globe and Mail*, has endorsed proportional representation as a way to sort out the increasing chaos of the party system. Interest in proportional representation has grown in the United States, too, but it is small by comparison.

Still another related proposal would give the tired party systems of Anglo-America — featuring six of the world's oldest continuously functioning parties — a vitamin supplement through injections of direct democracy like the initiative and referendum devices. Switzerland uses these devices more often and more successfully on a nationwide basis than any other country, but Australia, New Zealand, and the United States also use them, and participatory democracy may be about to develop its most important momentum in the English-speaking world.

Australia, with its populist heritage, has conducted almost fifty nationwide referendums since its federation at the beginning of the twentieth century. New Zealand has held about two dozen, most recently for voters to approve proportional representation. In the United States, where initiative and referendum devices have their widest use at a local level, independent presidential candidate Ross Perot made support of a *national* referendum system a centerpiece of his 1992 campaign, specifically recommending it for tax increases (as in Switzerland) and for approving or disapproving congressional pay raises. American voters embrace the idea by two to one, according to 1993 survey data. In Canada, the Perot-like Reform Party, which overwhelmed the establishment wing of conservatism in the 1993 elections, endorsed using referendums to resolve major national policy questions, as was done for the first time in 1992 when Canadians balloted, province by province, in a national referendum on the proposed special constitutional status for Quebec. Like Americans, Canadian voters also favored institutionalizing a wider use of the referendum.

British interest is also growing. Ireland's electorate votes occasionally on national issues from abortion to European unification. Scotland, Wales, and Northern Ireland have specially balloted on constitutional issues of local significance. It is the United Kingdom as a whole, the famous "mother of parliaments," where disgruntled voters may be most ready to upset tradition. Britain's sole national referendum to date came in 1975 on whether to stay in the European Community. But the current spark was struck in 1992, when Danish voters rejected the Maastricht treaty and a European monetary union. British voters, hitherto lukewarm on Maastricht, promptly crystalized around a populist sticking point: they, too, should get to vote on Europe. Former prime minister Margaret Thatcher added her voice, complaining that without a national vote, the government would "betray" the people's trust in the parliamentary system. Backup came from the Maastricht Referendum Campaign (MARC), which by mid-1993 claimed to be receiving thirty thousand signatures a day in its petition drive, as well as from the rival Campaign for a British Referendum (CBR). Popular sentiment is not much in doubt. Not only did 65 to 75 percent of voters endorse a national referendum on Maastricht (which the government refused to allow), but the debate also crystalized support for using referendums to decide major electoral reform questions.

Sentiments like these are being stoked by the weakness of Anglo-American institutions. National leaders are ineffectual, in part because parties and institutions are. Regionalism, ethnicity, and separatism are on the rise, and with them ungovernability. In the United States, wide-ranging reform is only a possibility, but Canada is in a crisis and Britain may be sliding toward one. Surveys throughout 1992 and 1993 recorded a sharp drop in Britons' confidence in almost all major institutions, from the prime minister and the judicial system to the monarchy and royal family. Moderate populism was rising as royalism was declining.

The unseemly behavior and separation of the Prince and Princess of Wales was a provocation, but the front-page scandals of the royal family soon crystalized a larger discontent: did Britain really need a monarchy, and could its overhaul be part of a broader reform? Back in 1984 the polling firm MORI found 77 percent of Britons saying the country would be "worse off" without the monarchy. By 1992 that had dropped to 37 percent. Support for simply abolishing the monarchy rose somewhat to 17 percent, but the telling number of those described as "indifferent" to its fate soared from 16 percent to 42 percent. Inasmuch as Queen Elizabeth was in her late sixties, with no successor able to command comparable respect, some observers saw a political revolution unfolding. Stephen Haseler, professor of government at Guildhall University,

London, published a book with a title unthinkable just a few years earlier: *The End of the House of Windsor — Birth of a British Republic.* He called for tackling Britain's increasing national obsolescence and uncompetitiveness through a crisis politics of replacing the monarchy and its feudal trappings with an up-to-date government.

Few politicians or commentators were prepared to go that far. But several weighed in with support for reducing the monarchy to the powerless Dutch or Scandinavian form. Downgrading the throne in this way would be important, because it is the British crown's lingering power that supports, and is supported by, the uniquely out-of-date House of Lords; and it is the crown in whose name ministers feel able to sign treaties (like Maastricht) lacking parliamentary authorization: "Replace its authority with that of a written constitution, dismiss the House of Lords and elect a senate," wrote one bold columnist, "and you have quite enough revolution for the average English family to stomach." For comparative purposes, chalk up Britain as possible political revolution number one.

Other portions of the British Commonwealth, meanwhile, were beginning to lay out more specific revolutionary timetables. Prime Minister Paul Keating announced that he planned to call a referendum in the 1990s to gain voter approval for Australia's becoming a republic. Exactly what kind of republic was not set out; various panels and commissions would deliberate that. The broad objective, however, was to eliminate any role for the monarch or reference to the monarchy in Australian law, thereby transforming the country into a republic by the year 2001, the centenary of Australia's federation. A majority of down-under voters told pollsters they agreed, especially young people and those citizens who traced their family origins to southern Europe and Asia.

Potential English-speaking political revolution number two? Probably, although not necessarily by 2001. Jamaica, Papua New Guinea, and even Canada and New Zealand could also leave the Commonwealth, according to Peter Lyon, head of Commonwealth studies at London University, even though unscrambling the Canadian constitution would be extremely complex, and New Zealanders would be unlikely to opt for a republic simply because nearby Australia had done so.

Canada, of course, faces its own constitutional crisis over the place of French-speaking Quebec in the Canadian confederation. By their rejection of the 1992 referendum giving Quebec special privileges, Canadian voters pushed disarray into a new dimension. Aroused Quebec politicians bolted from the Conservative Party and organized the new separatist Bloc Quebecois, which finished second in the 1993 national elections — and thereby became the world's only principal parliamentary opposition dedicated to splitting the country! Here the possibility of major national constitutional upheaval is more like a probability, albeit there is no countdown to the year 2000 or 2001, as in Australia. Are we looking at English-speaking political revolution number three? Each comparison — to Britain, Australia, and Canada — makes the idea of the United States making minor constitutional adjustments to its election system seem less radical.

Out-of-date internal boundaries and changing international alliances are two other signs of political old age and uncertainty. The United States, Britain, and Canada all face varying controversies over internal boundaries, ethnic self-government, and devolution of power. Many existing U.S. state lines are outdated, as we have seen, with odd geopolitical contours and an irrelevance to today's major metropolitan areas that makes them difficult frameworks for a federal system that works through local option in tax policy, health, and education. State boundaries dating back to the eighteenth and nineteenth centuries also provide dry tinder for recurring squabbles and secessionist flames. Will California divide into two states? Will the Idaho

Panhandle secede? Yet there is a potentially larger obsolescence in the east-west boundary that divides Canada and the
U.S.; many residents of the Canadian maritime provinces
would like to join with New England, while out in the Pacific
Northwest people on both sides of the border talk about link-
ing Washington, Oregon, Idaho, Montana, British Columbia,
and Alberta in a loose grouping called Cascadia. Supporters in
Vancouver and Seattle have already come up with green and
blue flags. Canada's internal boundaries, of course, are another
nineteenth-century framework waiting to unravel. If Quebec
secedes and breaks up Canada, the political geography of
twenty-first-century North America could take some interesting new twists.

As we have already seen, Britain is also handicapped by old
internal divisions and boundaries. After three quarters of a century of fading imperial glories, important political forces around
Britain's entire Celtic periphery — Northern Ireland, Wales,
and Scotland — are pushing for new arrangements. Many
Northern Irish Catholics want union with the Irish Republic;
many Welsh and Scots want local assemblies or subparliaments
to be allowed broad power over purely Welsh or Scottish affairs.
Vocal minorities want actual independence. Even some of the
smaller traditional boundaries get in the way. Government ministers had hoped to be able to simplify Britain's county and local
government by doing away with a two-tier structure of district
and county councils, but a tradition-minded population balked.
Residents said no in the historic counties like Durham and
Derbyshire. Only in the "artificial" counties invented and
mapped in 1974, places like Avon, Cleveland, and Humberside,
did the public have no objection to reorganization.

From Britain and the United States to Canada and even
Australia, the parallel is that out-of-date internal divisions
breed inefficiency. But even as the English-speaking countries
are being forced to look *inward* at archaic boundaries and diffi-

cult constitutional relationships, they are also being obliged to look *outward* in a direction which many find painful: unprecedented political and economic unions with non-English-speaking nations. Britain has joined the European Community, despite traditional English distaste for the French and fear of the Germans; Canada and the United States are entering into North American common market arrangements with Mexico; and Australia and New Zealand are drawing closer to their Asian and Pacific neighbors. Auckland, New Zealand's largest city, is already also the world's largest *Polynesian* metropolis. Each nation's new outwardness in part reflects its own changing internal demographics: ever-larger proportions of nonwhites, plus a diminishing ratio of descent from British ancestors. However, there is a sense, unimaginable even thirty or forty years ago, that Anglo-American global hegemony and ability to keep to its own circle of cousins is already a memory.

Let us state the problem baldly: the political and governmental systems of the English-speaking nations all show painful signs of age. For Americans rarely given to worrying about history, that adds another significant dimension to the interest-group barnacles and the governmental and political difficulties spelled out in the previous chapter. Unfortunately, we must also look at a second set of shared Anglo-American *economic* transformations — welfare-state burdens, high debt levels, overly speculative finance, and limited capacities for business-government collaboration — that complicate prospects for the twenty-first century.

The Shared Speculative Weaknesses of Anglo-American Commerce and Economics

Some of Wall Street's abuses are unique to the United States, but the broad framework of modern speculative finance is Anglo-American. As the lingering problems of the 1990s began to refocus queries about what went wrong with the Western economy during the late 1980s, several analysts offered an unusual suggestion: that ethnicity or shared culture was somehow involved. Anthony Harris, a columnist for the *Financial Times*, observed in February 1991 that "virtually the whole English-speaking world is in the same trouble, and, in most countries, it set in too early to be explained by the Gulf [war]." Two and a half years later, as the bust that followed Japan's earlier financial boom deepened, the editors of *The Economist* tossed out a parallel observation: "Japan is passing through a thoroughly Anglo-Saxon recession."

Even before Iraq's invasion of Kuwait in midsummer 1990, the Anglo-American nations, alone in the West, were slipping into downturns. Recessions were already under way in Canada, Australia, and New Zealand, and despite upbeat official insistences, Britain and the United States were heading down the same road. The National Bureau of Economic Affairs ultimately set July 1990, before the invasion, as the starting date of the U.S. downturn. Instead of the usual recession dynamics, a different explanation more or less works in all five nations: that monetary tightening or interest-rate pressures, typically because of unexpected inflation, led to falling property values, heavy banking losses, and widespread bankruptcies. This implosion of debt, coming on the heels of excessive 1980s speculation and borrowing, worked to collapse assets, expose careless and excessive lending, and produce a bankers' panic, which cut off credit and made things worse. By 1992 and 1993 the downturn had spread to the non-English-speaking pillars of the Group of Seven, Germany, France, and Japan.

What was so unusual, in retrospect, was that from the first tremors visible in Canada and Australia in late 1989 to the unfolding devastation of California home values and the early and mid-1990s "Anglo-Saxon" stock market, bank, and real estate debacle in Japan, there *was* an ethnic culture of sorts in

global economics. The critical weaknesses *were* most pro-
nounced in the English-speaking economies. Even Japan's predicament was indirectly Anglo-Saxon — in fair measure the
product of America's mid-1980s insistence that Japan expand its
money supply in order to let Washington carry out a trade-
related devaluation of the U.S. dollar. This expansion created a
speculative bubble which the Japanese alone might not have
permitted.

All of which brings us back to the shared-behavior premise.
The 1989-90 period was the first time since World War II that
the English-speaking nations, *ensemble*, had led the rest of the
world into a downturn. Was there some kind of pattern, some
common approach to economic affairs, that explained this con-
fluence? And did it also raise real questions about the twenty-
first century suitability of Anglo-Saxon finance and economic
management in general and U.S. practices in particular?

In a word, yes. Against the backdrop of the Dutch, English,
and American continuum that shaped the modern Western
political economy, the 1980s and 1990s have aspects of a speculative last hurrah. The evolution of Anglo-American politics
and government, the strengths of a century ago turning to
weaknesses, has a parallel in finance and economics.

In the late sixteenth century, individualism, Calvinism, entrepreneurialism, and speculation more or less went together.
Religion and cultural change were spurs. The organization of
public banks and bourses followed only a generation or two
behind Calvin, Luther, and the Reformation. By the seventeenth century, the Dutch and English had something of a corner on seafarers, maritime trade, merchant adventurers, and
commercial middle classes. Preeminence in finance and banking was not far behind. As for speculation, the best-known
frenzies of the seventeenth and early eighteenth centuries
were Dutch (the "Tulipomania" of 1636-37) and British (the
South Sea Bubble of 1719-20). The new United States soon

put its own abuses in the list, and of the twenty-four financial "panics" from 1720 to 1907 probed by Charles Kindleberger in his book *Manias, Panics, and Crashes*, eighteen principally involved Holland or Britain or the United States.

On one hand, cultures of economic individualism excel in producing navigators, engineers, entrepreneurs, and inventors, all essential to early commerce, manufacturing, and technology. The dark side is that they also breed speculators, at first critical to national risk-taking, but later increasingly parasitical. The point is simply that the English-speaking capitalism entered the twentieth century with different traits than the statist and mercantilist capitalism of continental Europe and Japan. The Anglo-American economies were open, bourgeois, consumerist, and innovative, and to Anglo-American businessmen, the cartels of Europe were largely an alien form of organization. Even more remote were Japan's *zaibatsu* — the unique alliances of banks, manufacturers, and trading firms that helped members out-maneuver rival alliances.

What stood out about Anglo-America was an entirely different economic genius. Whereas stock exchanges were only peripheral in Paris or Frankfurt circa 1910, two nations where corporations obtained their capital from long-term relationships with major banks, such markets were the heart and soul of Anglo-American financial centers like London, New York, and Toronto. Through the nineteenth century and well into the mid–twentieth century, innovative, entrepreneurial, and speculative Anglo-American capitalism was faster off the mark, and economic statistics proved it. By the 1950s, as we have noted, Britain, the United States, Canada, and Australia had boosted their 25 percent share of Industrial World GNP circa 1825 to a record two thirds of the total. Since then, however, that share has declined. And picking up where we left off in Chapter 4, it is time to frame a central question: has the speculative side of Anglo-American capitalism —

and U.S. excesses, in particular — now become a major weakness?

Despite the optimistic view that the Anglo-American share of the world economy of the 1950s was merely a brief artificial zenith, so that its decline is not critical, the figures put together by David Hale suggest otherwise. Even before 1900, Anglo-America had crossed the 50 percent line, and when World War I had ended, the four major English-speaking countries commanded almost 60 percent of Industrial World GNP. The retreat of the late twentieth century, in which the combined U.S., British, Canadian, and Australian GNP share fell below 50 percent, has carried the Anglo-American share of the world economy back to the level of the 1890s, hardly a normal postwar ebb. There is a more troubling probability: that the bloom is off the Anglo-American economic rose, and that the entrepreneurial and speculative capitalism that grew from the entrepôt of Amsterdam, Lloyd's Coffeehouse, and Wall Street to build the Suez Canal, bridge North America with railroads, and win two world wars is beginning to fade. The final verdict isn't in, but discomforting evidence — the economic traits and weaknesses that prestigious financial publications have started summing up as Anglo-Saxon — is piling up.

For the United States, what this means is that the speculative excesses spelled out in Chapter 4 are also part of a larger international transformation. Besides a shared penchant for voluntary associations and commercial interest groups, other common disabilities stand out in all of the four major Anglo-American economies. Most of them, moreover, represent the mutation of a one-time advantage. Yesteryear's individualism, as noted, has turned into a pursuit of entitlements, legal judgments, and ever-expanding "rights" that burden the economy and prop up the expensive mandates of the welfare state. Although the United States operates less of a cradle-to-grave system than Britain, Canada, and Australia, our evolution of rights and entitlements has also piled on relatively unique legal costs: the drag of the litigation and liability explosion, especially on business competitiveness, the insurance sector, and health care. The twin burdens of the welfare state and the litigation society have been well cataloged elsewhere, but they have a particular current bite — and threat — in the English-speaking world.

Anglo-America's second gathering peril — excessive budget deficits and public debt totals — is partly a function of the welfare state, but also partly the product of a tolerance and even taste for leverage, debt, and speculation. High national and international indebtedness is something the English-speaking nations share a proven ability to indulge, rationalize, and excuse. British credit ratings were devastated earlier in the century by the huge borrowings necessary to finance two world wars. The ballooning of the U.S. national debt from $1 trillion at the beginning of the 1980s to over $4 trillion by the early 1990s was shrugged off by three straight conservative GOP administrations. The Canadian and Australian national debts, in turn, soared during the 1980s and early 1990s, in large measure because voters in both countries didn't want the welfare state trimmed. The upshot, by the mid-1990s, was to saddle most of the Anglo-American countries with relatively large overall public indebtedness *and* annual budget deficits measured as a percentage of GNP.

The data on international borrowing also have overtones of ethnic indictment. Britain became dependent on foreign loans in the late 1940s and then again in the mid-1970s. The United States became a net international debtor in the 1980s. Canada and Australia have been routine overseas borrowers, so much so that Australia is now the world's fourth-largest international debtor. Large chunks of Anglo-America have been borrowing overseas to maintain their standards of living.

Developing nations can prosper as borrowers; witness Brit-

ain circa 1750 and the United States circa 1890. But once a
nation has become a great economic power and then topped
out, rising national debt and international indebtedness is a
poor augury. Each of the two leading Anglo-Saxon world economic powers successfully turned this fiscal corner during the
twentieth century. Their eras of Calvinist, bourgeois thrift are
long gone. No neat correlations exist, but there is almost
certainly a loose connection between broadly rising Anglo-
American indebtedness and declining Anglo-American share
of Industrial World GNP.

Caution number three is another shared Anglo-American
characteristic: the importance attached to owner-occupied
housing, dating back to the old English saying "A man's home
is his castle." Or, in the twentieth century, if not quite a castle,
it has been his prime investment and major capital asset.
Studies of home-ownership in twenty-five Western nations
have found all six English-speaking countries — Ireland, Britain, Canada, the United States, Australia, and New Zealand —
clustering in the top dozen, with at least 60 percent of households owning their own home. American and British tax codes,
in particular, have favored interest paid on home mortgages,
and home-transfer charges are also relatively low. But if home
owning has been a bulwark of cultural and political moderation, it can be an economic albatross. Both the U.S. and Britain lead the world in the speculative investing and trading
aspect of home-ownership. Economists point out several
downsides: first, sopping up large amounts of capital thus
made unavailable for industrial renewal; second, restricting the
mobility of workers who won't leave their houses, thereby
keeping unemployment higher than it might be; third, serving
as an engine of inflation, because home owners like to see their
largest asset gain value; and fourth, feeding a speculative approach to residential and commercial real estate that has
played a lead role in recent Anglo-American boom-bust cycles.

The caveat for U.S. public policy in this larger pattern is unmistakable.

Shared weakness number four, to which we have been leading up, is the broader, almost unquenchable Anglo-American desire to speculate. Market-focused Western economies have always had a more speculative bias than others, but the distinction has intensified over the last two decades as Anglo-America took the lead in financial deregulation, real estate speculation, tax cuts for the rich, electronic securities and commodity trading, currency speculation, and the introduction of new debt instruments and derivatives — all at least partial explanations of how the English-speaking countries were at the epicenter of the 1980s speculative bubble. And London and New York were the two cities where greed became a caricature. However, once the implosion of the 1980s bubble began, with over-leveraged companies unraveling, giant banks flirting with insolvency, and massive real estate empires going into bankruptcies, Canadians and Australians were also overrepresented. The entire Anglo-Saxon financial sector was in up to its red suspenders.

By late 1989, in fact, Australians were already watching with amazement as the first-stage collapse of the 1980s debt-and-speculative bubble pulled down their leading billionaires — men like real estate mogul Alan Bond, property magnate George Herscu, and financier Robert Holmes a Court. Local observers described them as products of the "supply-driven lending" that followed deregulation of Australia's financial system in 1983. Three years later, Canadians were even more stunned when the property crash in New York and Toronto pulled down their highest-flying real estate firm, Olympia and York, the multibillion dollar private preserve of the secretive Reichmann brothers. Toronto real estate was a particularly filmy part of the global Anglo-Saxon speculative bubble. Overall, one newspaper's capsule of what happened in

Australia would have served almost as well for Canada, Britain, or the United States. The eighties had been "a saga of greed and overambition, of eager bankers peddling expensive credit to insatiable borrowers in a newly unshackled financial system; and of corporate empires built on rising asset values, often lax and sometimes questionable accounting, and a hot stock market full of hungry investors." The indictment is most pointed for the United States, but it is a broader criticism of Anglo-America.

That is further true because of shared weakness number five — how the Anglo-American system of financing corporations relies on the avarice-prone stock market, in contrast to the bank orientation of the continental system. The English-speaking approach is sometimes dismissed as "short-termism" — Anglo-Saxons, Americans especially, think short; continentals and Japanese think long. That equation is actually much more complex. What we can now call the Anglo-American system clearly outperformed other systems in the late eighteenth and nineteenth and early twentieth centuries when regulation was minimal and the opportunities for fast decision making and the fruits of economic individualism were greatest. In the late twentieth century, however, that system may have started to lose its competitive advantage.

Too much speculation, as we have seen, can be dangerous to a national economic ascendancy. Anglo-America, after the successive financializations of Britain and the United States, with the junior mimicry of the Canadians and Australians, has become a series of national cultures in which the financial economy has gobbled up too much of the real or industrial economy. Deregulation and the advent of spectronic finance have only added to the momentum. The practice in continental Europe is different. These nations have proportionally fewer companies, smaller stock markets, and, interestingly, had faster growth rates for the 1970s and 1980s. Descriptions like French LBO, Swiss corporate raider, and German speculative bubble, while not quite oxymorons, are uncommon usages.

In 1992 the London Business School published a detailed comparison of the Anglo-Saxon or "outsider" system of corporate finance, in which the outside takeover threat — the stock market, in short — imposes the main discipline on corporate managers, versus the continental or "insider" system, which relies on linked companies, internal committee-style supervision of management decisions, and a web of cross-shareholders that gives incumbent managers protection from speculators and stock markets. The study, based on recent corporate data, concluded that the Anglo-American system works best for industries that require subjective assessments of future prospects and also for speculative endeavors like oil exploration, biotechnology, and pharmaceuticals. The continental system, in turn, was better suited to the more typical manufacturing situations in which there is a direct need to control quality of product, management, and employees, and in which it is useful to have performance monitored by a supervisory board including workers, bankers, and experts from related companies who have a direct stake in the company's future.

Our last caution lies in Anglo-America's poor record of government-business collaboration, plus the inability, stark in early twentieth-century Britain, to formulate and pursue a strategy to keep manufacturing and status as a great economic power from slipping away. Britain's economic coming-of-age overlapped with the supremacy of laissez-faire, from its late-eighteenth-century philosophic emergence in the writings of Adam Smith to its late-nineteenth-century crest and downturn. The United States was not far behind. Shaped in this free-market forge, business-government relationships in both countries have been standoffish and frequently adversarial. Management-labor relations have been mostly adversarial. Indeed, collaborative business-government-labor industrial strategies on behalf of manufacturing or key industries may run contrary to the Anglo-Saxon thought process. The British government never achieved anything in this vein during the critical early years of this century. Washington may do better, but the precedents are not encouraging.

These shared weaknesses add up to a considerable case that Anglo-America has peaked economically and now deteriorates in ways that will be hard to overcome. Optimists insist that none of these previous weaknesses will matter very much, because the twenty-first-century U.S. future lies less in manufacturing than in services — especially communications, entertainment, and financial services, in which the United States in particular and Anglo-America in general are still preeminent. The individualistic genius of Anglo-Saxon economics will be able to triumph again. Perhaps, but there are also historical reasons to be cautious about a services future.

"Post-Imperial" Overdependence on Services

Increased dependence on the service sector, in fact, is a familiar phenomenon of declining great economic powers. In seventeenth-century Madrid, as the reform-minded *arbitristas* pointed out, everybody was a bureaucrat, courtier, teacher, pupil, churchman, broker, or lounge-about. Hardly anybody manufactured anything, and when New World gold ran out, so did Spain. The Holland of 1750, which had lost most of its Leyden textiles, Delft ceramics, North Sea shipbuilding, fishing fleets, and once-proud navy, was increasingly an economy of financial and commercial services and government employment. Late-nineteenth-century pessimists concerned about Britain losing its manufacturing edge had a stock analogy: *the country might become another Holland.* By the 1990s that was not a bad description: both countries had become financial services centers with broad welfare states and a lot of government employees.

We cannot say the trend to services in the fin de siècle United States necessarily holds parallel prospects. Services *are* becoming steadily more important. And the hybrid nature of some of the new service industries, from entertainment (films, cassettes, discs, television programs, etc.) to fast food, computer software, and the 1990s "multimedia" rage of crossbreeding telephones, televisions, and computers for a personal communications revolution, could signal a new consumer age in which services effectively displace manufactures as a staple of world output, GNP, and prosperity.

Yet service industries are *already* firmly in place as our major overseas earners. That pattern, which dates back many years, has been emerging alongside the six Anglo-American economic negatives just reviewed. In 1992, when the United States had a $96-billion deficit in international merchandise trade, services produced a $59-billion surplus. True, over 40 percent of the surplus in services came from the money foreign tourists spent in the United States and from foreign enrollment in U.S. universities. The rest, however, came from sale to foreigners of business, professional, and technical services — accounting, investment, legal, insurance, brokerage, engineering, advertising, and banking — and from entertainment and technologies that earn royalties and license fees.

But Madonna cassettes and more advanced technology aside, the basic pattern is classic declining economic power in the Dutch-English mode. Both the Dutch, as their manufacturing and fisheries declined in the eighteenth century, and the British, as their steel, textiles, coal, and shipbuilding industries weakened in the early twentieth century, showed substantially similar trends as they slid. Merchandise exports might be slumping, but services were selling as well or better than ever — banking, money management, shipping, insurance, maritime brokerage, export-import services, and the like.

These are the accumulated skills and contacts of a great economic power, in a sense postimperial legacies.

The reasonably reliable data of twentieth-century Britain are particularly cautioning. At first, as manufactured exports slipped, they still produced a trade surplus, and rising service exports — so-called "invisibles" — made that surplus bigger still. Then manufacturing no longer produced an export surplus, but services kept the overall balance narrowly favorable most of the time. During the 1980s, however, Britain's trade deficit in merchandise became big enough that exports of services could no longer plug the hole — and by 1992 the merchandise trade deficit was a gaping £13.4 billion, the "invisibles" surplus only £4.8 billion. The OECD's annual policy review for that year came to a regretful conclusion: the growth in exports of Britain's skilled financial, banking, and advisory services didn't seem capable of making up for the deterioration in manufacturing.

In considering how much prosperity services can maintain in the United States, it is useful to point out a further parallel: the extent to which the late-stage Dutch, British, and U.S. economies have all had their greatest successes in the "imperial" service sectors built up by world political or economic leadership and connections. The repeaters over three centuries have already been mentioned: banking, trade brokerage, money management, insurance, and the like. Late-twentieth-century add-ons include engineering, travel, global construction, advertising, legal services, entertainment, and communications. The U.S., Canada, and Britain continue to do very well in these fields, partly because of Anglo-American leadership of the West, but also because of a related legacy: the English language as the lingua franca of multinational business, maritime affairs, aviation, banking, and investment, plus the current dominance of English-language entertainment, news services, and popular music. Global influence still also helps the U.S. in contracts for heavy construction, oil and oil services, and waste management and in politically influenced markets for aircraft and weapons systems. Britain still enjoys lesser versions of the same benefits — in aerospace and oil, for example. But if the next century *is* Asian, political and service-industry legacies enjoyed by Anglo-Americans could thin rapidly in two or three decades.

In short, some of the service-sector strength that Americans are counting on to reverse the analogies to troubled great economic powers of the past may be unreliable. Elements of the growth in services are actually *part* of our disconcerting analogy. The huge employment linked to government and the health/welfare sectors is as much burden as asset, and the sale of "postimperial" financial and commercial advisory services — while continuing to earn tidy sums and provide lucrative niches for upper-bracket Dutch and Britons — did not succeed in restoring either nation to the status and relative prosperity lost when its broader commercial and manufacturing success ebbed. No one can be *sure* that this failure will recur in the United States. But it may.

Chapters 3–6 have sought to lay out a series of troubling circumstances and aging processes that threaten U.S. ability to perform in the twenty-first century. From the entrenchment of speculative finance and Washington interest groups to the arteriosclerosis in much of the governmental and political system and the troubling signs of a larger obsolescence in Anglo-American values and institutions, these add up to a considerable obstacle to renewal. They also amount to a call for the equivalent of a political and governmental revolution. The hopeful aspect is that, over the next decade or so, Americans may have a rare, even unique, opportunity to make their country over. These opportunities — and some specific remedial recommendations — are the subject of Part III, to which we now turn.

Part III

The Revolutionary 1990s and the Restoration of Popular Rule in America

Chapter Seven

The 1990s: Converging Revolutionary Traditions and Post–Cold War Jitters

All democracies suffer from a common misery. The Germans unable to govern, the British unstoppably descending, . . . France paralyzed, seemingly crisis-tested Italy decaying with corruption. . . . The forty fat years are over and the entire political class from Boston to Berlin are helpless.

> —JOSEF JOFFE,
> *foreign editor,* Suddeutsche Zeitung,
> *1993*

Having now considered all the things we have spoken of, and thought within myself whether at present the time was not propitious in Italy for a new prince, and if there was not a state of things which offered an opportunity to a prudent and capable man to introduce a new system that would do honour to himself and good to the mass of the people, it seems to me that so many things concur to favour a new ruler that I do not know of any time more fitting for such an enterprise.

> —NICOLO MACHIAVELLI,
> *Exhortation to Liberate Italy, from*
> The Prince, *1532*

AMERICA'S CHALLENGE in the 1990s is to mount the political equivalent of a revolution to revitalize its institutions. Some such effort will occur. The scope may be sufficient, although more probably it will fall short. But for several reasons, the 1990s are the decade in which to try.

Claims of great opportunities for renewal in troubled nations usually deserve a skeptical reception. Machiavelli, the great political cynic of the Renaissance, was at his most naive when he contended, in a final chapter of *The Prince*, that the time was ripe for a strong leader to steer decayed, fragmented early-sixteenth-century Italy back to glory. The time was not ripe, and it didn't happen. Current-day prospects in the United States *are* better, but the warnings of the past also deserve respect. So far, leading world powers with extraordinary histories — two circumstances that usually go together — have been unable, when they later decline, to call up again those puritan and republican virtues, those revolutionary spirits, in which that earlier greatness was born.

Italy failed in Machiavelli's era, and then did so again four hundred years later when Benito Mussolini's revival of the salutes and insignia of ancient Rome ended as comic opera. Hapsburg Spain never managed, although its early seventeenth-century *arbitrista* reformers identified the problems well enough. Nor could the Dutch script a national renewal, although by the mid–eighteenth century a nostalgic

"Patriot" movement was decrying the loss of yesterday's cultural and commercial values and calling for their resurrection. And the early twentieth-century British were just as incapable of recapturing the revolutionary spirit and entrepreneurialism of their younger days.

Why should *we* be different, the reader will properly say. Isn't it more nostalgia than realism to suggest that the United States of the 1990s can transcend precedents and renew itself? Isn't it wishful thinking —understandable, but still wishful — to believe that the United States can reach back into its own revolutionary origins and stage yet another relatively bloodless political insurrection that revitalizes national institutions? And isn't it especially naive to think that yesteryear's Anglo-American political and economic hegemony can be restored for a twenty-first century already moving in Asia's direction?

Yes and no. Anglo-America *is* in decline, and the upcoming "Pacific Century" may well be disproportionately Asian. There *is* a certain amount of nostalgia in counting too much on America's revolutionary origins. Nations always want to thrill again to the trumpets of their adolescence, but few can. And yes, it certainly is unrealistic to think that the United States can reverse its historical trajectory and somehow duck the consequences of all these accumulating predicaments we have been describing — from a special-interest-ridden national capital and calcified governmental institutions to a tired party system, an overload of lawyers, speculators, and rentiers, a depleted Calvinism, and a plague of debt. Problems of this magnitude can't be dealt with easily or quickly. A price, presumably a large one, will have to be paid. The 1990s probably mark the beginning of several decades of upheaval and reckoning.

However, an affirmative viewpoint — that a significant national renewal is possible after several decades of upheaval and reform — also has merit. Compared to previous leading economic powers, this country's position is significantly better for several reasons: First and foremost, instead of being a peripheral European peninsula (like Spain) or a peripheral European maritime power (like Britain and Holland), the U.S. is the anchor of a whole continent with a large population, huge resources, and the world's richest internal market. This represents a more solid long-term foundation. If more efficient structures of government, better-handcuffed interest groups, and lower debt ratios can gradually replace the abuses of the last three decades, the United States should remain one of the two or three strongest and richest world powers through the first half of the twenty-first century. Second, the United States enjoys real population growth, which contrasts favorably with the demographic stagnation of past great powers, and the increase is strongest in just those regions — the Pacific Coast and the Sun Belt — that can serve as North American windows on the emerging political economies of Asia and Latin America. Advantage number three, almost as important, is that the extraordinary decade now unfolding may produce the sort of political and economic transformation opportunity rare in world history, a psychological framework for an institutional revolution. The "nineties" have always been a springboard of political and governmental reform in the United States. But now there is an additional factor that was unavailable to reformers in prior declining powers: the ultimate pro-change context of the approaching millennium.

The Radical Nineties: An American Tradition

To say that the world faces convulsive forces in the 1990s is an understatement. Besides the English-speaking nations, all the other leading economic powers are also caught up in political and governmental upheavals — from Japan, where a large part of the political and party system is being restructured, to the chaos of the former Soviet Union and the *angst* of a Germany stressed by reunification. The geopolitical unrest of the post–Cold War 1990s should match the century's other two great maelstroms: 1914–1920 and 1937–1950. For Americans, of course, those were the upheavals that put the United States on course to twentieth-century global leadership. The outcome of the millennial restructuring is a lot more precarious.

Internationally, end-of-the-century decades have often been eventful ones — the 1490s, 1690s, and 1790s come to mind. And even the less grandiose periods historically shared the hurry-up-the-future thinking typical of the last decades of centuries. As we saw in Chapter 3, Spaniards started getting worried about the future in the 1590s, and Dutch concern accelerated in the 1690s. British uncertainty, in turn, mushroomed in the 1890s, a decade in which people feared that the security of the Victorian era was about to explode in a new century of great steel battleships, socialist and communist risings, barely imaginable changes in technology, and movements from women's rights to anarchism. And they were right.

Now Americans are in another fin de siècle decade, in which it is our turn to be worried. Yet for citizens of this country the nineties have a second, more encouraging tradition — one already fulfilled twice. The nineties have been prime periods of American political and ideological revolution, as opposed to physical and military upheaval. The 1790s, which began with the essentially conservative triumph of the Constitution and its ratification, finished with something very different: the renewal of anti-elite politics, the election of Thomas Jefferson, and the "Revolution of 1800." A century later, the 1890s, which began with robber-baron capitalism and laissez-faire at its zenith, ended with populism and progressivism on the rise, with William Jennings Bryan barely defeated, with ideas like popular ballot initiatives and direct election of U.S. senators about to spread like a prairie fire.

Each time, the nineties in the United States have been a period in which American politics regrouped around its founding ideal of 1776 — that the rule of the people should triumph over the narrower assertion of aristocracies and elites. Popular success is never more than partial, because democratic politics can only reform, not uproot, the financial and commercial structures built up by the factions of privilege. Yet in the 1790s and again in the 1890s, rediscovery of responsibility to the people has served to renew a critical element of this nation's politics and government.

In his landmark book *The Radicalism of the American Revolution*, historian Gordon Wood underscores that the revolution this country carried out from 1776 to 1783 was not radical in the French sense; it was not at all a class-based uprising of the downtrodden. What it was — and what American politics has continued to emphasize ever since then — was a revolt against the misuse of government by elites to promote their own interests against the people's. So when the radicals talked about purifying corruption, eliminating courtiers, overthrowing the crown, and establishing a republic, they seemed mostly to be out to change political institutions; but they expected to change society, too — and they did. The upheavals of the 1790s and the 1890s were both about maintaining this revolutionary tradition.

The 1990s have much the same political and economic character and challenge. They, too, began with special-interest economic conservatism in power, then the tide shifted in a more popular direction, outlining a populist upheaval. And these present nineties, too, must raise up a new force of popular democracy to undo another interest-group supremacy, one even more crippling than its predecessors.

However, this decade's neorevolutionary spurs are not limited to familiar fin de siècle psychologies. The 1990s should produce an even greater catharsis, not merely as the end of the century, but as the threshold of the millennium. Some Christian leaders have been talking about the imminence of the "end times" referred to in the Bible. Yet even for the non-religious middle-aged man or woman, the century about to arrive is one that for twenty or thirty years has been associated with beings from other galaxies, flying saucers, intergalactic wars, and the most extraordinary breakthroughs in science and lifestyle. The millennium should involve a great sense of discontinuity. Powerful forces for upheaval are converging. Popular willingness to accept far-reaching change should be unusually high.

The Overlap of Post–Cold War Frustration

On a more practical dimension, the 1990s also overlap with yet another massive source of destabilization: the end of the Cold War and the need of most Western (as well as former Eastern bloc) countries to replace old political structures that have become outdated and to cut free of governmental arrangements and economic policies assembled around four decades of Cold War parties and leaders.

The changes since the toppling of the Soviet Union have been enormous, not least in economics. Germany is dislocated by the cost of reabsorbing the more primitive and less entrepreneurial East. Massive defense cuts have already taken place in the United States, especially in New England, Long Island, and California. However, most of the prosperous G-7 countries also face a deeper irony: even as the collapse of Communism and the Soviet Union has freed the Western nations to turn inward and concentrate on rebuilding their domestic economies, industries, and public services, the economic trauma of the 1990s has left most of them too strapped to do so, while holding out the added prospect of still higher debt, resurgent inflation, or both. Communism may have gone down in a blaze of failed statism, but the West, and especially its Anglo-Saxon portion, has spent years in a slump that partly reflects the excesses of the speculative side of capitalism. This is part of what must change.

By the early 1990s, as the population of the advanced Western nations became convinced enough of the end of Communism and the Cold War to take a new look at their own countries, public opinion polls began to report a widespread discontent. Incomes and wealth were polarizing as the rich got richer and average families lost ground. Unemployment across most of the European Community was back in the unacceptable 8 percent to 12 percent range, because most European countries rejected the alternative U.S. policy of getting unemployment down into the 6 percent to 8 percent range by letting real wages fall.

If worries about standards of living were justified, noneconomic trends were also threatening. Ethnic hostilities kept under wraps during the Cold War were mushrooming, not just in the former Soviet Union and Eastern Europe, but in the West. Large inflows of nonwhite immigrants stirred youthful violence and resentment politics in Germany, Italy, Britain, and France. The German state of North Rhine–Westphalia reported seventy acts of violence against foreigners in the ten days between May 29 and June, 9, 1993. Five Turkish women and girls were burned to death in a firebombing in the city of Solingen. In East London, a neofascist won a local council race despite intensive media coverage. Across Europe, ex-Communists gained new credibility attacking the excesses of capitalism, finance, and privatization. Italian neofascist candidates critical of immigration and permissiveness outscored the corrupt politicians of the discredited center to become the principal opposition to the left in the 1993 city elections in Rome and Naples. America's own middle-class radicalism had mushroomed in the surprise 1991–92 election showings of angry outsider candidates from David Duke in Louisiana to Pat Buchanan and Jerry Brown in the Republican and Democratic presidential primaries, followed by independent Ross Perot in the general election. All but Perot coupled criticism of the abuses of illegal immigration with attacks on vulture capitalism and multinational corporations. Canada's 1993 election was strongly influenced by national polarization on the issue of special political and linguistic rights for French-speaking Quebec. The overall message was sour: economic and cultural pressures might ease, but in situation after situation, the established parties seemed unable to cope.

As the Cold War sentries of Pax Americana and Pax Sovietica stood down, the forces of crime and anarchy rose up. Global demographic changes, meanwhile, were an explosion beginning to get its spark. The postwar world of 1950 had only ten cities with five million or more residents, and only thirty percent of the world's people lived in cities. By 1990, fifty-four cities had populations of five million or over — and six had over fifteen million residents! Half the planet's people now lived in cities, including most of the growing global underclass, with profound effects on unrest, crime, prostitution, drug use, and other corollaries of urban breakdown.

Experts acknowledged still another unexpected problem: globalization and the breakdown of the Cold War had led to a major growth in the *internationalization* of crime, a level more difficult to combat. A reduction in obstacles to trade and financial movement helped. So did the demise of police states in the former Soviet bloc and elsewhere. Cross-border movement of stolen cars, drugs, historic artifacts, and endangered species started rising rapidly. Banks in small new countries and in the former Soviet Union emerged as laundries for drug money, either out of willingness to do anything for hard currency or because their inept management made tracking funds impossible. According to the United Nations, "mass communications have facilitated contacts with [criminal] associates in other countries and continents, modern banking has facilitated international criminal transactions, and the modern revolution in electronics has given criminal groups access to new tools enabling them to steal millions and launder the huge illicit profits." Few national governments had solutions.

Even piracy was becoming a problem again — not just in the always-dangerous South China Sea, but in the sea lanes off Nigeria, Brazil, and the Philippines. The U.S., British, and Russian navies were a shadow of their old presence.

No wonder, then, that from the United States to Japan so many electorates had become so ready for new national directions and so contemptuous of politicians who had spent the 1980s deregulating finance, globalizing the economy, cutting taxes for the rich, ignoring the cities, and proclaiming that all was well. All was *not* well. Conservative politicians attracted more dislike because more of them were in office. But unsuccessful socialist governments were equally disdained (in France), while opposition parties, left or right, were perceived to be almost as out of date as the regimes they criticized.

Beyond America's own fin de siècle radical traditions, this is a further basis for seeing the 1990s as a revolutionary decade. Early 1990s polls in virtually every G-7 nation or English-speaking country charted the same phenomenon: fear on the part of the public that things were falling apart, mixed with disdain for the existing class of national leaders and political parties. In Canada and the United States, most polls showed 60–75 percent of voters dissatisfied with their nation's directions. The British were just as unhappy. Large majorities doubted that their country was "going forward along broadly the right lines." They said that Britain was no longer well governed and that "the mother of parliaments" was no longer something to be proud of. More than citizens anywhere else, a huge (49 percent) minority of Britons said they would go to another country if they could.

Italian and Japanese awareness of just how corrupt their governments had become produced angry descriptions in the opinion polls until the electoral revolutions of 1993, when new regimes replaced Japan's corrupt, ruling Liberal Democratic regime and Italy's tainted Christian Democratic and Socialist-run coalition. Sixty-one percent of French voters told pollsters that things in France "have a tendency to get worse." German voters were so disenchanted with their own leaders and parties that they invented another long Teutonic word to express themselves: *Politikverdrossenheit* — contempt for the political establishment.

The 1990s, in short, have been breeding an unexpectedly radical awareness in the West, rooted in the understanding that the end of the Cold War has left many nations in the clutches of corrupt and inept governments, arrogant specula-tors, and interest groups and political parties rooted in the status quo of a bygone era. In Europe and North America, concern was further intensified by awareness of how much in-ternational economic momentum has shifted to Asia and the Pacific. Not a few scholars speculated that the essentially Con-fucian values of East Asia — attention to the future, commit-ment to work, education, excellence, merit, frugality, and community — could give Japan, China, and Korea the chance to pick up where the depleted Calvinism and Protestant ethic of the Dutch-British-American continuum is leaving off.

With the 1990s a decade dominated by these worries and uncertainties, no one should be surprised to find so many ma-jor nations flirting with upheavals, even bloodless revolutions, in their governmental and party systems. But now that this multiple frustration context has been laid out, it is time to shift back to the principal focus of this book: through just what measures can the United States, walking where past great powers have stumbled, promote another national revolution to roll back some of its afflictions and rebuild its government, politics, and economy for the twenty-first century?

The Next American Revolution: Let the People Rule

The 1990s *should* be a revolutionary decade, perhaps the most notable in two hundred years. And for Americans, it must be a decade that reasserts the popular values of the 1790s and 1890s. Failure to seize this moment in history could cost the United States its critical opportunity to once again redesign national political institutions. This same volatility also means a real chance for populist politics to go astray in the 1990s, which was also a threat in the previous upheaval decades. Even so, standing pat is not an option. In quieter times, Anglo-American politics has had great luck with what the British call muddling through, but psychologies of the 1990s are too high-strung for that to work. Bolder clarions will be sounding.

For all these reasons, there is nothing contradictory about a near-revolutionary mood in the 1990s following the late-twentieth-century political crest of conservatism in the 1980s. The promises of that decade have not been kept, fanning concern about living standards at risk, excessive interest-group power, useless politicians, and a future possibly spinning out of control, whether or not the threat is real. And with Japan and Italy already caught up in political revolutions, the Germans coining terms like *Politikverdrossenheit*, Canada and Australia toying with splitting up or bidding farewell to Queen and Empire, and the British more dubious about the monarchy than at any point since Oliver Cromwell sent Charles I to the block, comparable restiveness in the United States must be taken seriously. The great disquiet in the public opinion polls — 60 percent of Americans see the country on the wrong track,

while half say Congress might just as well be chosen from voter lists or telephone directories — only confirms this country's abiding tradition of disrespect for authority and
establishments. This decade is tailor-made for the resurrection
of Jefferson's belief that revolutions in politics and government
are as natural as thunderstorms in nature.

Technologically as well as psychologically, the decade looks
ripe for direct democracy. Frustrated voters anxious to bypass
corrupt officials and exhausted political parties now have the
means. The Electronic Village is about to become the Wired
Electorate. New major parties *may* take hold, but if proportional representation keeps spreading, few parties will still be
majority based — and if the Wired Electorate simultaneously
insists on being fully connected to the terminals of power
through initiative and referendum mechanisms, the parties'
roles will shrink even further. Yet this same phenomenon also
creates a unique opportunity to give back to American politics
its genius of rule by the people.

Populism's history in this country is the world's most in-
tense. In the Revolution, the troops from New England, home
of the town meeting, were those most inclined to elect their
own officers. Similarly, for almost all of the last century, since
the various mechanisms were put in place after the populist
upheavals of the 1890s and 1900s, the United States has led
the world in direct democracy: the right of the people to initi-
ate ballot proposals and, assuming petitioners get enough signatures, to put those proposals in statewide or local elections
for the nation as a whole to say yes or no. Many more issues
face voters each year in the United States than in Switzerland.
By comparison, the referendum — a proposal put before the
people after being formulated by the legislature — is tame and
elite-controlled stuff.

The mechanics of achieving greater rule by the people instead of by the elites are likely to be a central agenda of the

1990s. As we have seen, plebiscitary demands have been sweeping through Europe and the English-speaking nations. The German people want to vote; the British want to vote. The leader of Britain's Labour Party proposes that an eventual 1990s package of major political and electoral reforms should be submitted to the electorate in a referendum. The leader of Canada's new Reform Party shrugs off questions about several issues; he'd have them decided by voters in a referendum. The prime minister of Australia wants to hold a referendum on becoming a republic. Part of the explanation, to be sure, is that politicians understand how easy these approaches have become to implement. We can readily imagine, in the United States of 2015, 30 to 40 percent of the eligible citizens signing in on their home computers to vote during a forty-eight-hour open period on a statewide ballot initiative. Besides, if Canada and half of Europe have begun holding referendums on major national issues, it is safe to assume that Long Island and Los Angeles will be requesting — or perhaps more accurately, *demanding* — the same privilege.

Would it be revolutionary? Yes. Is it far-fetched? No. The technology is a snap. The core of the debate will involve the *philosophy:* should ordinary voters rule? The entrenched influence-mongery of Washington — or, for that matter, of Ottawa, London, or Brussels — will cringe at the thought of their hard-won lines to power being disconnected in favor of people sitting in Sheboygan rec rooms. The absurdity of leaving serious tax decisions to the untutored will be proclaimed in mahogany-paneled executive suites from Back Bay to Beverly Hills, despite evidence that the Swiss electorate has been a model of seriousness in making sophisticated fiscal choices in nationwide referendums (including a two-to-one decision in 1993 to accept a 6.5 percent value-added tax to replace a more selective tax on goods only). But it may be telling that one of the most convincing and sophisticated arguments for the West using direct democracy and referendums to break the stranglehold of entrenched interest groups was set forth in an essay by Associate Editor Brian Beedham in *The Economist*, an eminently respectable weekly.*

Parts of the revolution *are* uniquely North American. The spreading U.S. effort to limit how many terms state officials, legislators, and even congressmen may serve has no parallel in foreign parliaments with their indefinite tenures. Meanwhile, the push to set up state and local mechanisms to permit U.S. voters to recall elected officials has spawned imitation only in Canada, where the Reform Party put a similar plank into the populist platform it used to wallop the established Progressive Conservative Party in the 1993 elections.

As for Americans' unusual willingness to bash official Washington and its perquisites, pay scales, law factories, and lobbyist colonies, who can doubt it? Canadians who loathe Ottawa, northern Italians anxious to send chariots with scythed wheels careening through the streets of Rome, Japanese wanting the Diet to move out of Tokyo, all of these are amateurs

---

* It may be useful to digress here for a personal explanation. Since the 1970s, I have had some sympathy for the populist devices of initiative and referendum, but until recently, I would not have supported them on the national level in the United States. Back in 1968, I had hopes for a more or less normal realignment in the U.S. party system, and I had some minor recurring hope for the multiparty election process in 1992. Now my doubts that the U.S. party system can overcome the bipartisan entrenchment of Washington have simply grown too great. Brian Beedham has reached the same point in his *Economist* essay "A Better Way to Vote: Why letting the people themselves take the decisions is the logical next step for the West." Then, just as I was finishing this book, I came across a column by political scientist Everett Carll Ladd, who explained why he, too, was modifying his orthodox faith in the U.S. political party system he had written about for decades: "Politics as usual inside the (Washington) beltway really has become an insiders' game. The interests that dominate it differ from those the Progressives battled, but are no less insensitive to popular calls for change. The old Progressive answer of extending direct authority and intervention to the citizens may be the only answer to present-day shortcomings in representative democracy." I have reached that same conclusion.

next to Americans. How many disgruntled Canadians count ancestors who forced Pennsylvania's capital to leave the Sodom and Gomorrah of Philadelphia for the more democratic air of Lancaster? How many Japanese have forebears like those who drove Georgia officials out of the perfumed salons of Savannah a hundred miles west to the piney woods and privies of Milledgeville? If the 1990s are to be a decade in which electorates rebel against entrenched special interests and political elites, U.S. voters will be in the van. Fail they may, but try they will.

American readiness to consider major constitutional reforms can also be assumed. Back in 1987, when several organizations tried to use the bicentennial of the U.S. Constitution to interest the electorate in giving the document an overhaul, the public yawned. The American electorate is bored when reform comes in an upper-middle-class good-government package. On the other hand, voters over the last fifty years have told pollsters of their support for dozens of constitutional amendments, from one to prohibit school busing for racial balance and another to ensure equal rights for women to perennial favorites like proposals to abolish the electoral college and balance the budget. Scores of state legislatures, meanwhile, have voted to petition Congress to call a constitutional convention to draft this or that proposed constitutional amendment. In sum, politicians and voters alike are quite ready to traffic in constitutional amendments when an issue moves them — and the 1990s should be a decade of movement.

The stunning willingness of the other major nations to consider or undertake significant constitutional changes may also be catching. Institutional radicalism can spread in the world as easily as financial deregulation. The Italians, having voted in a referendum to change their electoral system and structure of government, have installed a new coalition at the helm. The Japanese reform government elected in 1993 managed to replace that nation's old system of multimember parliamentary districts, blamed for corrupt one-party politics, with a mixed system of single-member districts and other seats filled by proportional representation. Canada's constitution is in flux, not only over the status of Quebec, but over proposals to reform or abolish the unpopular Canadian Senate. Germany has just reworked its constitution to bring in the former East. And as we have just seen, potential changes to Britain's unwritten constitution range from reform of the monarchy to implementation of some kind of proportional representation in Parliament and abolition of the current hereditary House of Lords in favor of an elected senate.

There is more constitutional upheaval abroad in these nations than at any time since the aftermath of World War II. American citizens, equally contemptuous of their politicians, just as convinced that their government no longer listens to the ordinary person, are unlikely to lag. What we don't know is how far change will go. Voters currently lining up behind state ballot initiatives to slap term limits on state officials, or to require all tax increases to be approved by voters, are at no more than 1767 or 1771 on a pre–Revolutionary War scale of political awareness. If Americans want far-reaching reform, the ultimate necessity is to take up political arms at the national level — against the forces of the Crown, so to speak, or in this case, against the essential mechanisms of misgovernment from Washington. The citizenry must be ready to amend the Constitution and even to weigh the possibility of a Second Constitutional Convention. Excessive caution has ceased to be a virtue.

The Imperative of Curbing Economic
Interest Groups

Any blueprint for a twenty-first-century America must shrink the role of interest groups, just as was done a century ago — and also a century earlier. In Chapter 8, we will look at specific proposals to break the hammerlock that special interests have gained on Washington. Once again, economic renewal demands it. The last thirty years have produced a national-capital influence structure that represents the multinational corporations who move jobs from Wisconsin to Taiwan, not the anonymous Americans who suffer, that protects the financial giants who run the bond markets and mutual funds, not the ordinary folk who are at their mercy, and that favors the professionals — the lawyers, lobbyists, accountants, stockbrokers, trade consultants, and communicators — who enjoy record incomes from the same globalization and polarization that has brought Middle America two decades of decline in real manufacturing wages. These trends would have happened anyway, but not to the same extent. It is foolish to expect the biases to change until the power structures of Washington are themselves transformed.

In the 1970s observers in the capital could still assign great, if no longer dominant, weight to the national lobbies of the old economic order that had presided over America's 1950s zenith — steel and mining, industrial labor, aerospace, oil, textiles, heavy manufacturing. By the 1990s, however, most of these were has-beens or relative has-beens. Of the strong new voices, many were foreign, from among the hundreds of overseas organizations with increasingly powerful representation in Washington, but more were American — *multinational* American. Gauged by who was spending what to hire whom, power in Washington had tipped toward a new profile of dominant economic lobbies concerned about the profits of floating a Mexican stock issue, establishing new bank branches in Brazil, selling computer systems and software to Belgium, securing Coca-Cola distribution in Rumania, and outsourcing manufacturing jobs to Taiwan, Honduras, or anywhere else where labor was half or one third the rate in Fort Wayne. During Congress's NAFTA debate, a particularly revealing vignette came from a comparison of lobbyists by the *New York Times:* the "war room" of the pro-NAFTA forces, on one side, was full of all the bipartisan talent and access money could buy, well-known lobbyists and ex-officials expensively turned out in Armanis, Guccis, Puccis, and Ferragamos. The anti-NAFTA headquarters, by contrast, was a polyester-central of aging labor officials, underpaid environmentalists, and Ralph Nader aides in baggy chinos.

But if emphasis on services and reduced-wage manufacturing is a political fashion in Washington and a workable vocational strategy for America's top 2 percent, 5 percent, or 10 percent elite, there is no historical precedent to suggest that it can achieve a broad national revitalization. None of the previous leading economic powers ever followed this pathway to new success. Once a nation's share of global manufactured exports began a long-term decline, often accompanied by declining real wages, no new approach to the world economy ever recovered anything like the old share of manufactured exports — or anything like the country's peak share of world GNP. The prospect that the United States, too, will fall short in any romance with globalization increases the likelihood of a political backlash by the large numbers of working-class and middle-class Americans losing ground.

Mounting criticism of interest-group Washington suggests growing public understanding of why government does what it does. Populist attempts to change economic policies through existing governmental processes and their allied interest-group networks can no more achieve victory in Washington than populist political pressures can succeed by working through the two-party system. Disruptions can be achieved, but not successes. To accept elite governmental structures and processes also means to accept elite policy decisions. Those who would change the loyalties of Washington policy making must weigh a revolutionary conclusion: it will first be necessary to overhaul the political and interest-group structures.

Here again, the evidence in Europe and Canada is supportive. Once the Cold War ended and establishment conservative parties lost their anti-Communist and national-security appeal, concerns about economic stagnation and receding prosperity surged to the fore. Typically, this drained the support of parties that had spent the 1980s deregulating finance, cutting taxes for the upper brackets, and proposing and implementing multinational economic and financial unions — all too often, these were the same parties allied with financial and business interests and the same ones that approached the 1990s with a program of austerity and consumption taxes. Not only were the Republicans driven down to 37.5 percent of the presidential vote in 1992 (an eighty-year low), but Canada's governing Progressive Conservatives were almost eliminated from Parliament in 1993, Japan's conservative Liberal Democrats were removed from office in 1993 for the first time since 1955, and the business-financial establishment Christian Democrats crashed in Italy. The governing conservative regimes in Britain and Germany sunk to new lows in the polls.

Moreover, the reaction, as we have seen, was not simply against the existing parties but also against the existing political system and the political and economic leadership classes. The Europe of 1992-93, instead of celebrating a planned economic and currency linkage, suddenly exploded against the Maastricht Treaty in a series of referendums, demonstrations, and demands for the issue to be put to the vote in countries where the government dared not do so, like Britain and Germany. Fear that so-called Eurocrat financial and planning elites might jeopardize national independence and living standards triggered a widespread push for referendums to take decision making back into the hands of the people. Canadians, too, rose against their elites in 1992 and 1993. The further acceptance and entrenchment of special-interest groups in the Washington of the Clinton administration — a breach of 1992 campaign promises — argues that a greater political revolution in the United States is still to come.

Bluntly put, there is a good case in the United States for the political equivalent of a revolution. Institutions and structures must change before policy can change. And the mixture of frustration and excitement abroad in the 1990s suggests that this decade, in the United States and around the world, is the time for action. But as we have seen, the term "revolution" carries a wide range of meanings and intensities in U.S. history. So let us turn to Chapter 8 for a description and proposal of the kind of upheaval that America needs.

Chapter Eight

Renewing America for the Twenty-first Century: The Blueprint for a Political Revolution

Each generation has a right to choose for itself the form of government it believes most promotive of its own happiness. . . . A solemn opportunity of doing this every nineteen or twenty years should be provided by the constitution.

— THOMAS JEFFERSON,
1816

I realize there are a lot of dangers in a constitutional convention, but I am more open-minded about it. Particularly if this president and this Congress cannot deal with some of these issues, the threat of a constitutional convention could be very useful.

— DAVID GERGEN
(before appointment as counselor to President Clinton), 1993

SERIOUS NATIONAL REVOLUTIONS are usually about politics, government, privilege, unresponsiveness, and anger. This is exactly what is simmering — and periodically boiling — in the United States of the 1990s. Debates over education, welfare, and other public policies are subordinate.

Revolutions can be renewing without being violent. Even an election can be a revolution of sorts when it brings sweeping change in politics, ideology, and the nature of the ruling establishment. Not many elections qualify, but a few do. Thomas Jefferson and Andrew Jackson both saw their watershed presidential victories of 1800 and 1828 in that light, as political revolutions or electoral reincarnations of the spirit of the American Revolution itself. In Chapters 1 and 2 of this book, however, we have seen that since the 1960s, revolutionary elections have been stymied by the interlock between interest-group power and the political system. Presidents can only govern by accepting, placating, and bargaining with the interest-group structure. And the public knows that its own voice is heard with only limited effect.

As a result, for any national political revolution of the Jeffersonian and Jacksonian sort to take place at the ballot box during the 1990s will require a new premise. No candidate can implement outsider changes through the current two-party system. It may even be necessary for any serious outsider seeking the presidency to assault that two-party system and its interest-group linkage. Which brings us to the critical question: what form must any potentially successful neo-Jeffersonian revolution assume? Some part of its emphasis must be on a new political movement or party. However, there is little chance of creating a new major party on the scale of the two formed back in the nineteenth century. Therefore, a second emphasis of any bloodless political revolution must be on ways of displacing the outdated party system with the emerging technology of direct democracy. But only in part — and carefully.

A few theorists contend that mobilizing direct democracy to counter the interest-group hijacking of representative government is becoming a central task of Western politics in the 1990s. It is a plausible thesis. But I have more confidence in the somewhat narrower argument that direct democracy has a particular usefulness for political renewal in the Anglo-American nations where interest groups are most numerous and entrenched, the populations are best trained in centuries-old democracy, and the parties are most geriatric. Proponents in the United States can take some heart from the Jeffersonian aspect of Canada's 1993 national election, in which a new movement, the Alberta-based Reform Party, swept past the governing Conservatives and became the dominant voice in the center-right of Canadian politics. In what leader Preston Manning described as a blueprint for a "quiet revolution," the Reform manifesto advocated not only breaking up the old party system, but also a whole series of constitutional reforms, including two key proposals for direct democracy — one to let Canadians decide major questions through national referendums and a second to establish mechanisms for recalling elected officials. Ross Perot, of course, had represented the same kind of insurgency in the United States.

Whatever happens to the Reform Party, some elements of this approach must be part of the next American revolution on *both* sides of the border. No North American political revitalization can succeed without greater emphasis on direct democracy. However, because the principal focus of this book is on the United States, this final chapter will use the weaknesses we have analyzed thus far in our own governmental, political, and economic systems — the accumulating damage of age, relative national decline, economic polarization, and the like — as a framework for identifying helpful or necessary reforms.

My assumption, set forth in the last chapter and then amplified at the end of this one, is that the United States has some unique renewal opportunities that must be seized. At the same time, current circumstances in this country broadly fit those of a leading world power declining from its peak, as set forth in Chapter 3. Anybody who disagrees with these characterizations and with the analyses of predicaments set forth in Chapters 1–7 will disagree with some of the proposed remedies. Let me also restate a second central premise: the frustration among Americans that has built up since the late 1980s is real and valid, and apparent revivals of national confidence will only be temporary without changes in the political, governmental, and interest-group system. This is the basis for a relatively radical blueprint. The chapter will also separate out a milder set of alternatives — half measures for the timid, as it were. But if the diagnosis is correct, the more radical-seeming approach would be a better corrective.

Skeptics will say that the bolder blueprint isn't achievable. Probably it isn't. Reformers, even *governments*, in the previous declining powers could not implement proposals to reverse predicaments we now know to have been all too real. The writings of Spain's *arbitrista* reformers, beginning in the 1590s and leading into the *desengaño* (national disillusionment) of the early 1600s, helped convince officialdom to propose sweeping changes, first in 1619 and then through the *Junta de Reformacion* in 1623. Remedies ranged from clearing the Madrid court of parasites to reforming the fiscal system and tightening moral standards. Most were blocked. The reformers of eighteenth-century Holland were not so organized or specific, and, as we have seen, little came of their complaints. As for Britain, the Conservative government of Prime Minister A. J. Balfour, fearful in 1903 that British manufactures were losing markets in part because other nations did not practice free trade, proposed the selective imposition of retaliatory tariffs to give Britain leverage. He, too, failed. Other reforms in the Britain of 1900–1930 were too little too late. In declining powers, even weak prescriptions are invariably disputed, while interest groups that feel threatened have the leverage to block controversial changes.

Nevertheless, what follows are ten sets of renewal-oriented proposals grouped by subject matter and designed to counter or contain the major trends, circumstances, and historical perils that the previous chapters have set forth.

> Proposal 1. Decentralizing or dispersing power away from Washington
>
> Proposal 2. Modifying the U.S. Constitution's excessive separation of powers between the legislative and executive branches
>
> Proposal 3. Shifting U.S. representative government more toward direct democracy and opening up the outdated two-party system
>
> Proposal 4. Curbing the Washington role of lobbies, interest groups, and influence peddlers
>
> Proposal 5. Diminishing the excessive role of lawyers, legalism, and litigation
>
> Proposal 6. Remobilizing national, state, and local governments through updated boundaries and a new federal fiscal framework
>
> Proposal 7. Regulating speculative finance and reducing the political influence of Wall Street

Proposal 8. Confronting the power of multinational corporations and minimizing the effects
   of globalization on the average American
Proposal 9. Reversing the trend toward greater
   concentration of wealth and making the tax
   system fairer and more productive
Proposal 10. Bringing national and international
   debt under control

Let us begin where Chapter 1 started: with how Washington's late-twentieth-century interest-group buildup has had a
pernicious impact on the integrity and performance of American democracy, and what we can do about it.

1. *Decentralizing or Dispersing Power Away from Washington*

Alas, the time is long gone when Americans could change federal and state capitals with the antiestablishment enthusiasm of
the late eighteenth century and early nineteenth century.
Abandonment is not an option. Too many people have put
down roots; too many interests have vested. Germany may be
in the process of downgrading Bonn to move its capital back to
Berlin, its longtime seat of government, but that is a unique
situation. And although Brazil could take its capital out of Rio
de Janeiro back in the 1960s and move it to the newly created
Brasilia, that situation also was different.

Washington cannot be dumped like Bonn, which is small
enough to revert back to a quieter status, or like Rio, which
was too big and too much Brazil's cultural heart to be hurt by
the exit of bureaucrats. The capital of the United States, by
contrast, is a metropolitan area of four million people essentially dependent on politics and government. The last serious
debate on leaving it behind and transferring the government

west to St. Louis came in 1870. Removal is now out of the question.

However, if one accepts the notion that Washington has become an overstuffed seat of government, crawling with parasites and wormed with interest groups, the possible answer lies in lesser, partial solutions to disperse the city's power and pressure groups. Decentralization is one approach — the idea of taking parts of the government and moving them elsewhere.

Some of this is under way, because other sections of the country are anxious for federal offices and payrolls. Yet the effect on Washington interest groups would be negligible if five thousand or even fifteen thousand largely clerical jobs were to migrate to nearby sections of Virginia and West Virginia. A bolder approach would be to relocate enough functions to force power and interest groups to migrate along with the portion of the federal establishment detached. The Interior Department could be moved to Denver or Salt Lake City, Agriculture to Des Moines or Kansas City, Housing and Urban Development to Philadelphia or Chicago. Uprooted lobbies would mean broken lines of influence.

Even greater benefit would come from splitting or rotating the capital between Washington and some other city, most plausibly in the West — Denver, say. Two or three federal departments could be substantially relocated, and Congress could sit in the shadow of the Rocky Mountains from late May until the August recess, enjoying a better climate in more ways than temperature and humidity. Countries *do* split national government functions between two capitals — for example, South Africa between Pretoria and Capetown, Bolivia between Sucre and La Paz, Israel between Jerusalem and Tel Aviv, Holland between The Hague and Amsterdam. And in Japan, which has been considering how to disperse functions now concentrated in Tokyo, one proposal is that the Diet meet in another city, beyond the capital's corruption and dominance. No one can seriously propose the *year-round* removal of Congress from Washington, but lawmakers' reputations — and, indirectly, the capital's — would profit from a ten-week annual House and Senate sojourn in the West. The discomfort of lobbyists could also be beneficial: dividing sessions of Congress between two cities would spread the influence mongers distinctly thinner.

A less predictable but potentially important breakthrough could come from a minor technical proposal. Several legislators have introduced bills to allow members of Congress to cast votes from their home districts in case of illness, emergency, or a local disaster. Technology is obviously no problem; remote voting on everything from motions to final passage could take place by secure electronic device. What has congressional leaders both doubtful and hostile is a longer-term implication. If members of Congress could vote from their districts, the public would want them to do so — to stay in their districts listening to ordinary citizens instead of hearkening to party leaders and hobnobbing with Washington interest groups. In short, the electronic revolution that has aided pressure groups to blitz Washington officials with information and communications from the grass roots has now begun to create a *counter*opportunity: to let congressmen and senators function from their districts while interest-group Washington shrivels in the hot democratic sun of the ultimate dispersal of power. This is *not* imminent; nevertheless, repatriating congressional vote-casting back to the grass roots from Washington may, by the year 2010 or 2015, be a better way to break up concentrated interest-group power than regulatory attempts that run afoul of constitutional protections. And, of course, if representatives and senators were spending most of their time in their states and districts, Congress's huge Washington-based staff of fifteen thousand, many of them K Street influence-peddlers-in-training, could be cut back sharply. We will return to this possibility shortly.

2. Modifying the U.S. Constitution's Excessive Separation of Powers Between the Legislative and Executive Branches

For good reasons, Americans have mixed views about the separation of powers. Our system of checks and balances makes the government in Washington less effective, but voters know that a recalcitrant Congress constitutes an excellent check on a president with a dubious agenda — a frequent description of chief executives over the last three decades.

However, much discussion of modifying the separation of powers is also linked to the desirability of strengthening the party system. The Committee for the Constitutional System, in which I participated for some years, is a group of present and former public officials and scholars who have outlined reforms to modify the separation of powers. One proposal would amend the constitution to let members of Congress serve a friendly administration in executive branch posts without giving up their House or Senate seat. A second would elect the president and members of the House for parallel four-year terms instead of House members being chosen every two years. A third would have voters pick presidents, senators, and representatives in mandatory straight-ticket voting to insure a government in which the president has a strong support base in Congress.

Most of these proposals, as noted, have been developed with an eye to reinforcing a standard Anglo-Saxon two-party system, in which members of the House are elected on a winner-take-all basis in single member districts. Moving into the twenty-first century, though, this is not a safe assumption. Also, if citizens were obliged to cast a straight-ticket vote for president-senator-congressman every four years, that would weaken the prospects of *broad-based* minor parties — Perot's in 1992, for example, with its 19 percent support more or less spread all over the country — while helping those with narrow *regional* bases. The 1968 George Wallace ticket, which carried five states in the Deep South, would have pulled in Wallaceite congressmen from perhaps a dozen districts.

On balance, the idea of further entrenching the Republican and Democratic parties with mandatory straight-ticket voting is contrary to the national interest. The electoral reforms discussed in Proposal 3 will tilt in a different direction. They assume that the two-party system needs to be *opened up*, not *protected*. Yet several non-party-related curbs on the separation of powers *do* seem compelling. For one, let us amend the constitution to allow the president to appoint members of Congress to serve in federal positions — i.e., as secretary of defense or attorney general — without these individuals having to give up their seats. That would promote better ties between the two branches irrespective of changing party roles. Secondly, a specific case can be made for a new administration selecting as its federal budget director the House or Senate budget committee chairman from the president's party. The critical advantage is that if he or she could hold both offices simultaneously, parliament-style, a more collaborative budget process could then be formalized. A third useful reform would establish a mechanism for dissolving the government if the separation of powers between a particular White House and a particular Congress had become too debilitating. The president would be able to call a special national election to get a fresh start. None of these prescriptions is exactly a call to arms, so let us move on to a grander aspect of any political revolution: reconfiguring the electoral system to strike at the crippling interlock between interest-group Washington and the two-party system.

3. Shifting U.S. Representative Government More Toward Direct Democracy and Opening Up the Outdated Two-Party System

Futurists Alvin Toffler and John Naisbitt emphasize two reasons for rightly calling our system of representative government outdated: First, what used to be true representative government is being swallowed up by the Washington presence of more interest groups than the world has ever before seen in one place. Representative government has become interest-group government. Second, new electronic technology now gives governments an unprecedented wherewithal to empower the ordinary voter directly. We should use it.

Foremost, the United States should propose and ratify an amendment to the Constitution setting up a mechanism for holding nationwide referendums to permit the citizenry to supplant Congress and the president in making certain categories of national decisions. Arguably, the procedure set up by the amendment should be less sweeping than the Swiss system, in which the public votes on just about everything. Some kind of prior national advisory commission, citizens' group, or both should consider specific details: for example, whether the public should be given the chance to decide on major national electoral reforms (of course) and also to rule on major federal tax changes (arguably), as well as whether Congress should be given a veto over any such voter decision. It will also be necessary to decide whether to couple an initiative provision with the referendum so that three million to five million signatures (or more) could put a proposal on a yearly or special ballot. Finally, any such amendment would have to authorize a national referendum as an alternative method of amending the U.S. Constitution.

Although this would be a major reform, a depth of historical and public support already exists. As we have seen, the referendum mechanism is gaining acceptance globally, not least in the Anglo-Saxon countries. Myron Goretzky, chairman of the Coalition for a National Referendum, has pointed out that a proposal was introduced in Congress prior to the Civil War for a national advisory referendum to try to find a compromise in the face of the impending sectional crisis. Theodore Roosevelt supported populist empowerment devices in his 1912 Progressive Party platform because "it is often impossible to establish genuine popular rule and get rid of privilege without the use of new devices to meet new needs." Then, just before World War II, the House of Representatives only narrowly defeated a proposed constitutional amendment to require a national referendum before the U.S. could declare war. In 1981 a Gallup poll asked Americans whether they favored or opposed a proposal being considered by the U.S. Senate to require a national referendum on an issue when 3 percent of the number of those voting in the most recent presidential election signed petitions requesting one. Fifty-two percent said yes, 23 percent were opposed. Revealingly, among those admitting they had not voted in the previous general election, 48 percent would have been more likely to participate had important national *issues* as well as *candidates* been on the ballot. In 1992, a nationwide poll by the Gordon S. Black Corporation found 72 percent voter support for a constitutional amendment to require any federal tax increase to be voted on in a national referendum by the general public. Then in 1993 a national survey by the Americans Talk Issues Foundation found nearly two out of three respondents in favor of having binding national referendums on policy questions, and another by the *Los Angeles Times* found 65 percent of Americans in favor of making some laws by national referendum. The public is ready and waiting.

Then there are the related issues of imposing term limits on state officials and legislators and establishing mechanisms by which officeholders, once they have served for at least a year, can be recalled by the voters. Whether the states can impose the same restraints on the congressmen and senators they send to Washington is still a matter of constitutional debate. And few observers expect Congress to be willing to impose term limits on its own. However, *both* constraints, term limitation and recall, would push members of Congress closer to the role of citizen legislators and eliminate their ability to spend sixteen, eighteen, or twenty-two years in Washington prior to retiring (and remaining on hand) as powerful, well-paid lobbyists.* The toughest term limitation — a proposed cap of three terms or six years — has a particularly populist logic: enticing more non-traditional people into Congress for brief tenures by making turnover so rapid that no power elite really has time to entrench. New freshmen could develop influence impossible today. Would-be Washington careerists, in turn, would not find a mere six years of incumbency worthwhile. In early 1994 a group of congressmen favoring term limits proposed holding a national advisory referendum to spell out the public's lopsided two-to-one or three-to-one support.

Besides term limits, the recall, and the referendum, the other far-reaching reform that deserves more attention is modifying our electoral system in the direction of proportional representation with an eye to opening up the parties and increasing voter participation. By the end of the century, the four other English-speaking nations may be using proportional representation to elect one or both houses of their parliaments in a broader and more inclusive party system. That could put a debate that is now just embryonic in the United States into full swing.

---

* Even if the states cannot act, a special Gallup poll in 1987 found 67 percent of Americans in favor of changing the U.S. Constitution to establish recall elections for members of Congress.

In order not to remain the only member of the Group of Seven relying solely on the restrictive first-past-the-post system of choosing legislators, Americans should at least begin *thinking* about how to modify our system in a proportional direction. This could be done boldly at the federal level by congressional action — or piecemeal at the state level. Many possible variations exist, most of which sound complicated on first reading. Discussion will not mushroom overnight. Even so, one plausible approach would be to keep electing members of the Senate, two from each state, on today's single-winner basis because proportionalism would be unworkable, but to reorient the House of Representatives by enlarging its membership to, say, 650 members from the present 435 and then by establishing some variation of proportional representation. Small parties would get little or no benefit in small states electing only two, three, or four House members. But in large states, the effect of proportional selection would be considerable. For example, in California, where minor parties are already making some impact in congressional races, a changeover would make the state's potentially enlarged House membership of seventy-five House members elected in 2002 come in a wider variety of flavors. As one hypothetical approach, the state could be divided into five large regional districts, each of which would elect fifteen House members. Any party that crossed (say) a 7 percent threshold would get one House member. So the San Francisco Bay region, for example, might elect eight Democrats, three Republicans, one Nationalist, one Rainbow/Peace and Freedom, one Green, and one Gay Rights. Diversity would flourish. The nature of interest-group access to the House would change: voters and voter blocs would at least partially replace lobbies and hired guns.

There are other approaches to proportional representation. One is the "additional members" system, by which a nation's voters elect a fixed number of legislators from single-member districts but then also vote for a national candidate list, from which winners are selected in proportion to overall support for their party. Still other related variations are not quite proportional representation, like "alternative preference" voting and the "single transferable vote" system. Alternative preference, used to select Australia's lower house in ordinary single-member districts, simply requires voters to rank candidates as their first, second, or third choices. If one candidate secures 50 percent of the first preferences, he or she wins. However, if nobody does that well, then the weakest candidate is dropped and his supporters' second-choice votes are distributed among the remaining contenders. Sooner or later someone will get 50 percent. But an opening-round plurality is not enough. Even for the mathematically inclined, these systems can seem cumbersome and thus undesirable. Yet all are used efficiently in some country or other, and, in the computer age, all are now easy to manage, which allows national attention to focus on their other merits — promoting a broader representation of parties and minority viewpoints, as well as the much greater turnout of voters that this breadth almost always encourages.

Were the United States to move toward partial proportional representation for these reasons, the major change, as we have seen, would concentrate in the House of Representatives, not in the Senate or in the presidency. But although the presidency isn't an obvious candidate for proportional representation, there *are* several possible indirect approaches. John Anderson, the 1980 independent presidential candidate (and subsequent proportional representation supporter), has suggested that he and other third-party contenders would have been helped by the use of an Australian-style alternative-preference system of popular voting (without the electoral college). In this system, as noted, voters rank the top group of candidates by preference. In 1980 an independent Republican voter choosing Anderson would presumably have marked his ballot Anderson (1), Reagan (2), and Carter (3). Had this option existed, Anderson contends, his support would not have sunk from 20 percent in the September polls to 7 percent on election day. People could have voted for him and still have cast a backstopping second-preference vote for Reagan or Carter, precluding any possible constitutional malfunction. That might indeed have allowed the third-party vote to remain high instead of being forced back into a two-party preference. This option, too, is worth considering.

Interestingly, even the unpopular electoral college unfolds avenues to proportional representation. Either legislation by Congress or enactment of a constitutional amendment could require states to split their electoral votes. But the states do not need to approach Washington to allocate their electoral votes any way they want. Each can cast them en bloc for its winner, award one for each congressional district carried, or allocate its electoral vote proportionally. And the itch is spreading. Maine now splits electoral votes by congressional district, Florida has considered the same approach, and in 1993 the state of Washington held hearings on a bill to allocate its eleven electoral votes proportionally. Had this last system been in place in 1992, Bill Clinton would have won five electoral votes in Washington, George Bush three, and Ross Perot three. Indeed, had the electoral votes of all fifty states been awarded on this basis, no 1992 presidential candidate would have won a majority in the electoral college, sending the choice of the president to the House of Representatives. To take that one more step: were the House forced to choose the president with any frequency, our system would start to turn quasi-parliamentary.

The reader may sense that the previous five or six paragraphs have not produced firm recommendations. Just so. I am inclined to think that *some* form of proportional representation makes sense for the House of Representatives, not just because of its disruptive effect on existing interest-group relationships but because it would also reduce or eliminate the flagrant racial gerrymandering of the early 1990s. It is no coincidence that after the U.S. Supreme Court cast doubt on the legitimacy of using grossly distorted boundaries to create black-majority districts in 1993, interested parties and federal judges began discussing the alternative usefulness of proportional representation and related approaches like cumulative voting; if a county board, for example, had five seats, each voter would be allowed to make five choices, with the option of picking five different candidates or cumulating all five votes for one contender. As for abolishing the electoral college and choosing the president through popular vote, that option would gain merit if the process also involved selecting first-, second-, and third-place choices so that the second-place votes of the weakest candidate could be redistributed if nobody got over 50 percent. Declaring a winner based on a 38 percent popular-vote plurality is unwise and unnecessary. But then again, some of the possible changes in the electoral college could also make that ancient mechanism more friendly to twenty-first-century circumstances.

Still another intriguing possibility — anathema to professional politicians — could involve states' creating "None of the Above" lines on the ballot, where voters, in essence, would have a chance to vote against the candidates listed. Proponents of NOTA range from Ralph Nader and the *Nation* magazine to the *Wall Street Journal*. Depending on what statute a state might enact, a large enough NOTA vote could be used to force a new election with new candidates. Incumbents could conceivably be vetoed even if they had no serious opposition. In 1990, 52 percent of Texas voters told a Gallup poll that, given the choice, they would have voted for NOTA instead of that year's GOP and Democratic gubernatorial contenders. And in 1991 a Mason-Dixon poll found that 66 percent of

Louisiana voters wished the state had a NOTA line on its ballot. Unfortunately, Nevada is alone in offering that option to its voters. More states should do so, because a NOTA line on the ballot adds another safeguard against the present excesses and unreachability of the two-party system.

Having a bipartisan commission of major-party appointees study these five reforms would be a waste of time by definition. But on the matters of proportional representation and the role of the electoral college, there is no rush. Public support for reform will depend on how much parties and independent candidacies proliferate in the presidential elections of 1996 and 2000. Continuing electoral fragmentation in the United States, while the other English-speaking countries deal with their own party changes by adopting some degree of proportional representation, would turn this country's preliminary discussion into a full-fledged national debate. Then the various alternatives, ranging from basic proportional voting to Australian-style alternative preferences, could be matched to more concrete circumstances and challenges.

4. Curbing the Washington Role of Lobbies, Interest Groups, and Influence Peddlers

Precedents for directly purging bloated great power capitals — from Rome and Constantinople to Madrid and The Hague — are so inauspicious that indirect, high-tech reforms like electronically returning power to the people and to the congressional district level may be the best hopes. Congress, in particular, is barely credible on proposals to restrain lobbying and clean up federal campaign finance. Even when proposed reforms start out with teeth, these usually fall out before the legislative bite becomes statutory.

The real interest-group problem in the capital doesn't

come from the largest numerical categories: trade associations, corporate offices, and think tanks funded by special pleaders. The first two groups mostly include open representatives of legitimate interests. True, Washington has lured far too many, but because the capital city now serves as a virtual chessboard of national interests, many arrivals had no choice. As for the think tanks, they are essentially beyond reach because of political speech protections.

The greater danger is the emergence over the last two decades within Washington of a mercenary or hired-gun culture — a mentality that reaches far beyond admiration for the half dozen Wyatt Earp lobbying equivalents whose quick draws add notoriety to any Capitol Hill shoot-out. As research by the Center for Public Integrity and other groups has shown, most of the House and Senate members who stay on in Washington, as well as most of the former Republican and Democratic party chairmen along with a majority of the former senior trade officials, quickly gravitate to the capital's well-paid and high-expense-account lobbying niches. That's where the money and more and more of the real power has concentrated. The One-Hundred-and-Third Congress, as we have seen, became the first ever to have two senior House members resign their seats *during the session* to take up positions running major lobbies. The public understands that influence peddling along the Potomac has become more than a profession; it is the mark of Washington success. Small wonder six out of ten Americans see lobbyists and interest groups controlling the city.

Lobbying for foreign governments and interests, in particular, has reached a magnitude never before seen in a capital city. The economic patriotism of London circa 1910 was not very high, and investors sent their money to every part of the world but the decaying parts of the United Kingdom. And the eighteenth-century Dutch were worse; their merchants and traders would sell to anybody, even nations at war with the Netherlands. In the current-day United States, the hundreds of former senior officials helping foreign governments and economic interests outmaneuver domestic industries or shut down factories in California or Ohio rarely seem embarrassed either.

Corrective measures must strike at this culture. In 1991 I was asked by the chairman of the Senate Finance Committee to testify at committee hearings on legislation to deal with foreign lobbying in the United States. Stricter restraints on ex-officials lobbying after they leave office are well and good, but I suggested that senior lawmakers could accomplish just as much or more *without* legislation. Were most senators and presidential candidates to refuse contributions from foreign lobbyists or interests, and then further refuse to let lobbyists for foreign interests raise money for them or serve on their campaign committees, the Washington lobbying community would receive a powerful message. This, however, was not an idea anyone ever wanted to discuss. Striking at an accepted culture is not how things are done. But a year later George Bush's willingness to have foreign lobbyists playing prominent roles in his reelection campaign mushroomed into a major debate. And grassroots politicking, in addition to blueprints to remove decision-making power from Washington, is probably the way in which serious reform must be pursued: by turning clear excesses of Washington interest-group and lobbying power into a grassroots frustration and debate in every plausible election battle.

A significant overhaul of campaign finance, unlikely through federal legislation, could also come, if it can come at all, from a broader uncorking of populist politics. To be sure, the occasional bold reform can emerge — like the idea of raising money to underwrite a partial public financing of elections by imposing a new tax of 30 percent or thereabouts on contributions to political campaigns (although it might not be constitutional). But such proposals are rare. There is also a question of parallelism. If term limitations are pursued to keep congressmen and senators from serving more than six or twelve years in office, that could increase the opinion-molding role of the lobbies and political contributors unless emphasis is put on limiting *their* power, too.

Still another useful change, already mentioned in the section on dispersing power away from Washington, would be to cut back the huge staffs of the House and Senate. The power of senior staff members, especially longtime veterans, would also be increased by any term limits on senators and representatives, making new congressional staff guidelines important. Five or six times as large as the support structures of other major national legislatures, a large part of this huge staff spends much of its time interfacing with the capital's huge corps of lobbyists and preparing for its own vocational graduation into that corps. The numbers we saw in Chapter 2 — some twenty thousand congressional staffers and as many as ninety thousand persons engaged in lobbying or lobbying support — feed on one another. Force the staffs of Congress to shrink by 30 to 40 percent over the remainder of the 1990s, and the odds are that the ranks of Washington lobbyists would also shrink by a meaningful percentage. Legislation of this sort would carry a double benefit.

Overall, then, several specific reforms do seem wise. But attempts to change campaign finance and regulation of lobbyists too often resemble shooting paper clips at a tank because the system is so resistant. Massive infusions of direct democracy and blistering public discussion are the most plausible flamethrowers of change.

5. Diminishing the Excessive Role of Lawyers, Legalism, and Litigation

America's curse-of-the-one-million-lawyers will be a hard one to shake. Too much of the nation's current overabundance of lawyers, legalism, and litigation is the product of a two-century evolution. Moreover, reversing the situation faces a slight technical hitch: the lawyers in the White House, Congress, the courts, and the state legislatures are the people who make the laws.

A central dilemma is that there are simply too many attorneys, which forces them to keep generating legislative, regulatory, and litigational subject matter and opportunity. When seventeenth-century Spain had too many scholars, bureaucrats, and clergymen, the government proposed to shut down a number of the colleges and universities that turned them out. It was blocked, but it was not a bad idea. Shutting down half of the nation's law schools might be another good idea, but how — through the vote of what legislative body? Texas professor Stephen Magee, a lawyer-basher, may have a partial solution in arguing that the United States, following the example of Germany and Japan, should limit the number of lawyers admitted each year to the bar in order to bring down their numbers slowly. Unfortunately, bar admissions are a state responsibility. As Proposal 8 will discuss, a so-called progressive flat tax version of the federal income tax would put a lot of lobbyists and tax lawyers out of work, which probably ensures that it will never be considered.

The mid-nineties are also witness to an interesting new phenomenon: the emergence of nonlawyer — and in some cases *anti*lawyer — candidates for the House of Representatives and the Senate. Medical doctors, drawn by heated legislative controversy over health care, became especially conspicuous. However, there was also a growing public awareness that both houses had too many lawyers (fifty-six out of one hundred senators, for example), most of whom were also, almost by definition, legislative and political insiders. Non-lawyers, by contrast, would be more likely to be outsiders rather than architects of the omnibus legislative achievements cynically nicknamed "The Lawyers' and Accountants' Full Employment Acts." In Queen Anne's County, Maryland, State Delegate Ronald Franks, a dentist, announced his candidacy for higher office by pointing out, "There are fifty-six lawyers and not one health provider in the U.S. Senate." The self-interest of lawyer-legislators, in short, is becoming a topic of discussion, which is constructive.

Meanwhile, more direct opportunities exist to curb the litigation and liability explosions. On the federal level, proposals include limits on punitive damages in product liability lawsuits, expert-witness reform, increased use of arbitration, and others. And on the state level, where many of the legal profession's best opportunities exist, constraints are growing. Indiana, for example, is one of the few states that has capped both medical malpractice awards (at $750,000) *and* the amount lawyers can take as their cut (15 percent). And in California the business-backed Association for California Tort Reform talked for some time about a ballot initiative that would limit contingency fees to personal injury lawyers to 25 percent of the first $100,000 awarded to their clients, 15 percent of the next $100,000 and 10 percent of anything over $200,000. The caveat is that consumerists worry that such reforms could jeopardize plaintiffs' rights.

For countries with too many lawyers and too much litigation, alas, there are never easy solutions.

6. Remobilizing National, State, and Local Governments Through Updated Boundaries and a New Federal Fiscal Framework

Aging great economic powers usually have archaic internal divisions to deal with — we saw the unfortunate precedents of Spain, Holland, and Britain in Chapter 5 — and the United States is no exception.

Proposing remedies is easy enough, but assuming their success is not. Such changes do not come easily. Here are four that would be helpful, beginning with an obvious one: that most of our fifty states would profit from holding state constitutional conventions or otherwise setting out to modernize state government by eliminating as many unnecessary units as local opinion will tolerate. Proud old townships can't be expected to give up centuries of existence without a fight, but many largely anonymous governmental units, from newly created townships to special tax districts, could easily be dispensed with.

It also makes sense to consider new types of official and ad hoc structures to reach across outdated state boundaries. Romantic concepts like Cascadia are probably impractical, but columnist Neal Peirce's proposal to emphasize city-states might work. He would treat some of the emerging weaknesses of the nation-state, especially our own, by elevating the roles of key metropolitan areas — city-states — as national political, economic, and cultural building blocks. The Italian parliament, Peirce notes, voted in 1990 to give all of its major metropolises — from Rome and Milan to Turin and Bologna — the sort of powers hitherto reserved for provinces. The critical inhibition is that the United States, unlike most major European nations, is stuck with the current political structures and boundaries of our fifty states because there is no political mechanism for redrawing them. Congress has little relevant power. Creating such a mechanism would require a federal constitutional amendment (and even if one were to pass through the Senate and House, it's hard to imagine ratification by the necessary number of states). The most important outdated boundaries, in short, are incurable.

Practical reform, then, probably will have to come in fiscal federalism. As economist Alice Rivlin has written in her book *Reviving the American Dream*, the fiscal self-determination of the fifty states — they can impose as many or as few taxes as local officials choose — represents a significant obstacle to the overall cohesion of U.S. domestic policy making. Programs like education, and now health care, largely funded by whatever state and local resources are available, fatten or starve accordingly. What Rivlin proposes is for the federal government to come up with a two-part approach: part one would give much local social program responsibility back to the states, while part two would establish a single common tax or set of common taxes to be collected all over the country and distributed back to the states on a per capita basis. For example, this would take away Texas's option to have a tax system that encourages business but provides little money for education. Some version of Rivlin's idea is needed, but the catch is that any legislation would need a magic wand to get through Congress, where many members would oppose its fiscal interference with states' rights. Nevertheless, consideration should begin.

Another broad opportunity may exist for improving outdated internal boundaries and governmental relationships — the possibility that the new North American common market could be a framework for developing some new boundaries and relationships and for clearing away regulatory cobwebs. As we saw in the heady coming-together periods of the United Provinces, the United Kingdom, and the United States, these geopolitical fusions create a new momentum that transcends older parochial divisions even though many are still left in place. Nineteen-nineties Europe is realizing some similar benefits from its partial unification, and the North American Free Trade Agreement could create some comparable opportunity. The catch lies in NAFTA's giving its principal benefits to investors while workers may lose ground. Such a North American economic union might not progress far enough to reshuffle boundaries and interest-group alignments. But in the abstract, the economic union of the United States and Canada, in particular, could produce an opening to reorganize boundaries and governmental relationships on both sides of the border.

7. Regulating Speculative Finance and Reducing the Political Influence of Wall Street

These two objectives, antispeculative and political, go together. For a late-stage great economic power like the United States, both reforms are imperative. Oversized, speculative financial sectors have unfortunate histories; they suck the juices of broader national renewal opportunity.

A third related agenda, the question of how to bring the very richest Americans under more political and fiscal constraint, is discussed in Proposal 9. So these immediate pages are confined to the two remedies directly relating to finance: curbing runaway electronic speculation and also subduing Wall Street's excessive political influence.

The potential speculative dangers, even some Wall Streeters acknowledge, pivot on the inadequacy of piecemeal regulation of spectronic finance, especially the so-called derivative contracts and instruments discussed in Chapter 4, with their extraordinary $14-trillion face value. Not only were the 1980s a decade of unenthusiastic regulation, but as derivative instruments emerged, they fell under no particular regulatory body's sole jurisdiction. Indeed, because derivatives combined traditional assets in new ways, they slipped through the individual-product jurisdictions policed by commodities, bank, securities, and insurance regulators. And because they were nobody's regulatory baby, no one agency maintained an adequate profile of who was doing what where, with what stakes, and with what institutions on the other side of the many, many transactions. This regulatory vacuum became important because the exotic contracts and interrelationships of derivatives spread quickly enough into mutual funds and the pension system, where the public's stake is enormous. In no way has involvement been limited to a handful of consenting adults in the big banks and investment megafirms.

Worry in 1994 that derivatives were adding to the instability of financial markets reinforced the case for stricter supervision. Congressional regulators, beginning to get involved, dismissed many of the assurances offered by financiers. The previous year, a few had commented that it was déjà vu all over again, that another speculative house of cards was being built into the global financial system. Congressman Jim Leach of Iowa, ranking Republican on the House Banking Committee and author of many reform proposals, was especially blunt: "There is no escaping the circumstances that derivative activities in the '90s must be examined in the context of the decade of the '80s, when America overleveraged itself with junk bonds, junk real estate, and junk S&Ls." That examination should have occurred years ago.

The issue of reform is not *whether*, but *how much*. Certain changes are almost beyond dispute, namely, that much closer federal scrutiny is necessary and regulators should use existing securities and banking laws to force greater disclosure of derivatives trading. Congressman Leach's proposed Derivatives Supervision Act, which would create a Federal Derivatives Commission to establish principles and standards for capital, accounting, disclosures, and suitability of institutions dealing in the products, makes sense as a start. Most banks and investment firms involved objected to critics' analogies to the S&L crisis and opposed demands for tougher regulation to impose a restraining framework on derivatives and slow down the evolution of new techniques. However, this may be exactly what the circumstances require. Partly because the 1980s speculative bubble was not followed by a new regulatory crackdown, derivatives have swelled to a precarious face value of many trillions of dollars. The amount actually at risk was much less, of course, but calculations by the comptroller of the currency indicated that Chemical Bank and Bankers Trust, both very active in derivatives, had exposures to potential defaults ranging from 2.68 times to 5.71 times their capital. Moreover, because no one was quite sure of the many complicated ways in which firms have become interconnected by these gambits, no one could be sure what dominoes would fall and where.

The political-historical rule of thumb, though, is that any such speculative buildup usually produces a major shakeout, reinforcing the case for serious regulation. Even large-scale discomfort and severe losses by overly speculative banks and investment firms would be preferable to losses by the public or a federal bailout costing ten, twenty, or fifty times as much. There is also merit — and not a little potential Treasury revenue — in a federal tax on financial transactions that would simultaneously reduce the profitability and volume of speculative trading. Which brings us to the second area of concern in this proposal: getting the financial sector under control and curbing its political influence.

The genius of American political finance, as we saw in Chapter 4, has been to follow up speculative implosions with eras of populist and progressive reform in which financial sector transgressions were dragged into the spotlight of congressional hearings and then subjected to substantial new regulation. Both times, to varying degrees, the political power of finance shriveled as its reputation sagged. However, the opportunity for a repeat of that pattern was lost in the early 1990s, and it will be difficult to indict the financial sector in mid-decade without a new wave of market difficulties and speculative failures.

There is a partial exception — widespread support for more serious auditing, monitoring, and regulation of the largely independent Federal Reserve Board. During the 1980s and early 1990s the Fed emerged as a reliable ally of the banks, the financial markets, and speculative finance at the expense of consumers, farmers, small businessmen, and homeowners. But the added vulnerability it has developed in the mid-1990s comes from conducting its affairs in secret, without outside scrutiny or even financial audit, as well as from allegations that it has used its funds to buy futures to prop up the stock market. The Fed has also openly, and quite legally, given money in so-called overnight loans to rescue some shaky banks but not others, based on its own yardsticks and favoritism.

This is unacceptable. In an era of increased governmental openness, critics rightly demand that the Fed should be required to open its deliberations to public view and its finances to regular public audit. Moreover, the regional Federal Reserve Bank presidents who sit on the monetary-policy-making Federal Reserve Open Market Committee should be appointed by the White House and confirmed by Congress. They should not be picked as they are now by local bankers and businessmen. Shaping this country's monetary policy must become a public responsibility and cease to be a private opportunity. Reform is in order in each instance.

In a similar vein, and even lacking any major catalyst, elected officeholders must start representing the public and the "real economy" rather than the financial system and the financial markets. *The Economist*, no bomb-throwing publication, has suggested that while the 1980s will be remembered for the deregulation of finance and the emergence of a global capital market, the 1990s will be the decade of the world's struggle to cope with that emergence. In Belgium and France, finance ministers — prime ministers, even — have started attacking currency speculators. From Brazil and Venezuela to Russia and New Zealand, politicians have begun to scoff at the notion that their responsibility is to stock markets rather than to voters. Even ex-communists have been able to win elections by appealing to voters' economic frustration. In Brazil acting president Itamar Franco, criticized for rejecting his predecessor's banker-driven policies, told the *Jornal do Brasil* he wasn't concerned about falling stock prices: "I don't worry about the stock market. I'm not here for them." If the financialization discussed in Chapter 4 is to be brought under control and the real economy is to reassert itself in this country, similar words may have to come from a president of the United States.

8. Confronting the Power of Multinational Corporations and Minimizing the Effects of Globalization on the Average American

The United States can no longer sidestep a familiar problem: how the elites of great economic powers invariably, in later years, pursue interest-group internationalist values at the expense of ordinary citizens who would profit more from economic wagon-circling to nurture markets, industries, values, and lifestyles of their nation's heyday. This country's transition to finance, services, and lower-wage manufacturing is unfolding fast enough; it should not be artificially favored to serve the interests of a small elite.

Protecting redundant steel capacity or unnecessary shipyards is not the issue. History recommends a different group of suggestions. First, it makes sense for leading economic powers starting to decline to restrain their wealthy citizens from shifting their investments overseas — the previous behavior of the Dutch and British pattern is now repeating in the United States — by tightening tax policy. Economic patriotism, quite simply, requires making individual and corporate investments overseas less rewarding than domestic ones. Second, and in a related vein, Washington should rewrite its corporate foreign tax credit and foreign tax deferral provisions to discourage U.S. multinationals from investments that move jobs overseas. These loopholes also cost the Treasury too much revenue. A 1993 study published by the National Bureau of Economic Research showed that in 1986, the year of the most recent available data, a sample of 340 U.S. parent corporations had foreign source income of $47.3 billion and paid U.S. taxes on that income of just $1.6 billion. Third, politicians, especially the president, should jawbone major corporations against slashing their U.S. employment base, especially when the motive is not survival, which is compelling, but raw pursuit of higher profit and a higher stock price. When companies discharge five, ten, or twenty thousand employees, everyday events in the 1990s, the effect, invariably, is to increase the burden on communities, employees, and other local taxpayers while favoring company shareholders who see profits go up. Policies to shift more of this burden back to companies and shareholders should be explored. Our fifty states, in turn, should revisit their late 1980s efforts to put employee and community "stakeholder" rights on a closer statutory par with those of shareholders. Last, Washington policy makers should move very cautiously in negotiating agreements to open this market to cheap manufactured goods in return for greater overseas access for U.S. financiers, bankers, and other professions. Old manufacturing jobs are already too periled. And the economic polarization involved is already too advanced.

Karl Marx, who loathed nineteenth-century capitalism, commented in an 1848 speech, "The free trade system is destructive. It breaks up old nationalities and pushes the antagonism of the proletariat and the bourgeoisie to the extreme point. It is in this revolutionary sense alone, that I vote in favor of free trade." The destruction would occur, Marx argued, because capitalists would use free trade to push wages down. That later happened in turn-of-the-century Britain, prompting much of the British working class to forsake the old pro-free-trade Liberal Party to join the new socialist Labour Party. Now similar patterns are visible in the United States, and qualified thinkers should be convened to look into two pivotal issues: First, does free trade have a historical sequence of *benefiting* great economic powers as they are rising toward their peak — the Dutch, the British, and then Americans — but then *working against* those same countries and their workers as their great industries fade? There is some evidence in this direction. Second, is there a connection between the expansion of free trade in the 1970s, 1980s, and early 1990s and the decline of real manufacturing wages in the United States? Until we can clarify or reject those linkages, the American workforce should not be needlessly exposed to further "globalization."

This decade has also seen the postwar social contract between business, government, and labor break down over stagnant wages and unprecedented job cutbacks by corporations excusing themselves because of "international pressures" and "unavoidable responses to global competition." Half of the excuse, at least, is elite self-interest; "globalization" should be stalled where it involves pushing less-educated Americans into ruinous competition with Asians and Latin Americans who ride bicycles to work and live four to a room. Those economics are too unfair — and also too politically explosive.

9. Reversing the Trend Toward Greater Concentration of Wealth and Making the Tax System Fairer and More Productive

Taxes on the really rich — as opposed to taxes on the not-quite-rich — must rise to a more equitable level. Leading economic powers at their zenith or past it have been notorious for concentrated wealth, just like the United States of the 1990s. Gaps between the rich and the middle class invariably widen, as do gaps between the rich and the poor. Worse still, the monied classes include a high ratio of rentiers and speculators, and their taxes are usually relatively low. In retrospect, the rich of eighteenth-century Holland and Edwardian England should have been taxed more heavily, so that the public sector would have had funds the private sector refused to allocate to rebuild each country's manufacturing economy and neglected infrastructure.

That is in *theory*, of course. In practice, those higher taxes probably weren't achievable — and kindred proposals may be fruitless in the United States, given the enormous power of the financial sector and upper-bracket interests in Washington. Parenthetically, the Clinton tax increases of 1993 did not concentrate on the high-income, high-political-influence, investment-dollar rich, the people making $4 million or $17 million a year. Instead, self-employed $300,000-a-year doctors and $400,000-a-year executive vice presidents of midsized manufacturing companies not only got burdened with the 39.6 percent top rate, in Clinton's 1992 campaign promises to be reserved for millionaires alone, but the phasing out of their exemptions and deductions often pushed their marginal federal rates to 45 percent or 46 percent. Then, in addition, a Medicare tax of 1.45 percent (2.9 percent for the self-employed) was imposed on all *earned* income. The multimillionaire speculator, by contrast, had a nominal 39.6 percent top rate, but he paid only 28 percent on his capital gains, and because most of his income was unearned, that portion was untouched by the Medicare tax. He might also come under the Alternative Minimum Tax, with its backup rate of 28 percent.

Back in 1935 when Franklin D. Roosevelt had put through the so-called Wealth Tax Act, that label was accurate in a way that wasn't at all true in the early 1990s. New Deal tax policy had distinguished between upper-middle-class earners just inside the top one percent — their income tax rate was about 15 percent — and the millionaire Rockefellers and Mellons who had to pay about 70 percent. In 1993, by contrast, Clinton and his congressional collaborators imposed the highest marginal rates on the upper-middle-class, while the truly rich kept a 28 percent to 39.6 percent rate structure that still retained much of the pro-investor favoritism of the 1980s. This comparison is set out to underscore a point: not only did the 100,000 American families in the top tenth of one percent enjoy by far and away the greatest wealth and income gains in the 1980s, but they also came through the 1993 tax overhaul in much better shape than the $250,000 or $300,000 earners clustered at the bottom of the top one percent category. The richest 100,000 families — million-dollar-a-year folks or close to it — are the group that, by historical yardsticks, has too much money and influence in a declining great economic power. The several million dollars a year and up speculator's tax rate should be much higher than that of the $300,000-a-year doctor or manufacturing executive. Fairness will be mocked and revenue potential neglected until it is.

Of course, as we have seen in Chapter 4, this investor group and their allies in Washington have a bold offensive strategy: to shift federal tax policy away from taxing income in general to simply taxing *consumed* income and ignoring *invested* income. But any such reduction of the burden of the top 100,000 families, which would add to speculative pressures and unequal outcomes, is not the way to go. Equity and sensibility both lie in trying to raise some serious additional revenue — perhaps $30 billion to $40 billion a year — from the top one tenth of one percent so that their payments are fairer before it becomes necessary to raise some further money from the ordinary Americans. No shared-sacrifice theme can resonate nationally while the truly rich remain so much better off than they were in 1980. Here are some of the possible options:

• *Progressive Flat Tax:* Politicians on left and right have toyed with a "flat tax" — a levy on income above a certain threshold that would allow virtually no deductions or exclusions and that would impose a single common rate on *everyone*. Proponents say that a 19 percent across-the-board rate would raise enough to match present revenues. What makes that or a similar rate unacceptable, though, is that it would force low- and middle-income Americans to pay much steeper taxes while the rich got off more easily. More intriguing is a variation called the "progressive flat tax," which would borrow the concept of taxing all income *without* allowing deductions, but would do so by applying five different brackets: 14 percent, say, from $15,000 to $30,000; 20 percent from $30,000 to $85,000; 28 percent from $85,000 to $200,000; 36 percent from $200,000 to $1,000,000; and 40 percent over $1,000,000. It would raise more money than the present system, coming down hardest on loophole beneficiaries and the rich.

• *Progressive Expenditure Tax:* Two very different versions exist, which gets confusing. One, widely backed by influential Washington lobbies, would be substituted for the federal income tax, and because it would tax only income spent on consumption, not money "invested" (as defined, no doubt, by Washington's best-connected tax lobbyists), it would be a treasure trove for the top one tenth of one percent. Version number two, however, would not *substitute* for the present income tax; it would *supplement* the income tax and would be aimed at the top 900,000 taxpayers (those with $200,000 a year and over), who are estimated to consume about $180 billion a year. The first $75,000 of each household's consumption would be exempted, and then a 20 percent tax would be applied to the rest. This could raise $25 billion to $35 billion a year, although because it would fall heavily on yachts, antique Bugattis, beach homes, and the like, such a levy could convince some of the rich to pursue more serious outlays.

• *Inheritance Taxation Rather Than Estate Taxation:* Taxing the *estates* of the rich produces only about $6 billion a year, thanks to so many loopholes, and some experts say it would be better to tax the *recipients* — the inheritors. Individuals could be allowed to inherit up to $1 million tax-free, but beyond that, any receipts would be taxable. At a 30 percent or 35 percent rate, that would raise a lot of money, perhaps $15 billion to $20 billion a year. Proponents argue that this would also reduce the concentration of wealth by giving the middling rich a reason to split up bequests.

• *Taxing Capital Gains at Death:* Right now, if someone dies and leaves to an heir stock bought at $1,000 but now worth $10,000, no capital gain is realized at death. The heir, however, gets a new $10,000 basis on his or her assets. And the missed capital gains tax becomes a de facto loss to the Treasury that some other taxpayers have to make up. Mandating that capital gains be taken (and taxed) at death would be tricky administratively, but were Congress to enact such a tax, the revenues could hit $5 billion to $6 billion a year.

• *Capital Gains Favoritism to the Middle Class:* If capital gains taxes can be increased in the top one percent, they should be selectively decreased on the middle class, where the savings crisis is real. For example, an exemption from the capital gains tax could be given each year for up to $2,500 or $3,000 of gain on assets with a sufficient U.S. national identity.

• *A Wealth Tax:* This is the (faint) hope of the left, and recent proposals for a U.S. wealth tax have come from the Institute for Policy Studies and individual economists. This is not as extreme as it sounds. A survey by the Organization for Economic Cooperation and Development (OECD) found that eight of the eighteen most advanced OECD countries had annual net wealth taxes — defined as a tax levied at a percentage of the taxpayer's wealth (beyond a certain exempted amount and typically applying to real estate, securities, financial, and business assets). Yet in these countries, France being the most prominent, the tax has been used as a secondary tool for progressivity rather than as a major revenue-raiser. However, the Institute for Policy Studies calculates that even with an allowed exemption of $1 million per family, a wealth tax at a low one percent rate could raise $40 billion a year in the United States.

Some combination of one, two, or three of these approaches could probably tap another $30 billion to $40 billion in annual revenue for the U.S. Treasury without raising hackles among ordinary Americans. But the reader can fairly ask, What chance would measures like these have of being approved by Congress? Not much. Even at risk of grassroots anger, Congress would be more likely to accept a consumption tax that put the new burden on the broad mass of the voters. Challenging America's richest 100,000 families is not good for campaign contributions. But, of course, if the United States ever decided to imitate Switzerland or take the advice of Ross Perot and put tax decisions before the electorate for a nationwide vote, the context of U.S. tax policy would change overnight. Tax law made by the *electorate* could begin to move in any of these directions.

On the other hand, the record of past great economic powers favoring the rich in tax policy doesn't tell the entire story. As Britain's economic decline intensified, especially after

World War II, reaction against the rich became punitive in terms of inheritance taxes and income taxes. The excesses of 1950 were worse than the inadequacies of 1910. Fortunately, there is little risk of that happening in the United States. During the period from 1935 to 1980, the top income tax rate in the United States for million-dollar-a-year earners was in the 70 percent to 91 percent range, and no one expects that kind of top rate to be reached again in the foreseeable future. The irony, of course, is that the half century during which those rates were in effect was this country's economic zenith. Perhaps the symbolism of once again demanding more from the truly rich, pursued in moderation, could have a surprise element of national renewal.

10. *Bringing National and International Debt Under Control*

It was fashionable in the late 1980s for economists to describe the United States with a new horrific: the world's biggest debtor. The numbers and implications were often exaggerated, but the description was true. The national debt of the United States, which had been $1 trillion at the beginning of the 1980s, moved across the $4 trillion mark and prepared to hit $5 trillion in the mid-1990s. By 1992 the country had a net international indebtedness of $600 billion. Cassandras identified rising debt as the nation's top crisis and called for draconian solutions.

At the very least, debt is a major *symptom* of America's problems. But blueprinting a successful remedy is something else again. Declining great economic powers usually let debt continue to build, because dominant interests either profit from it or cannot agree on a compromise for raising taxes or cutting spending to bring it down. In the United States of the 1990s most of the major debt-reduction groups, lobbies, and congressional activists represent conservative or financial constituencies that want to slash middle-class entitlements, means-test Social Security, or saddle the average family with some variety of new consumption tax. At the same time, these interests, far from proposing that the financial sector or America's richest 100,000 families accept any of the higher levies we have just discussed, favor a whole set of new tax cuts or tax policy overhauls to benefit investors. There is no reason for the average citizen to accept any such unfair deficit-reduction blueprint.

On the contrary, because large-scale deficit reduction, if it can be achieved, would give its greatest profit to financial-market investors, that is where a significant portion of new revenue should be raised. This is further justified by how a significant portion of the deficit and national debt reflects the several hundred billion dollars spent in the late 1980s and early 1990s on the federal bailout of savings and loan institutions, commercial banks, and other trembling financial dominos. If a major improvement in the deficit occurs, bond investors will see interest rates decline and the value of their bonds climb, which should also strengthen the stock market. Thus the fairness of substantially funding the tax-increase side of deficit-reduction with three levies aimed at the investment and financial sectors: The first ingredient would be a special surtax on the capital gains realized on bonds or other financial assets, which could be set high enough to push the special capital gain rate up to 39.6 percent, the same maximum rate that applies to ordinary income. Component number two would be some version of the excess profits tax on banks and financial institutions proposed several years ago by the late publisher William Randolph Hearst. He suggested a 25 percent excess profits tax on any financial institution that sold junk bonds or made bad loans until taxpayers were reimbursed for the cost of the bailout. Because financial-sector profits have been high in the 1990s, this tax, which should have been imposed as the decade began, could produce $2 billion to $4 billion a year. The third logical levy would be a small but significant federal tax on financial transactions — on everything from currency swaps, exotic derivatives, and all varieties of electronic speculation to more humdrum stock and bond purchases. Even a few small decimal points of those whirling, swirling trillions, along with other financial transactions, could put $10 billion to $15 billion a year into the Treasury. Instead of means-testing Social Security recipients, Washington could means-test speculators.

Is the financial sector likely to accept contributing $20 billion to $25 billion a year to deficit-reduction this way? Probably not. But if attempts to put the burden on the middle class stall deficit reduction, then after a certain period debt problems will again start weighing on the financial markets — and those pressures might induce serious financial-sector concessions. No fiscal program on the national table as yet justifies middle-class sacrifice.

The cautious observer will say that this agenda will not be pursued and that, besides, it is too haphazard. My response is that part of it will be pursued, but perhaps not enough. And, whatever these proposals are, they are *not* haphazard; they are designed to curb or contain critical recurrent problems of late-stage great economic powers, along with the biases, imbalances, and elites those nations produce as their historical trajectories flatten and turn downward.

Could such an agenda help turn the United States in a new, more successful, direction? Yes, because if most of these changes were pursued by an administration during this decade or early in the next one, the effect on public opinion would be enormous. There would, once again, be the sense of a revolution — of the sort of popular upheaval that has twice before revitalized a turn-of-the-century United States. Once again voters would feel that they were being listened to and that special interests were no longer running the country.

If this chapter and indeed this book has emphasized political and governmental reform rather than social reform, there is good reason. From the American Revolution on, that has been the premise of this country's most successful changes: to revitalize government and politics and to curb elites, special interests, and the emergence of privileged classes. Succeed in this, and much of what else is necessary — changes in specific policy areas — must follow as the United States renews itself economically, culturally, and socially.

Thus if I had to choose a half dozen reforms from the ten proposals just sketched, they would include 1) dispersing the capital and having Congress meet in another city for part of the year; 2) allowing congressmen and senators to vote from their home states and districts; 3) establishing a mechanism for national referendums; 4) concentrating a major attack on the hired-gun culture in Washington; 5) reining in abusive finance and its political influence by regulating electronic speculation, curtailing the nonaccountability of the Federal Reserve Board, and establishing a federal financial transactions tax; and 6) funding deficit-reduction largely by taxing its obvious beneficiaries. The impact of these six changes alone would be powerful.

But we can do best by putting even more trust in the public and pursuing two thirds or three quarters of the recommendations this chapter has made, most of which have been — or would be — supported by national majorities in public opinion polls. The sooner that debate begins, the better.

As for the larger national opportunity, because the United States is not a second Britain or Holland but rather a continental power with much greater resources and historical staying power, reforms aimed at cleaning out the nation's clogged political, governmental, and economic arteries have a genuine potential. A present and future great power is waiting for renewal, not a fading maritime periphery. *Even if this decade and the next are periods of a painful transition, the point is that such a transition ought to be possible.* The 1990s ought to be able to record the same sort of revitalization through popular democracy — the electricity of once again empowering the general public — that the United States experienced in the 1790s and 1890s and their following decades.

If that hope is no longer justified, gambling on it will still have been justified. Letting the people rule is the political genius and governmental raison d'etre of the United States of America, and if it no longer works — if that capacity for renewal is no longer there — then, as Thomas Jefferson asked two centuries ago, what else could we expect to work better? And for that question there is no answer.

Notes and Sources

ONE: Washington and the Late-Twentieth-Century Failure of American Politics

1. The reference here is to how America's leaders of 1787, 1801, and even 1829 exemplified not just one but *two* revolutionary traditions. In addition to the obvious one rooted in the success of the American Revolution, men like Washington, Adams, and Jefferson had themselves drawn on the historical importance only 90 to 130 years earlier of England's two most influential revolutions — Oliver Cromwell's overthrow of Charles I in the mid–seventeenth century and the "Glorious Revolution," which replaced Catholic James II with Protestant William and Mary in 1688. Through these events, the legitimacy of revolution had a broad philosophic base in the eighteenth-century American colonies, and with the added celebration of the success of the American Revolution, the politics of the early nineteenth-century United States — up to the Civil War — continued to draw on revolutionary thinking and rhetoric.

The quotations of Jefferson speaking of the election of 1800 as a revolution and Henry Clay describing Andrew Jackson as a tornado come from James MacGregor Burns, *The Vineyard of Liberty* (New York: Alfred A. Knopf, 1982), pp. 155 and 327. The vivid impressions of the Bryan campaign expressed by Clarence Darrow and John Hay come from Louis Koenig, *Bryan* (New York: Putnam, 1971), pp. 214 and 250, while the computations of how small a vote-shift might have elected Bryan come from the same source, p. 252.

TWO: Imperial Washington: The Power and the Glory — And the Betrayal of the Grass Roots

2. Obtaining information on congressional payrolls is not as easy as it should be for several reasons, and the numbers given in the text are slightly

deceptive in saying that a congressman's budget for hiring staff — clerk-hire, it was called — rose from just several thousand dollars a year in the early 1930s to $20,000 a year in 1957, and then to $255,000 in 1976. For a number of years, Congress used a deceptive scheme which I experienced first-hand as a congressional aide from 1965 to 1968. Pay scales were quoted in old dollars: being carried on the books for $3,000 a year meant you were getting $12,000 or some such. This helped ensure that voters back home didn't get upset over the capital city's pay scales. The system caught up with reality in the 1970s, when pay was stated in current dollars.

3. The essence of "transfer seeking," as pursued by lawyers, lobbyists, brokers, and other professionals, is to gain by transferring wealth rather than creating it, sometimes retaining the amount transferred but more often gaining a fee or commission.

The data about the rise in the number of trade and professional organizations, as well as the percentage choosing to locate in Washington, comes from Jonathan Rauch's article "The Parasite Economy" in the April 25, 1992, *National Journal*. So does the increase in Washington representation of health policy organizations. Professor James Thurber's estimate of the number of lobbyists and people associated with lobbying activities in and around Washington was cited in "80,000 Lobbyists — Probably Not, But Maybe . . ." (*New York Times*, May 12, 1993). The commentary by Arizona senator John McCain on the number of ex-congressmen and senators turned lobbyists appeared in "Let's Close the Revolving Door," *Washington Times*, December 16, 1993. The sentence about Bill Clinton trying to keep the press from describing a closed function at which he consorted with all the lobbyists he denounced in 1992 was in "Oh, That Party of Change," *Washington Post*, October 6, 1993. Professor Mancur Olson's observation that purging interest groups does amount to a marginal argument for revolution appears in his book *The Rise and Decline of Nations* (New Haven: Yale University Press, 1983), p. 140. As for the portraits of the parasites in the capitals of past great economic powers, these have been drawn from Michael Grant, *The Fall of the Roman Empire* (New York: Collier Books, 1990), pp. 92 and 103; J. H. Elliot, *Imperial Spain 1469–1716* (New York: Mentor, 1966), p. 311; and Simon Schama, *Patriots and Liberators: Revolution in the Netherlands 1780–1813* (New York: Vintage Books, 1992), p. 45.

THREE: The Crisis No One Can Discuss: U.S. Economic and Cultural Decline — And What It Means

4. Not enough has been written about the pseudoaristocratic or neo-aristocratic pursuit of things French in the early years of the Reagan administration. Lewis Lapham, the editor of *Harper's*, has described the first Reagan administration (not least the inaugural) as an American rerun of

France's shallow Second Empire. But it is also worthwhile to note a book by Debora Silverman entitled *Selling Culture: Bloomingdale's, Diana Vreeland and the New Aristocracy of Taste in Reagan's America.* Silverman describes the fashionable exhibits at the Metropolitan Museum of Art and elsewhere devoted to recapturing the world of eighteenth-century France and the Belle Epoque of pre–World War I France. In 1985 Nancy Reagan worked to convey, according to *Time*, "an ancien régime air" and to cultivate, in the words of a former aide, "an element of Louis XIV's French court and *les precieuses* — the precious ladies." It is extraordinary how these tastes recurred in eighteenth-century Holland, then in Edwardian Britain, and then in Reagan-era America.

There are endless examples of conservative insistence that U.S. problems are cultural and social, not economic. The statement by Milton Friedman came from *Florida Trend* magazine, June 1993. Myron Magnet's comments appeared in "The Misery of Our Cities," *Wall Street Journal*, April 22, 1993. The insistence by David Blankenhorn appeared in "Good News: Signs of Truce in Culture Wars," *Wall Street Journal*, April 9, 1993.

The Evolution of Risk Management Techniques

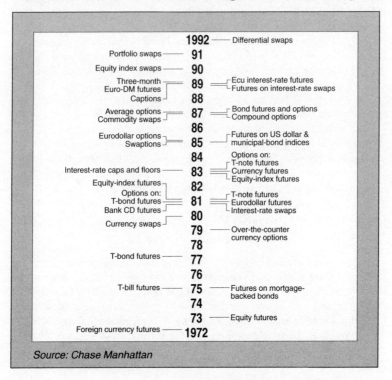

FOUR: The Financialization of America: Electronic Speculation and Washington's Loss of Control over the "Real Economy"

5. For those interested in a more precise chronology of the emergence of financial derivatives, the chart on the previous page — from *The Economist* of April 10, 1993 — captures it well, albeit under a too-kind description: "the evolution of risk-management techniques." The innovation from 1972–79, while significant, was nothing next to what followed after 1981.

The comments on how corporate and financial America were surviving at the expense of the average citizen originated as follows: Floyd Norris's came in his "Market Watch" column in the *New York Times* for August 30, 1992; the comments of *Business Week* came in that magazine's "Business Outlook" section for August 12, 1992; and the column in *U.S. News & World Report* by about-to-depart commentator John Liscio was dated July 20, 1992. Joel Kurtzman, executive editor of the *Harvard Business Review*, has elaborated his critiques of the financial economy and the biases of U.S. finance in a recent book entitled *The Death of Money: How the Electronic Economy Has Destabilized the World's Markets and Created Financial Chaos* (Boston: Little, Brown, 1994). The descriptions of financialization in eighteenth-century Holland and early twentieth-century Britain come from, respectively, Fernand Braudel, *The Perspective of the World* (New York: Harper & Row, 1984), p. 245, and Aaron L. Friedberg, *The Weary Titan: Britain and the Experience of Relative Decline, 1895–1905* (Princeton: Princeton University Press, 1988), pp. 75–76. The criticism of Clinton economic appointee Robert Rubin by Cato Foundation official Stephen Moore appeared in "Insight," *Sunday Washington Times*, January 24, 1993. The calculation of the enormous rentier wealth of top-one-percent America by Edward Luttwak can be found on p. 337 of his book *The Endangered American Dream: How to Stop the United States from Becoming a Third-World Country and How to Win the Geo-Economic Struggle for Economic Supremacy* (New York: Simon & Schuster, 1993). James Carville's wish that the stock market might fall so that real incomes could rise was quoted in "The Carville Market," *Wall Street Journal*, April 5, 1993.

FIVE: The Principal Weaknesses of American Politics and Government

6. Several early and mid-1990s polls have shown solid public support for having a third major party emerge to compete with the Republicans and Democrats from presidential elections right down to grassroots contests for Congress and state legislatures. But among the various national surveys, this question has been asked most often by the *Time* magazine poll conducted by Yankelovich Partners. Here's their data for three 1992–94 dates:

Would you favor or oppose the formation of a third political party that would run candidates for president, Congress, and state offices against the Republican and Democratic candidates?

	All Voters	Republicans	Independents	Democrats
FAVOR				
January, 1994	54%	54%	63%	47%
October, 1992	63	62	76	58
June, 1992	58	59	65	56
OPPOSE				
January, 1994	35	36	27	42
October, 1992	28	28	17	33
June, 1992	32	35	20	32

The small shift in 1994 came principally from a falloff in support for a third party among Democrats, whose attitudes presumably reflected increasing acceptance of the Democratic president in the White House. But overall support for adding another major party to increase voters' choice remained lopsided.

The comments by author David Osborne on the implausibility of renewing government in Washington came from "The Man Who Wrote the Book on Reinventing Government Tries It," *Boston Globe*, April 11, 1993, and "The Case for Reinventing Government," *Christian Science Monitor*, May 20, 1992. The quote about the lawyers and bureaucrats playing a major role in Roman decline comes from Michael Grant, *The Fall of the Roman Empire*, pp. 98–99.

SIX: The Fading of Anglo-American Institutions and World Supremacy

7. The chart on the next page, prepared in May 1987 by David Hale, chief economist of Kemper Financial Services, shows the combined GNPs of the industrial nations during the nineteenth and twentieth centuries, along with the Anglo-Saxon share of the total. Since 1985 the Anglo-Saxon share of the total has dipped further by most calculations (see next page).

GNPs of the Industrial Countries 1820–1986

	Percent of Total Industrial Nations' GNP					
	1820	1870	1913	1950	1979	1985
Australia	0.1	1.6	1.9	2.0	1.9	2.0
Austria	2.6	1.8	1.6	0.8	1.0	1.0
Belgium	2.5	3.3	2.4	1.7	1.5	1.4
Canada	0.4	1.6	2.5	3.4	3.8	3.8
Denmark	0.8	0.7	0.7	0.8	0.7	0.7
Finland	0.6	0.5	0.5	0.6	0.6	0.7
France	23.9	16.9	10.8	7.3	8.1	7.6
Germany	9.6	9.1	9.4	7.1	9.2	8.7
Italy*	14.1	11.2	6.6	5.2	6.1	5.9
Japan	14.7	6.1	5.4	4.9	15.5	17.2
Netherlands	1.9	2.1	1.6	1.9	1.9	1.7
Norway	0.6	0.6	0.5	0.6	0.6	0.6
Sweden	1.6	1.2	1.2	1.6	1.2	1.2
Switzerland	1.2	1.5	1.1	1.1	0.9	0.9
United Kingdom	18.2	20.5	14.5	10.8	6.7	6.4
United States	7.2	21.4	39.0	50.2	40.4	40.2
U.K. and U.S.A.	25.4	41.8	53.5	61.0	47.1	46.6
Anglo-Saxon total**	25.9	45.0	57.9	66.4	52.9	52.5
TOTAL	100	100	100	100	100	100

*Italy was not a unified nation until 1870.
** (U.K., U.S.A., Canada, and Australia)

Looking into the present decade, calculations by the International Monetary Fund in 1993 gave the U.S., U.K., Canada, and Australia about 47 percent of Industrial World GNP/GDP at that point. An even larger perspective, though, was that the industrial countries were no longer a very useful category because so much of world economic growth, computed by new purchasing power criteria, was in the so-called *developing* countries. Count them in the "Industrial World" for purposes of figuring the Anglo-Saxon share, and the latter plummets. The Anglo-Saxon share of the combined industrial-nation and developing-nation economies is clearly not just a little below its late-nineteenth-century levels but far below.

The observations about staging a minor British political revolution through downgrading the monarchy to the powerless Dutch or Scandinavia form come from the Joe Rogaly column entitled "Bicycle Ride to a Revolution" in the *Financial Times* for May 18, 1993. The speculations on the future status of Jamaica, Papua New Guinea, Canada, and New Zealand appeared in "Britannia Finds Less to Rule," *Christian Science Monitor,* September 22, 1993. The several references to the Anglo-Saxon genesis and character of the first-wave international downturn in 1989–91 came from "Economic Wisdom: A Casualty of War?," *Financial Times*, February 4, 1991, and "Japan in the Bankruptcy Court," *Economist*, November 6, 1993.

SEVEN: The 1990s: Converging Revolutionary Traditions and Post–Cold War Jitters

The material on the upsurge in international crime comes from "Crime Without Borders" in the *Los Angeles Times* of April 27, 1993. The urban buildup of population and socioeconomic pressures was set out in detail in "L.A. Riots Called Symptom of Worldwide Urban Trend" in the *Los Angeles Times* of May 25, 1992.

EIGHT: Renewing America for the Twenty-first Century: The Blueprint for a Political Revolution

More detail on Neal Peirce's views on the city-state phenomenon can be found in his book *Citistates: How Urban America Can Prosper in a Competitive World* (Washington: Seven Locks Press, 1993). The comments and proposals by U.S. Rep. Jim Leach with respect to regulating derivatives are from his press releases. The suggestion by *The Economist* that the 1990s will be the decade of national governments struggling to cope with the emergence of a global capital market came in its World Economy Survey of September 19, 1992.

Index